Applied Theatre: Aesthetics

The **Applied Theatre** series is a major innovation in applied theatre scholarship, bringing together leading international scholars that engage with and advance the field of applied theatre. Each book presents new ways of seeing and critically reflecting on this dynamic and vibrant field. Volumes offer a theoretical framework and introductory survey of the field addressed, combined with a range of case studies illustrating and critically engaging with practice.

Series Editors

Michael Balfour (Griffith University, Australia)
Sheila Preston (University of East London, UK)

Applied Theatre: Development
Tim Prentki
ISBN 978-1-4725-0986-4

Applied Theatre: Resettlement
Drama, Refugees and Resilience
Michael Balfour, Bruce Burton, Penny Bundy,
Julie Dunn and Nina Woodrow
ISBN 978-1-4725-3379-1

Applied Theatre: Research
Radical Departures
Peter O'Connor and Michael Anderson
ISBN 978-1-4725-0961-1

Related titles from Bloomsbury Methuen Drama

Performance and Community: Commentary and Case Studies
Edited by Caoimhe McAvinchey
ISBN 978-1-4081-4642-2

Affective Performance and Cognitive Science: Body, Brain and Being
Edited by Nicola Shaughnessy
ISBN 978-1-4081-8577-3

Applied Theatre: Aesthetics

Gareth White

Series Editors
Michael Balfour and Sheila Preston

Bloomsbury Methuen Drama
An imprint of Bloomsbury Publishing Plc

B L O O M S B U R Y
LONDON • NEW DELHI • NEW YORK • SYDNEY

Bloomsbury Methuen Drama

An imprint of Bloomsbury Publishing Plc

50 Bedford Square
London
WC1B 3DP
UK

1385 Broadway
New York
NY 10018
USA

www.bloomsbury.com

**BLOOMSBURY, METHUEN DRAMA and the Diana logo are trademarks of
Bloomsbury Publishing Plc**

First published 2015

© Gareth White, 2015

British Library Cataloguing-in-Publication Data
A catalogue record for this book is available from the British Library.

ISBN: HB: 978-1-4725-1387-8
PB: 978-1-4725-1355-7
ePDF: 978-1-4725-1177-5
ePub: 978-1-8496-6455-4

Library of Congress Cataloging-in-Publication Data
A catalog record for this book is available from the Library of Congress.

Typeset by Deanta Global Publishing Services, Chennai, India
Printed and bound in India

Contents

List of Figures

Notes on Contributors

Mojisola Adebayo trained with Augusto Boal and is a specialist in Theatre of the Oppressed with a master's in physical theatre. She has worked in theatre, radio and television, on four continents, over the past two decades, performing in over 40 productions, writing, devising and directing over 30 plays and leading countless workshops, from Antarctica to Zimbabwe. Her publications include her plays in *Mojisola Adebayo: Plays One* (2011), *48 Minutes for Palestine* in *Theatre in Pieces* (2014) and *The Theatre for Development Handbook* (with John Martin and Manisha Mehta 2010) is available through www.pan-arts.net. She is a part-time lecturer at Goldsmiths and PhD student at Queen Mary, University of London, UK.

Ananda Breed is an applied arts practitioner and scholar. Breed is the author of *Performing the Nation: Genocide, Justice, Reconciliation*, in addition to several publications that address transitional systems of governance and the arts. She has worked as a consultant for International Research Exchange Board (IREX) and UNICEF in Kyrgyzstan on issues concerning conflict prevention and conducted workshops in the Democratic Republic of Congo (DRC), Indonesia, Japan, Kyrgyzstan, Nepal, Palestine, Rwanda and Turkey. Breed is co-director of the Centre for Performing Arts Development (CPAD) at the University of East London, UK.

Brian Heap is a senior lecturer, staff tutor in drama and head of the Philip Sherlock Centre for the Creative Arts at the University of the West Indies, Mona, Jamaica. Heap studied with Dorothy Heathcote at the University of Newcastle upon Tyne, and has worked in the fields of drama and education for over 35 years. With Pamela Bowell he co-authored *Planning Process Drama: Enriching Teaching and Learning* (2001, 2013) as well as several conference papers and articles for refereed journals. He is an international consultant and served as conference director and convener of the Fifth International Drama in Education Research Institute (2006) in Kingston, Jamaica.

Anna Hickey-Moody is a senior lecturer in educational studies and head of the Centre for The Arts and Learning at Goldsmiths, University of London, UK. Her work focuses on disability, arts practice, gender and cultural geography. She is developing a cultural studies approach to youth arts as a subcultural form of humanities education. She is the author of *Youth, Arts and Education: Reassembling subjectivity through affect* (2013) and *Unimaginable Bodies: intellectual disability, performance and becomings* (2009), co-author of *Masculinity Beyond the Metropolis* (2006), and co-editor of *Disability Matters: pedagogy, media and affect* (2011), and *Deleuzian Encounters: studies in contemporary social issues* (2007).

Kirsten Sadeghi-Yekta is a assistant professor in applied theatre at the University of Victoria, Canada, Sadeghi-Yekta completed her PhD at the University of Manchester in 2014. Her research interests focus on the field of applied theatre, aesthetics, global economics, developing settings and (post) conflict contexts. She has been involved in projects with different communities and in a variety of countries. For instance, she has worked with children in the Downtown Eastside in Vancouver, young people in Brazilian favelas, disabled young women in rural areas of Cambodia, adolescents in Nicaragua, and students with special needs in schools in The Netherlands. She publishes research on internationalized applied theatre and global economics.

Nicola Shaughnessy is a professor of Performance in the School of Arts at the University of Kent, UK, and founder and director of the Research Centre for Cognition, Kinesthetics and Performance. Shaughnessy's research and teaching specialisms are in the areas of applied theatre, contemporary performance, dramatic auto/biography, cognition and performance and practice based pedagogies. She collaborates with researchers from other disciplines to explore the processes of making performance and its affects on participants. Her current research explores the potential of drama to engage with autism, performing psychologies and interdisciplinary modes of performance training. Recent publications are her edited collection *Affective Performance and Cognitive Science: Body, Brain and Being* (Bloomsbury Methuen Drama, 2013) and *Applying Performance: Live Art, Socially Engaged Theatre and Affective Practice* (2012). She is a series editor with Professor John Lutterbie for Bloomsbury Methuen Drama's *Performance and Science: Interdisciplinary Dialogues* series.

Gareth White is a senior lecturer in applied theatre and community performance, at Central School of Speech and Drama, UK. White's research is concerned with the aesthetics of participation, in a variety of settings and senses, including work on audience participation in contemporary practices from applied performance to live art to immersive theatre. Publications include *Audience Participation in Theatre: Aesthetics of the Invitation* (2013); 'On Immersive Theatre', in *Theatre Research International* October 2012; and 'Noise, Conceptual Noise, and the Potential of Audience Participation' in Kendrick and Roesner's *Theatre Noise* (2011).

Introduction

The title of this book brings together two problematic terms, which then have a problematic relationship to each other. *Aesthetics* is a common word with many overlapping meanings, while *applied theatre* (or *drama*) is an umbrella term for a collection of overlapping practices. A little further into this introduction, I outline some of the ways that ideas of aesthetics are used in connection with the theatre practices that gather under the *applied*; but first looking at the notion of *appliedness* will illustrate why exploration in relation to *aesthetics* might lead to useful insights. The re-examination of the core term is a feature of publications on applied theatre with which many of its scholars and students would prefer to dispense, and yet it contains contradictions that are not easily ignored and which are provocative in this context; I shall be brief.

Helen Nicholson's often quoted outline tells us applied drama is:

> A shorthand to describe forms of dramatic activity that primarily exist outside conventional mainstream theatre institutions, and which are specifically intended to benefit individuals, communities and societies.[1]

Here are two aspects which might indicate that applied theatre is an exception to what theatre usually is: it happens in different places, and for different ends. *Applied* is different to *pure* theatre, we might easily suppose, which happens in its proper places, and is properly focussed on its excellence as a work of art rather on its intention to give benefit. Pure theatre (real theatre, for some) is focussed on its aesthetics, rather than its effects. This is a simplistic and unfortunate misconception, one that is frustrating to practitioners who value artistic skills – their own as well as those of people they collaborate with – as highly as the ability to work sensitively in different situations and with an understanding of how the arts are beneficial to people and society. Applied theatre can create occasions of theatre as *pure* as any other; indeed for many practitioners it is the potential of these settings and intentions for creating powerful art that is the attraction. Attending to aesthetics might serve to bring this potential back into mind.

But there is another issue with 'applied theatre', as Mojisola Adebayo argues forcefully in her chapter in this book: in collecting a number of disparate practices under its apparently neutral umbrella term, it may obfuscate a political impetus of those practices which is more overt in terms like 'community theatre', 'theatre for social change', and most stridently 'theatre of the oppressed'. Adebayo also suggests it carries an implication of work done by one group *to* another, of theatre applied *to* people, where there is a clear distribution of power and authority;[2] and that the growth of applied theatre as a subject in universities (which is where the term is used, far more than anywhere else) is collusive in creating a class of professional 'applied theatre practitioners', rather than artists motivated to make work with people in alternative settings. Thus, re-focussing on artistry goes hand in hand with a return to the political origin of most of the practices under the applied theatre umbrella, rather than distracting from it. This suggests teaching, and conceiving, applied theatre as a way to *apply oneself* as a theatre maker, and thus placing artistry, skill, and creative ambition at the core, alongside critical thinking and political awareness.

This book is not a manifesto for the above approach. A reader looking for such a manifesto will find my own chapters theoretical rather than polemical, and those that follow disparate, perhaps contradictory, rather than presenting a coherent position. Nevertheless, it offers a set of examples of theatre and performance put to the service of social and personal change, along with rigorous analysis of the artistic forms doing this work, of conceptions of participants' engagement, or of the value of the artistic practice in its context – in other words, analysis of the specific aesthetics of a practice, the model of aesthetic engagement in question, or a return to the core aesthetic question of the purpose of art. By turning our attention to questions of aesthetics, in the various senses of the word and theories it makes available, the writers in this volume attend to applied theatre as art, and to practitioners as artists, sometimes working with the same tools as other artists and sometimes with different materials and techniques at their disposal. These diverse uses of 'aesthetics', while not a problem to be solved, need to be acknowledged, and noting how they manifest in writing about applied theatre will begin to unpack the complexity that can be entailed by invoking the word.

Applied theatre, aesthetics and the aesthetic

Eugene van Erven's conclusion, in *Community Theatre: Global Perspectives*, presents a commonly held perspective, and expresses the dilemma that applied theatre practitioners of all kinds find often themselves in:

> Judging community theatre by social welfare criteria alone . . . makes it susceptible to control by the institutional obsession for immediately measurable 'results' or the politician's desire to quickly 'score', thereby more often than not blatantly ignoring the artistic merits.[3]

The practitioner whose work is predicated on the social good that it can achieve is inevitably bound to the material systems that sustain it, but sometimes struggles to identify how the work has a value that is not easily measured in instrumental terms. Practice in applied theatre and other interventionist art has always embodied a kind of theory of art, particularly in its orientation towards process as much as product, towards redistribution of creative initiative and towards demonstrable worldly outcomes. At points the explicit rejection of conservative and oppressive values found in high art has entailed a rejection of the values of beauty, creative genius and artistic autonomy that are associated with it, in favour of a radically political model of continuity between art practice and social struggle. But more recently the challenge that arises from commentators on applied theatre is to beware of over-instrumentalizing, and to develop a more nuanced understanding of the role that the special capabilities of art – particularly beauty – have to play in social change, or of art experience as something that people have a right to in itself, that needs to be available to all as a matter of principle. In this writing the *heteronomy* of art – its interconnectedness with the world around it – is essentially taken for granted, the matter of artistic autonomy which is often in dispute in conventional academic aesthetics takes a different shape: to assert that within this heteronomy there is a need for a recognition of the distinctive contribution of the aesthetic.

Jan Cohen-Cruz, in an interview with Robert Landy, suggests that the instrumentalizing tendency is implicit in the umbrella term itself:

> The problem with Applied Theatre is that it is often understood as being too operational. You learn it and then you apply it to a situation. It's treated as the second cousin of real knowledge. And the notion of application doesn't communicate how reciprocal such relationships tend to be.[4]

She emphasizes the relational aspect of interventionist practice by calling it 'engaged' rather than 'applied' performance; the engagement and the relational influences face in both directions, so that the art and the artist are transformed by those they engage with, as well as being the catalyst for change themselves. And an understanding of aesthetics that serves this purpose needs to face in two directions too: it needs to show how art can be 'real knowledge' in its own right, and at the same time remain a tool of social and personal change. As van Erven puts it, there is a struggle for 'artistic legitimacy' in which the power structures of art worlds need to be reformed along with the social problems of applied theatre's various settings.[5] Asserting this legitimacy has often involved using a language of aesthetics drawn from its academic manifestation as well as in less precise everyday terms, and has sometimes developed specific theories of beauty, quality and autonomy. The next section outlines some ways in which the language and ideas of aesthetics are put to use in relation to applied theatre.

Terminological drift and clarity

The word 'aesthetic' in applied theatre literature is not used with neat differentiation. Most often it stands for a broad category of the artistic or the art-like, but there is also usage related to the specific aesthetic languages at play, and references that suggest aesthetic attitudes, or continuities with an aesthetic experience that extend beyond art. Even where the term is a considered part of the subject matter, as in Peter O'Connor's excellent chapter 'TIE: The Pedagogic as the Aesthetic' in the 2013 edition of Anthony Jackson's *Learning Through Theatre*, it drifts across meanings.[6] In his account of a TIE (Theatre in Education) project in the wake of the 2011 Christchurch earthquakes, he notes the opposition between instrumental aims of practice and other priorities:

> There has been a growing appreciation of the tensions that exist between the political, pedagogic and aesthetic imperatives of TIE. . . . Yet what is clear is that TIE's aesthetic and pedagogic dimensions are inextricably linked. . . . Exciting theatre and powerful learning are the true potential of TIE when the aesthetic truly acts as the pedagogic.[7]

The aesthetic here is evidently something other than political or pedagogic, in this context it could be read simply as a synonym for 'artistic'. However, the close association of the term with 'moments of beauty' – which are a key feature of the work he describes, suggest that 'the aesthetic' is something more specific; the 'alternative aesthetic statements' that children were able to create are not diverse artistic responses to their traumatic experiences, but examples of the beautiful.[8] O'Connor argues convincingly for the importance of 'moments of beauty', and I am not sceptical of his conclusion. But developing his argument in relation to the binary of instrumentality and artistry, he uses the term in a different way:

> If the project had had neat plans, with easily identifiable and measurable goals, linked specifically to narrow curriculum guidelines, it might

have gained the Ministry of Education's support. Yet by introducing these pedagogic constraints, it would have changed the aesthetic of the programme.[9]

Here the aesthetic is the form or style of the work, the aesthetic-as-language, rather than its use of one important quality, beauty.[10] I do not intend to suggest that it is incumbent upon writers using the word 'aesthetic' to closely define its meaning, but it is useful to note how, in the context of this key problematic for the field, its different uses come into play. Even writers who make significant progress with this problematic – for example, James Thompson or Nicola Shaughnessy, as I will discuss below – have not found it necessary to define the term or to work with discrete distinctions. However, there are some instances where more precise definitions bring the kinds of distinctions and nuances that academic aesthetics trades in, into the discussion of applied theatre.

In the introduction to the themed edition of *Research in Drama Education* of November 2010, Joe Winston and Brad Haseman define the word in a way that positions it more carefully. In an essay of only ten pages, they do not examine the variety of meanings available to the word; and the essays that follow largely adhere to their interpretation of it. They characterize the aesthetic as 'a meta-narrative of the enlightenment',[11] invoking the critique of meta-narratives that is characteristic of postmodernism. They note the term's origin in Baumgarten's *Aesthetica* and Immanuel Kant's decisive development of the idea of the aesthetic towards a theory of a kind of judgement that combines pleasure and disinterest. In their words the aesthetic in this tradition is: 'A specific form of knowing but along with it, a particular type of experience, one quite different from the normal business of everyday perception.'[12] Applied theatre, they say, makes use of deep and rich experiences of this kind, and depends upon the complexity of this way of knowing for its impact. They highlight the problem of disinterestedness as a key characteristic, both for its legacy in inspiring a 'hierarchy of taste' based on the education and leisure needed to discern and appreciate the appropriate works, and for its demotion of work that has evident and important interests and effects. They quote Clifford Geertz[13] on the cultural specificity, historicity and ultimate impotence of this version of the aesthetic in the face of art traditions and practices that defy its logic, and offer Brecht, Boal and Rancière as the sympathetic reference points for activist and interventionist theatre makers. They allow, however, that Kant had made some inconclusive effort to define a relationship between beauty and morality, and that there is something in common between the notion of a disinterested pleasure and the kinds of psychical distance that is important to the pedagogical aspect of political aesthetics from Boal to Rancière. In their emphasis on 'forms of knowing' and 'types of experience' that are quite different to those that belong to everyday life, they suggest an experiential definition of the particularity – and therefore autonomy – of the aesthetic.

Cohen, Varea and Walker, in *Acting Together, Performance and the Creative Transformation of Conflict*, offer an even more precise definition, one in which the experiential aspect and what it facilitates is most important:

> We use the term aesthetic to refer to the resonant interplay between expressive forms of all cultures and those who witness and/or participate in them. There are several defining features of 'aesthetic experience' – or aesthetic interaction with artfully composed expressive forms, such as songs, images, gestures and objects. First, aesthetic experiences involve people in forms that are bounded in space and time (e.g. by the frame around a picture, or the lights fading to black at the end of a play). Secondly, aesthetic experiences engage people on multiple levels at the same time – sensory, cognitive, emotive and often spiritual – so that all of these dimensions are involved simultaneously in constructing meaning and framing questions. Thirdly, aesthetic experiences engage people with forms that are able to acknowledge and mediate certain tensions, including those between innovation and tradition, the individual and the collective. Because of these defining features, an aesthetic experience is one in which an enlivening sense of reciprocity arises between the perceivers/participants and the forms with which they are engaging.[14]

In this admirably consistent definition aesthetic experience (in all but one case the two words are paired together) is clearly artistic experience, or in their words 'expressive form', and the boundary between it and the everyday allows simultaneous engagement on multiple levels and the mediation of tension that resides in the extra-aesthetic situation. The facilitating boundary is a familiar trope in writing about theatre education, where drama is said to offer a 'no penalty area' or 'safe space' for children and other students to take risks. Their definition is concerned with describing a limited autonomy of the art work: the separation that enables connection.

Beauty and engagement

Conventional academic aesthetics perceives a contradiction between artistic quality and efficacy, in contrast to various progressive aesthetics which would not (and sometimes disavowing aesthetics explicitly, because of these associations). Critical theory has tended to demote beauty, the most celebrated aesthetic quality, because of the ways it has been appropriated by and supported sexist, elitist and colonial values. A relatively recent development, (as I shall discuss in more detail in Chapter 1), has been the attempt to recuperate the power of beauty for progressive ends. Some applied theatre theorists have explicitly taken this approach, incorporating this version of 'the aesthetic' into their conceptualization of pedagogical and interventionist practice, so that the beautiful, especially, becomes a facilitating quality rather than one that exists apart from efficacy. Joe Winston, for example, champions beauty as an educational experience and its contribution to individual growth and a good society. Although his argument in *Beauty and Education*[15] is about contemporary schooling, he is a key figure in the growth of applied theatre theory, as his editorial contribution to *Research in Drama Education* evidences. James Thompson, in *Performance Affects*, insists that the affective dimensions of performance, especially those of joy and the perception of beauty, have to be given a place alongside – or even in precedence to – the effective dimensions that are much easier to analyse or quantify.[16] Even in the most challenging of circumstances, in the wake of natural disaster or conflict, where measurable improvements in relationships or clarity of communication between troubled communities may seem most urgent, he tells us, the excitements and pleasures of the work itself must be valued and allowed to do their work:

> Participatory theatre should focus on affect rather than effect. This would seek to avoid the anticipation or extraction of meaning as the primary impulse of an applied theatre process. . . . Working with affect awakens individuals to possibilities beyond themselves without an insistence on what the experience is – what meanings should be attached.[17]

'Awakening to possibilities beyond ourselves' consciously echoes Elaine Scarry's arguments about the potential of beauty; Thompson also discusses her thesis in *The Body in Pain* concerning the relationship between beauty and suffering, its useful palliative effects as well as its guidance towards better actions in the world.[18] He contrasts the tendency for narratives of oppression or trauma to be used as the starting point for applied theatre explorations, with the potential to 'collaborate in making something beautiful as the very point of departure',[19] instead. The 'call to beauty', a manifestation of a Kantian imperative to share our judgements of taste with others, is a call to some sort of good, indefinable but indicative that something better is possible, and with the potential to ameliorate painful circumstances or to critique them, while providing pleasure rather than re-enacting pain.

Thompson's use of the affective asks for a distinction that recalls the 'esthetics' of John Dewey,[20] which is more than experience associated with aesthetic objects or phenomena: it is the consummation of daily experience made possible by art. It is the experiential dimension which is defining, rather than the object itself or the tradition in which it is located. In other words aesthetic expression is a thing we do, rather than a thing we encounter:

> Dancing, and other forms of aesthetic expression, might be places of respite, but the argument here suggests something more radical – they are also integral and necessary parts of change itself. In a world of inequality, social injustices and endemic violence, they could be acts of resistance and redistribution, made in an intimate and sensory key.[21]

Nicola Shaughnessy, in *Applying Performance: Live Art, Socially Engaged Theatre and Affective Performance*,[22] develops the idea of affective and bodily dimensions of participatory practice, making use of Josephine Machon's concept of (syn)aesthetics,[23] along with neuroscience, cognitive philosophy and Hans Thies Lehmann's post-dramatic theatre.[24] In (syn)aesthetics both audience reception and performers' experiences of performance are considered to consist of overlapping and interweaving dimensions of conscious perception and physical sensation. Shaughnessy finds this appropriate for participatory practices where the subject in question – neither audience member nor autonomous artist – is physically as well as emotionally and cognitively involved in performance, and particularly apposite to what she calls the 'neurodiverse aesthetic' that is called for in creating work with people on the autistic spectrum. The aesthetic, as beauty in Thompson's treatment, calls us to relate to each other, invites us to participate, and it has radical potential. For Shaughnessy the aesthetic aspect of applied practice is found even more emphatically in bodily engagement.

An applied theatre aesthetic?

When Shaughnessy proposes a neurodivergent aesthetic 'where language, logic and rationality are delightfully suspended',[25] she is concerned with an aesthetic in the sense of a form or style of making, and its associated practices of attending to a work of art, what we might call an aesthetic-as-language, because it concerns the material that makes up the particular lexicon of the style, how it is used and how it can be understood. At other points in the same text she mentions a 'digital urban aesthetic', a 'popular participatory aesthetic', the aesthetic of objects presented in museums,[26] and 'the aesthetics of the piece' in relation to several examples of performance practice (the aesthetic-as-language is indicated just as often by a plural as a singular). Although it may be related to the manifestation of 'the Aesthetic' as a faculty or a mode of experience, it is dependent on context in quite a different way. The aesthetic of a single work, a set of related practices or a recognizable tradition draws on shared understandings between all of those taking part – as audience members, or artists of whatever kind – about how the elements of a performance are to be attended to and how they relate to each other and to the things they refer to, represent or re-shape in performance.

It would be possible to describe the aesthetic-as-language of a range of applied theatre practices: of the Theatre in Education of different times and places, of Theatre of the Oppressed in more or less rigorous forms, or of process drama led by classroom teachers; and the selection and evolution of an aesthetic by a practitioner or group of practitioners is an important process. But I would be very sceptical of any distillation of a singular aesthetic of applied theatre in general, as an artistic language that prevails across these practices, or ought to prevail, in order to effectively satisfy the demands of efficacy, ethics and politics. Applied theatre is a discourse around theatre and performance, that allows us to see things in common between practices and the contexts in which they happen, rather than a coherent set of practices in itself. It is important in several respects not to put boundaries around what 'the practice' of applied theatre is: because we might thus miss activity that does not fit within these boundaries; because we might produce an orthodoxy, and thus restrict innovation and initiative; and because we (probably) come to applied theatre with the perspective that all theatre has the potential to have effects upon its world, and therefore of being viewed through the lens of 'the applied'.

What does aesthetics have to offer applied theatre? This question will be useful if the responses to it allow deeper understandings of what practitioners and participants do. If, as I have suggested, the concerns of aesthetics take interesting shapes in applied theatre settings, then there should be something in this. For all that interventionist art appears to take for granted some obvious positions in these central debates (*for* heteronomy, *against* normative or elitist definitions of quality), the questions remain relevant, though they may mutate. Questions about autonomy and quality might appear as: What makes art activity special? What is quality in the absence of a high level of expertise? Applied theatre practitioners are hardly ignorant of these questions, in practical terms, but may nevertheless have something to gain from in depth reflection on them, hopefully in terms that offer something new. Richard Shusterman describes his pragmatist aesthetics, which I shall draw on at some length in Chapter 2, as 'meliorist': that is, he intends to 'direct inquiry away from general condemnations or glorifications so that attention may be better focussed on more concrete problems and specific improvements.'[27] He proposes that aesthetic theory should aim not to define the borders of worthwhile art and experience, but play a part in developing the way we make, respond to and make space for art, via a re-thinking of its dynamics. If these chapters are to play such a part they will do so not by providing more principles for practice, but by inviting practitioners already focussed on using their art form to address concrete problems and to make specific improvements. These chapters perhaps offer practitioners some more encouragement to think of themselves and their participant allies as artists, and to enjoy the different kinds of focus that might encourage.

The chapters

Chapter 1 introduces some key themes in the philosophical field of aesthetics, principally to distinguish the specific questions that it is concerned with from everyday language, and how these questions both investigate and define the way we make, say and think about 'art'. I take Immanuel Kant's theory of taste and aesthetic judgement as a key example, both because it takes such a seminal role in the inauguration of the field, its concerns and its prejudices, and because it is a theory that I work with in some detail in Chapter 2. The chapter concludes with a proposal for the concerns of an 'aesthetics of participation' that is concerned with matters that are important to applied theatre thinking, while also relevant to other kinds of participatory performance practice.

Chapter 2 is in two parts; the first returns to Kant and the problem of aesthetic judgement as the inspiration for an idea of 'the Aesthetic'. I give a reading of two aspects of Kant's theory (genius, and dependent beauty) that makes it amenable to an aesthetics of participation. Using Kant might seem perverse, but it is deliberate, as a strategy to employ an apparently unsympathetic theoretical architecture which has for a long time reflected what many people value in art. I explore it here not as a straw man to demolish along with the arguments for aesthetic autonomy, but to see what can be learnt from it; and also in part to demonstrate how far there is to travel from some of the core concerns of aesthetics, to the practical concerns of interventionist and participatory theatre. The second part moves on to some contemporary aesthetic theory that is inspired by Dewey's pragmatist aesthetics, approaches that are more obviously sympathetic to a heteronomous aesthetics and to interventionist practices. Between these chapters is an 'interlude' where I describe a project that is used to exemplify and illustrate my argument throughout Chapter 2: Access All Areas' creation and performance of *Eye Queue Hear.*

Chapter 3 is by Nicola Shaughnessy: 'Dancing with Difference: Moving Towards a New Aesthetics' challenges dualisms between the aesthetic and non-aesthetic through an analysis of the work of two contemporary performance companies whose practices are situated on the threshold between applied theatre and performance by virtue of working within the liminal spaces 'in between' art and life, practice and research, dance and theatre. Fevered Sleep's 'Men and Girls Dance' explores interactions between mature professional male dancers and young untrained female dancers, drawing upon cognitive neuroscience to explore kinesthetic empathy. The Kent-based company StevensonThompson also explore intergenerational dance based work in a series of projects between older women (50+) and younger generations of men and women experiencing the early stages of adulthood (18–22 year olds). This is and isn't 'applied' theatre, drawing upon personal and collective experience as the dancers perform their own stories and their relations with the company through the choreography. Shaughnessy reflects upon the company's work in care and community contexts, working with people with dementia whose experiences were source material for the first production, and subsequent pieces which build upon this foundation. The chapter also refers to Shaughnessy's work on neurodivergence and outsider art in discussion of an emergent new aesthetics and a reconceptualization of beauty, creativity and imagination.

Chapter 4, by Mojisola Adebayo is a critical reflection on *I Stand Corrected*, a performance with participatory workshops and post-show discussions, developed in collaboration with members of the black lesbian community of Cape Town, visual artist Zanele Muholi, and devised by Mamela Nyamza and Adebayo herself, an actor, playwright and facilitator. *I Stand Corrected* is a response to so-called 'corrective' rape against lesbians in South Africa and the virulent anti-gay marriage rhetoric in Britain. In spite of its horrific content, *I Stand Corrected* has been repeatedly described by audience members, participants and critics alike as 'beautiful'. The chapter asks: what do people mean when they say a work of art is beautiful? What, if anything, can beauty move you to do? What are the problems and limitations of beauty in activism? How far is beauty a crucial feature of 'applied theatre', and can beauty be applied? Adebayo explores questions of the senses, the sacred, sex, representation, race and ritual. However, she begins her chapter by challenging the notion of applied theatre in itself. Just as Shaughnessy describes work that is at and beyond the borders of 'applied' practice, *I Stand Corrected* would not sit comfortably within most definitions of what characterizes the applied. Adebayo's objections are manifold, but she questions particularly the implication that an 'applied' art is an exception to what makes art forms what they are, that is their 'aesthetic' character. Her interrogation and celebration of beauty amount to a defence of aesthetic value in activist art.

Kirsten Sadeghi-Yekta's 'Competing International Players and their Aesthetic Imperatives: The Future of Internationalized Applied Theatre Practice?' returns to a key area of practice normally covered by the 'applied' umbrella, but again with a critical perspective. She presents the aesthetics of a theatre initiative in a development setting: the multi-disciplinary arts centre Phare Ponleu Selpak in Cambodia. By focussing on how different judgements of social and aesthetic worth meet, conflict and interact within the programmes, processes and outcomes of this theatre organization, the chapter articulates the different kinds of 'values' attached to the (at times) competing aesthetic criteria for practitioners, government bodies and national and international non-governmental organizations that have stakes in this work. After exploring social and aesthetic binaries at play in the art centre's work, this chapter points out the many ways in which international economics and global governance – manifest in funding decisions of international interveners and cultural policies of national governments – participate and intrude into both the aesthetic and social constructions of applied theatre's artistic value, framing its aesthetic sphere. Sadeghi-Yekta frames the impact of economic and international actors on discourses of aesthetics in applied theatre through Arjun Appadurai's concept of the ethnoscape, which offers an analytical framework for investigating the meaning of aesthetics of applied theatre in development settings. She argues that the massive global pressure coming from the United Nations and the international humanitarian community seeking to shape applied theatre companies and make them respond to certain dynamics serves neither art nor community, and that applied theatre practices globally are becoming too uniform as a result, existing in an environment partially organized according to international agendas. As a result, this chapter proposes a more politicized, historicized kind of practice, critically aware of these influences.

Chapter 6, Ananda Breed's 'Aesthetic Play: Between Performance and Justice', is about performance in a 'development' context, but not theatre for development: the performances here belong to a local tradition, rather than being 'applied' by outsiders. What Breed describes is how traditional performance has been used and reconstructed for instrumental purposes; the performance in question is the *gacaca* court, as deployed by the government of Rwanda to resolve charges related to the genocide in that country in 1994. She examines how the aesthetic of these juridical performances is connected to processes of law, while also reinforcing varied narratives of justice and reconciliation, and argues that in the case of post-genocide gacaca courts an aesthetic frame of justice has been used to perform international norms and to provide legibility to local level courts, while the actual courts themselves were eventually manipulated for purposes ranging from revenge to extortion. She makes the correlation between this and the historic use of the arts by the current governing Rwandan Patriotic Front, while in exile, as a mode of survival, employing performance for its reconstructive attributes to preserve Tutsi culture, to imbue the historic past to the next generation who were born in exile, and to fuel a militarized return to Rwanda. The implication of Breed's argument is not only that traditional performance practices are distorted by history, becoming not modes of mediation but protective strategies for the political parties of an ascendant ethnic group, but also that this is an aesthetic process, where performance helps to convince and to define a sanctioned point of view.

Anna Hickey-Moody, in 'Technologies of Imagination', adopts Peter Brook's description of holy theatre as a way of thinking about rendering the invisible visible. Brook's proposition is that holy theatre is a living example of 'the notion that the stage is a place where the invisible can appear',[28] a means through which the virtual is made actual. Holy theatre, in this sense, shows a world that is always present, yet hidden, usually because of power relationships that render things unspeakable. Her chapter draws on Brook's ideas of holy theatre and rough theatre to explore C&T[29] Theatre Company's work, framing their transnational political theatre project *LipSync* as a vehicle of holy theatre and rough theatre. Building on the concepts Brook holds at the heart of his theory, she argues that *LipSync* is a practice animated by what she characterizes as technologies of imagination, a concept developed both in relation to *LipSync* and as a theoretical device that translates Peter Brook's ideas into contemporary scholarly terrains.

In 'The Aesthetics of Becoming; Applied Theatre and the Quest for Cultural Certitude' Brian Heap reflects on his own practice and that of student teachers in schools in Jamaica. His chapter concerns itself primarily with the recognition of aesthetics as an essential organizing principle in drama education, but in the context of post-colonial societies where national goals of citizen empowerment and the realization of individual and communal creative potential might be well served by applied theatre. He argues that participants frequently take responsibility for shaping the aesthetic qualities of their own personal encounters with performance while they are situated inside the drama, such that social and personal skills develop as a result. Heap's earlier writing with Pamela Bowell emphasizes the attention which must be paid to the development of competences in the art form of drama if these claims for the efficacy of applied theatre are to be fully substantiated. His chapter evaluates the use of applied theatre, particularly in the context of the cultural pluralism of the Caribbean. It draws on some of the ideas of Caribbean theorists like Rex Nettleford, Eduard Glissant and Kamau Brathwaite as well as those of theatre practitioners such as Augusto Boal and Dorothy Heathcote, to interrogate issues of national and cultural identity in a globalized world.

These chapters could be organized according to different principles or agendas: there is a strong thread of interest in the issues of post-colonial countries and populations, that runs through the chapters by Adebayo, Breed, Sadeghi-Yekta and Heap. Where Heap is concerned with the part that classroom drama can play in the exploration and assertion of identity, we might see the use of performance to assert a narrative in situations where identities remain contested and in conflict, in both Breed and Sadeghi-Yekta's chapters, though with different problematics in each case, and again for Adebayo, where the identity in question is not a national or communal one. Though examined in different ways and to different degrees, the aesthetic aspect of subjectivity, culture and identity features in each of these chapters. The theatrical, and performative aesthetics that are closely examined are in each case expressive of a culture, and in tension with that culture; the outward expression of identity and the inward experience of subjectivity are aestheticized in ways that do not stop at the end of the drama.

Heap's chapter overlaps with others too, being like Hickey-Moody concerned with the techniques of performance pedagogy and young people's aesthetic engagement with self-expression. The children that Shaughnessy refers to are certainly also learning, but in work where the attention is as much on the older people they perform with; and in her other examples even older performers play unexpected roles, as aestheticized dancing bodies, again framed in contrast with younger bodies. Youth and age, in these cases, are investigated and experienced through aesthetic means.

There are other threads of technique, from Heap's unpacking of some well-known techniques in the 'applied' arsenal, through Hickey-Moody's critique and celebration of techniques of technology, to Shaughnessy's advocacy of genre-spanning dance and performance, and my own account of the acquisition of performance technique as an aesthetic experience in itself. But we could contrast with this Adebayo's challenge to applied theatre as a body of technique devoid of politics, Sadeghi-Yekta's analysis of the internationalized and instrumentalized technique of a Theatre for Development aesthetic, and a traditional performance transformed into a governmental technique in Breed's chapter. If aspects of each chapter may answer Adebayo's concerns that the applied theatre umbrella itself has no politics, by exercising political questions of different kinds, several ask awkward questions about the politics of practice or present practices that are politically questionable. In none of these does the aesthetic become detached from the political, in most it is shown to be in a profound relationship to it, either as a dimension of political action or in some cases imbricated in conflict or subjugation. In Nicola Shaughnessy's words applied arts may be best seen as having a relational and socially situated aesthetics, to reveal the artistry of the arts practitioner, as one who with collaborators of different kinds gives form to life experience, puts beauty to work and exploits both the distinctions and connections between art and life.

Part One

Aesthetics and the Aesthetic

What do we mean when we talk about 'Aesthetics'?

Consider these statements:

- We don't care about the aesthetics, our work is about the process.
- The process in this project is highly aesthetic, as much as any end product could be.
- It's politics that matter for this community, not aesthetics.
- My participants are just as capable of an aesthetic experience as anybody else.
- The aesthetic I work with is inherently political.
- Aesthetics has nothing to tell us about what matters in this kind of work.
- Aesthetics are always political, they're about the way people understand their world.

Do the words 'aesthetic' and 'aesthetics' mean the same thing in each of these sentences? We could imagine the speakers to be talking about the same work, and to be taking opposing views of that work and what is important to it. But when they use the word 'aesthetic' or 'aesthetics', are they talking about the same things? I hope it is immediately clear that they are not. Perhaps it is immediately clear what might be understood by each of these usages; or there may be some ambiguity, or fuzziness, around the edges; or perhaps it is a complete blur. The purpose of this chapter is first to unpack some potential fuzziness and ambiguity around the use of the words 'aesthetic' and 'aesthetics', and the second chapter builds on this to propose some (relatively) distinct concepts that can be useful in discussion of applied theatre.

The reason I think it is important to note these contrasting uses is that it is possible to imagine people speaking and listening to each other using the statements above, and misconstruing each other's meaning, either because of imprecision about the sense intended, or because of simply mistaking one sense of the aesthetic for another sense entirely. Where usage and understanding are imprecise, the danger of misunderstanding is perhaps as great as in a complete mismatch of meaning: with a complete mismatch it will become clear soon enough to a listener that they do not use a word in the same way as they hear it spoken; but where two speakers are vague about what they mean or what they understand by a word, they may blunder on regardless, attempting to adjust what they understand and mean to fit what they imagine the other might mean and understand, bluffing and eliding their way towards appearing to know what they speak about. 'Aesthetics' and 'aesthetic' are among those words that we (that is people in general and I myself) tend to use when we don't know precisely what we mean, and perhaps when we want to sound like we mean something sophisticated and astute.

However, there is a long-established discourse in academic philosophy which is based on secure understandings of these terms – though with different nuances and parameters associated with different schools of thought. Students of this discourse are not likely to misunderstand each other in this way or, one hopes, expend much energy bluffing about their terms; but this discourse does not, except in perhaps the most global sense, address everything suggested by everyday use. And everyday use, because of the attitudes and prejudices implied in it, is important. While the academic field of aesthetics is concerned with sensuous experience and the purpose and understanding of art, everyday uses of 'aesthetic' and 'aesthetics' approximate ideas about these things as they are relevant to ordinary life. And these everyday uses carry and perpetuate attitudes, some of which may derive from the more nuanced and contested values of the academic field, some of which betray prejudices about what should and shouldn't be considered beautiful or 'artistic', or what can safely be ignored because it belongs to that world and not to the practical concerns of everyday life. A lack of rigour in the definition of our terms is not a fault in everyday life, though when expert theatre practitioners use imprecise terms when discussing their work they may lead themselves astray. Everyday uses, therefore, are important both because they may play a part in important conversations, and also because they betray and evidence attitudes and values.[1]

The confusion around these words is particularly important for applied theatre and other applied art practices because they inhabit a peculiarly problematic territory for academic aesthetics, and because the values betrayed in everyday uses of the words are troublesome and unresolved for practitioners. Applied theatre is a problematic territory for academic aesthetics because (as I have outlined in the introduction) it takes for granted a heteronomy, a connection with that which surrounds it, whereas much of academic aesthetics is concerned with the autonomy of aesthetic judgements and of the art that gives rise to them. The values implied in uses of the words are troublesome to applied theatre because they can suggest a conservative understanding of art and its purposes: a concern with beauty, with the universality of artistic value, with forms of art that have a narrow historical and cultural pedigree, and a privileging of the visual and aural over other sensual and somatic experiences.

'Aesthetics' can be a plurality of ideas under the remit of an academic discipline, or something less obviously plural, a qualitative dimension of a practice and its associated objects. 'Aesthetic' as a singular can designate a shared understanding appropriate to such a practice, or something much broader, a category of experiences, perceptions or relationships to the world. 'Aesthetic' can also be an adjective, to differentiate things and their properties, according to these categories, dimensions and disciplines.

An aesthetic, expressed as a singular noun, is most often a style that a work of art belongs to, or an artistic language that it uses – a productive way of thinking about this, indicating that it is not only the artist who must be fluent but audiences too. An aesthetic language often invokes an implicit or explicit definition of what art is: in the simplest sense it guides us towards what to pay attention to and how to value the things we do pay attention to. In other words, this singular aesthetic, as a convention to which a set of art practices belong, has its own theory of art, its own aesthetics. This theory of art may also contain an implicit or explicit definition of the human faculties that art addresses, or the realm of being to which art experiences belong: a sense of a general category of the aesthetic. These are three interconnected but different things, each called by the same word.

But this should not be a book about words, or if it is, it should be about what the words can do for us and what we can do better with them. These words do good work for us, in each of their guises, which is why they wander so much across vital and troublesome territory. It is the territory that matters, a conceptual territory that may map across the human, historic and artistic territory of applied theatre practice, helping us to see where we stand, and where we want to go. To employ a different metaphor, the ambition is not to remove the disguises of a single coherent idea of aesthetics, but to examine how aesthetics has many faces, which may mask productively diverse ideas.

Applied theatre transgresses and re-shapes the relationships between performers and audiences, putting active participants at the heart of the performance experience. However, this sense of transgression assumes a relatively conservative conception of those relationships: the attitude that the division of roles in performance is essential and sacrosanct seems very old fashioned, for all that there are some exponents of it still living.[2] Aesthetics (as a field of philosophy concerned with art in particular) tends to engage in debates about the *ontology, phenomenology* and *judgement*[3] of works of art from a fairly conservative position, partly because these questions themselves are so difficult to answer and novel ways to approach them continue to be found, while in other fields the heteronomy of art is taken for granted. This is one of the reasons why the core questions of aesthetics, as they seek to define the particularity of art phenomena, don't feature heavily in the literature of applied theatre and socially engaged art in general. They ask the wrong questions, and start from the wrong place.

But what might be gained from re-framing some of the questions at the heart of the field of academic aesthetics? We might, for a start, be better able to argue that participatory art is art, and in what particular ways it is. The argument here is less about a need to convince the art establishment of the character and quality of any piece or project, than it is to persuade those partners and advocates of the work who see its effectiveness but habitually see benefits in terms of definable, measurable and predictable outcomes. This is a genuine problem for practitioners working with people for their benefit: there is an understandable and probably inescapable need to evidence and convince ourselves and others that scarce resources should be spent on making art in situations where art is not usually made.

As a snapshot of this issue, we might imagine a set of characters. There are the good people of the grant-making committee, eager to share their limited resources where they will do the most good, but obliged to gather evidence for that good. There is the applied theatre artist, compiling a funding application, juggling evidence and ambition. There are other competing projects that use other means, perhaps with more ample evidence, or more direct connections between input and output. There are the participants, members of a community or individuals pursuing their own interests, wanting to 'get something out' of making art. As we shall see, the connection (and the distance) between input and output, between art and its influence on the world, between autonomy and heteronomy, remains one (if not the) central puzzle of aesthetics; it is one of the questions that will be asked again throughout this book. But an input/output model of artistic work runs the risk of neglecting another important character: the art work itself.

To put it simply (and simplistically) if art is being used as an instrument (as Anthony Jackson puts it),[4] we should judge it alongside other instruments; but if art is allowed to have its full range of art-like characteristics (unpredictability, experimentation, intuition, for example), then its efficiency as an instrument is unreliable. Can art compete on these terms, with interventions that are more amenable to a precise equation between input and output? It does compete, evidently, because people in positions of power have faith in its outcomes, and because artists pursue opportunities doggedly and make their own sacrifices to ensure that work goes on, one way or another. What will pursuing this particular aesthetic question offer? A more rigorous way to argue for applied theatre's position as art, but in places where we need effect? Perhaps. Or perhaps it will allow us to ask the question in a better form.

Finally, a note about these confusing terms and how they are presented through these two chapters: as the argument progresses I distinguish 'aesthetic', 'the Aesthetic', 'aesthetic-as-language', and other variations which are explained as they appear. My aim is to make explicit what I have proposed here, that the web of meanings around the word is complex, and can benefit from some differentiation in a discussion of this kind. I do not imagine that the distinctions I employ here will *solve* this problem or expect them to be adopted elsewhere (they are not, for example, in the chapters that follow this opening section)

Philosophical aesthetics

Consider these potential definitions, in relation to the statements at the beginning of this chapter. Something is aesthetic which:

- Has an attractive, but superficial quality.
- Has a substance based on its unified, sensuous and affective properties.
- Is 'good' according to a limited set of criteria belonging to an art milieu.
- Is a particular kind of heightened experience or moment of perception.

Or an aesthetics is:

- An artistic practice, style or form, and the practices of reception associated with it.
- A theory of art, and the values that belong to that theory.
- A theory of sensuous experience in general.

If philosophical aesthetics is captured by either of the last two of these definitions, it seeks to understand the phenomena of the other five. Where it is taken as the philosophy of art primarily or exclusively, certain questions come to the fore. They might be summarized, once again, as overlapping questions of ontology, phenomenology and judgement, each having relevance to applied theatre, as each is concerned with a fundamental aspect of art phenomena that is not easily resolved, and is brought into a distinct manifestation when art is put to work in social situations. It is beyond the scope of this book to give the ontological foundation of applied theatre, its particular modes of phenomenological experience, or to reassess the grounds on which we should judge it. So I will do none of these things, though what I do say may be relevant to anyone brave (or foolhardy) enough to attempt such a thing. What I shall do instead is to map some ways in which these questions take shape in conventional aesthetics, and I shall attempt to present some alternative ways of forming the questions for the purpose of interpreting applied theatre situations. The field of aesthetic theory is so vast that to even survey it effectively is not possible here; so instead, I will draw two threads from a foundational text in the discourse, Immanuel Kant's *Critique of Judgement*, briefly outlining how he articulates aesthetic autonomy and value, suggesting how later theories are influenced by his thinking. My aim is not to comprehensively explicate the ideas, but to demonstrate the dilemmas that inhere in these matters, and in order to be able to draw on them in Chapter 2.

However aesthetics, in philosophy, also sometimes indicates a concern with something much broader, a thread – that can once again be followed from Kant through continental philosophy into contemporary critical theory – which is concerned not only with the way that human subjects experience art, but how we have experiences in general, and are constituted as subjects that can have experiences at all. As a concern with sensuous perception, aesthetics attempts to grasp aspects of human being and experience that cannot be understood through logic, ethics or metaphysics: it is about the immediate experiential dimensions of inhabiting the world. Art may be where we have some of our most intense sensuous experiences, but by seeking an understanding of its intense moments aesthetics opens up questions and approaches to the everyday sensuous realm, when it does not achieve this pitch or power. Again, beginning with Kant's approach will help to delineate these questions, though I will fall far short of resolving them.

Immanuel Kant and the emergence of aesthetics

John Carey's argument in *What Good Are the Arts*[5] is that the preservation of the distinct and specialist field of Art, abetted by much of academic and philosophical aesthetics, obscures the interconnections that it depends on and fosters as a social practice:

> Most pre-industrial societies did not even have a word for art as an independent concept, and the term 'work of art' as we use it would have been baffling to all previous cultures, including the civilisations of Greece and Rome and of Western Europe in the medieval period. These cultures would find nothing in their experience to match the special values and expectations attached to art that make it into a substitute religion, the creation of a spiritual aristocracy called geniuses, and the arena for the display of a refined discriminatory accomplishment called taste.[6]

The aim of applied theatre, and other interventionist participatory arts practices, is diametrically opposed to cultural practices and inheritances which would celebrate a 'spiritual aristocracy', or elevate 'refined discriminatory accomplishment'; instead, it seeks to promote cultural democracy in arenas that value diverse creative accomplishments.

Exploring the part that aesthetics as a discipline plays in this inherited structure, and some of the reasons for which the separation of art and life has been defended, does however reveal some conceptual tools that can be used to deepen understanding of art that seeks out and exploits its connections with life.

Although the theory of art, in the sense of careful and precise thinking about poetry, drama, painting and other activities that we now consider to belong to a realm of art, is much older, the idea that art was a category that needed its own distinct theory emerges in Europe in the eighteenth century, along with the idea of the aesthetic. As Carey tells us, through most of history, people have considered the activities of art to take place alongside and have a continuity with other 'arts': arts of cooking, fighting, religious ceremony, or government, for example. And it is the hegemony of Western culture and the academic attitudes that associate with it that has supplanted other ideas of what these techniques of making and performing and relating to the world might mean, around the non-European world. It is ironic, then, that the word that stands for this study of art as a special category derives from a Greek word with a different and broader meaning, and which was first appropriated for less narrow purposes. The word *aesthetics* was adopted for the Western philosophical tradition by Alexander Baumgarten, in 1750, in his two-volume treatise *Aesthetica*, a work that is more famous for the coining of this word than for its content.[7] The word's original Greek meaning is related to sensory perception, in opposition to rational or conscious understanding. Although Baumgarten was responding to questions about taste and judgement that were current in writing about art, for him this became part of an enquiry into 'sensitive knowing', and its autonomy from rational knowledge. Despite some objections and alternative offerings, over the next two centuries, the study of aesthetics per se drifted away from sensation in a broad sense, and towards art theory more particularly.[8] As we shall see, the recuperation of non-art aesthetics, to incorporate responses to the natural and everyday world, or to reassert the importance of sensory perception, has been proposed several times. Some contemporary approaches have suggested very strong re-definitions of a holistic aesthetics and consequently an alternative view of the ontology of art that emphasizes its heteronomy at the expense of autonomy – and I will consider some of these in Chapter 2. But for the majority of aesthetic theory, the task is to define what it is that gives art and its objects their distinctiveness and to define the autonomy of art from other realms and concerns, often in the interest of being able to give a strong account of what it is that is valuable about art, its works and its activities: in other words, to define artistic qualities.

Rather than explore the formulation of autonomy particular to each of these trends, I shall look at one theory in more detail, one which has played a huge role in installing autonomy as a key feature of aesthetic theory.[9] Among those who initiated this kind of enquiry in the Western philosophical tradition after the enlightenment there was a concern to find a basis on which thinking about beauty and art could be undertaken with the same rigour as in other branches of philosophy, but which nevertheless recognized what was distinctive about those phenomena and our experiences of them. Most significantly in the 'Third Critique' of Emmanuel Kant, the *Critique of Judgement* (1790) is found a rigorous and systematic – although still persistently controversial – account of judgements of taste, and in it a very influential idea of the aesthetic in general.[10] In this section, I will outline the basis of this judgement, concentrating on responses to beauty, and I will follow this by discussing the motivations for his approach, and what the consequences of his ideas have been, so that in the next chapter the discussion can move on to what we might draw from it to the advantage of applied theatre. I will neglect, due to constraints of space and in the interests of clarity, Kant's treatment of the sublime, which would be necessary to a full exposition of his argument; the summary I will offer here is inevitably far short of a full account of its complexity that this may not be a significant drawback.

Famously, Kant's 'Analytic of the Beautiful' is composed of four 'moments' of the judgement of taste: disinterest, universality, purposiveness and necessity. Each of these is to some extent a paradoxical characteristic because what distinguishes judgements of taste as a special class of mental operations is that *they aren't based on concepts.* Kant tells us that these judgements are important and consequential, they matter to us to the extent that we feel that others should share them, but they neither reflect ideas that we can articulate and use to persuade other people, nor depend on how useful a thing is to us, how it might benefit us, or give us pleasure. They are unlike the ideas that we entertain through our faculties of understanding and practical reason in that we can't deduce them through careful thought, nor through observation of the empirical world; nevertheless, in the four moments, we find (he says) the ways in which these judgements appear to us like mental operations that are based on concepts. This 'conceptless' character is very important to Kant's schema, and has consequences for all of the aesthetic theory that follows after him; in the first instance, however, it is the key element of his claim for what is distinctive about 'the aesthetic'.

Each of the moments of the judgement of taste is related to their manifestation to us as if they are important and consequential, but without having the usual basis on which we would understand that importance. When we encounter things that will bring material benefit to us, that are sensually pleasant to us, or are evidently good for other people as well as or instead of us, the satisfaction we feel from them is *interested*. Though the pleasure we feel in response to something beautiful may feel similar subjectively, it is distinct because it is not provoked by any of these kinds of interest. Instead, Kant says: 'Taste is the faculty of judging of an object or a method of representing it by an entirely disinterested satisfaction or dissatisfaction. The object of such satisfaction is called beautiful.'[11] As a consequence of this, judgements of taste also behave for us as if they were *universal*: if we feel satisfaction in something where that satisfaction doesn't depend on our particular circumstances, we 'must believe that [we have] reason for attributing a similar satisfaction to everyone.'[12] Kant allows that people have preferences for different things: colours or musical instruments, for example, much as we do for different food and drink.

But this alternative (and more common in contemporary language) conception of taste cannot be applied to the beautiful; it is laughable to Kant to claim that something is 'beautiful for me', and absurd not to feel that we should demand that others should agree with us when we perceive something beautiful; even though we know that when others disagree, we have no rational argument to draw on to persuade them that our judgement is right. *Purposiveness* is the sense that a thing is aimed towards some kind of an end, that it will result in something and is formed in order to achieve that result. In aesthetic judgements, however, there can be no ends in this sense, as they would amount to interests of some kind or another. And yet beautiful things present themselves to us *as if* they have purposes; Kant finds that this subjective experience of purposiveness is at the basis of aesthetic judgement. We cannot help but think of beautiful things as if they had purposes, although if we examine them and find that they do have actual purposes, we will have undone their aesthetic nature, and reduced them to mere ordinary objects. Because it replicates the pleasure we experience when we contemplate things that are perfectly suited to their ends, although it has no such end in this case, purposiveness is the source of the pleasure we find in beautiful things.

The fourth moment is the aesthetic judgement's *necessity*, not a practical necessity which we could articulate with recourse to concepts, but a subjective necessity (and as with the other moments, the contradiction here is quite deliberate). It occurs to us in a process, which is undeniably subjective as it cannot derive from an objective cognitive judgement, but which again compels us to assent to it, and as before with universality, to expect that others do too. And as we do expect other people to share our pleasure in beautiful things, we must be aware of something that connects us to those other people: Kant calls this a 'common sense', or *sensus communis*. It is not common sense in terms of the practical reasoning that might tell us to put on a coat on a cold day, but something in the faculties of rational beings which ensures that ideas of this kind can come to all of us. I will return to this kind of common sense in Chapter 2.

Important to all these 'moments', which are effectively all different ways of describing what must logically be in place if we are to give value to an idea that is not based on concepts (which we could be forgiven for reading as 'an idea that is not an idea'), is that they all show aesthetic judgement as *something that happens to us*,[13] rather than something we arrive at through consideration or debate.

There are many more subtleties and complexities (and contradictions) in the *Critique of Judgement* that Kant has to do considerably more work to prove the distinctive givenness[14] of Aesthetic judgements. The moments of the beautiful are described as much in relation to the natural world as to human made objects, but there is more work to do to take account of art, or Art, as Kant styles it, to make the distinction between that which provokes aesthetic judgements in us, and lesser achievements. The arts in general are imbued with interests, purposes and content, and belong to their local conditions, so the aesthetic aspect of an art work is that which defies all these evident facts. The aesthetic and Art emerge out of art works, or rather out of our encounter with them, because of the genius of the artist, the capacity to create something that awakens the 'free play' of our sensible and cognitive faculties. Genius is that capacity for this free play, when it is harnessed to technique. Fine Art is the arena where we can find this free play, and as viewers of art, release it in ourselves.

Kant was motivated to define a 'faculty' that would unite the faculties of understanding and practical reason, the subjects of his two earlier *critiques*. His reasoning in this work takes on a central role in his overall philosophical thinking, not just about the theory of art (although that is where it has been most influential), but about subjectivity's relationship with the objective world. It is possible that his definition of the aesthetic is given such prominence so that it could serve as the exemplar of this faculty, and thus resolve what would otherwise seem to be two mutually exclusive realms of philosophy. His confidence that judgements of taste take the shape that he describes seems to be based on little other than his own conviction that this is how they are 'given' to us. The result of the emphasis on the autonomy of this faculty is a similar emphasis on autonomy in aesthetics. Because his writings on aesthetics, judgement and the beautiful have been read in relation to art more often than in relation to everyday or natural objects, variations on or responses to this perspective have been widely adopted ever since. In this derivation, art is art because it is somehow detached from the world. Disinterest and universality become key values in the art world, the necessity of judgements and the purposelessness of art (as the basis of its peculiar purposiveness) are taken for granted, and other characteristics of art works fade from view or are discounted as non-aesthetic and therefore not belonging to the realm of Art at all. This idea, consequently, has been associated with the field of aesthetics, so that in situations where the heteronomy of art is considered vitally important, either to creating art or to critiquing it, aesthetics and its perspectives have tended to be thrown out, and along with it respect for the beautiful.

Kant's aesthetics can be seen as a kind of formalism in that it is based on the formal structure of the relationship between the object and the subjectivity perceiving it; or perhaps to put it more correctly, it is based on the relationship among parts of that subjectivity. The imagination and sensibility, in a kind of free play, overcome the rational mind and convince us that what we have encountered conforms to a satisfying concept, even though it is absent. The apparent fit between what our mental structure and the objects which it is never entirely able to grasp, suggests a symmetry between the two (in the sublime, the other variety of Aesthetic experience that he deals with in detail, it is the overwhelming asymmetry, our inability to grasp the scale or power of the objective world that makes an impression). Ostensibly this theory says nothing about the content of an artwork. But the effect of this close and restrictive definition of judgements of taste, of the beautiful, and of the aesthetic itself, is to place a very high value on these experiences and on objects that we expect to provoke them. The common sense shared by all human beings can all too easily become, in the face of everyday evidence that some people have more in common than others, especially in relation to the cultivated life that is required in order to give time to these objects, an exclusive community rather than a general and plural one. The genius that is able to draw on the faculty of taste in the making of objects becomes a special class of individuals rather than a capacity of people in general. These are not necessarily what Kant intended, but they are among the consequences of his work.

However, in the autonomy of judgements, particularly their capacity to occur to us without our willing them or reasoning them out, I see both the limit and the continuing power of what Kant proposes. He admits at several points in the *Critique of Judgement* that beautiful things are found in situations where interests and purposes are plain and obvious: artists are dependent on their work, as are collectors and tradespeople; beautiful plants and animals can also be valued as food or as goods to trade; beautiful poetry, speeches and performances are used to mark important occasions and to enact rituals. But Kant insists that there is a kernel of something beyond and not dependent upon these ends and interests, that is worth our attention and worth his painstaking investigation; that the Aesthetic has its own truth. Contemporary readers might find his moments of aesthetic judgement counter-intuitive. Being accustomed to a more relativist world view we might prefer to say that things are beautiful to us individually, and instinctively resist imposing our judgements on others, or we might see how our perceptions belong to our class and culture, and always embody interests that are subtly disguised. And as arts practitioners we may have purposes in mind that we do not want to make extrinsic to what we do and its status as Art. But with a little moderation of the language – or an allowance that more than one concept of beauty and the aesthetic might be at work in the same situation – we might also find that the pure, rare and illuminating experience of beauty is something that occurs to us in addition, and in supplement, to the social character of art and all its undeniable complex connectedness. We might benefit from ways of thinking about this work that secures its value without reducing it to the moral, ethical and political.

The critique of aesthetics and progressive alternatives

The autonomy of the Aesthetic (and of Art) remains an important theme from Kant up to the present day. Questions of artistic quality depend upon whether art can claim its own truth as a basis for that quality; and questions of artistic ontology, for example whether the essence of a work resides in an object or in the perceiver of that object, depend on the relationship of objects or processes of perception to other objects and processes. In the nineteenth century, Romantic views of art predicated on the potential to express things inexpressible in other ways were contrasted with the Hegelian[15] view of art as valuable, but ultimately subordinate to philosophical enquiry. In the twentieth century, writers such as Theodor Adorno[16] proposed that the autonomy of works of art is what gives them their political potential, standing as a critique of repressive social reality, while others such as George Dickie[17] developed institutional, or 'art world' models which made the autonomy of any work a product of the practices that go into its production, circulation and reception. Most importantly for our purposes, critical theory has attacked the principle of artistic autonomy, on the grounds that, in creating space for art to have independence from other ways of knowing or finding truth, it absolves it of ethical responsibility, and reifies certain bodies of work and their content as above political concerns.

Raymond Williams, in *Keywords*, briefly outlines the history of the term *aesthetics* up to his own vantage point, and observes of its focus on the subjective experience of beauty:

> It is an element in the divided modern consciousness of art and society: a reference beyond social use and social valuation which, like one special meaning of culture, is intended to express a human dimension which the dominant version of society appears to exclude. The emphasis is understandable but the isolation can be damaging,

for there is something irresistibly displaced and marginal about the now common and limiting phrase 'aesthetic considerations', especially when contrasted with practical UTILITARIAN . . . considerations, which are elements of the same basic division.[18]

Thus, disinterest becomes a problem, and the language of aesthetics betrays a dysfunctional separation of art from life. For many progressive theorists, like Williams, this separation preserves art as a bourgeois institution, serving to exclude the majority of people from either enjoying the 'fine arts' or using them to reflect or change their own lives. Pierre Bourdieu's sociological investigations, for example, demonstrate how the appreciation of art, along with other cultural activity, serves the reproduction of privilege for those who are raised to gain the habits of and dispositions for art, and using it to connect and communicate with others of the same social class; the title of his *Distinction: A Social Critique of the Judgement of Taste*[19] is a direct reference to Kant, and a challenge to his transcendental model. For Bourdieu, the separation and purity of the fine arts make them a particularly useful tool in this regard, in contrast to popular arts which are more intrinsically connected to life, and therefore more easily excluded from the refined field of the aesthetic.[20] The dynamics of the different art forms, their traditions and the ways they are produced and used are manifestly historically specific, and perpetuate themselves as long as they serve interests. Terry Eagleton, in *The Ideology of the Aesthetic*, traces the conservative tendency of the discipline as it emerged and mutated from Baumgarten through to Michel Foucault, and articulates the very idea of the aesthetic as a prop to bourgeois subjectivity.[21] In the later twentieth-century critical philosophy and progressive theorizing about art and culture, aesthetics went out of fashion. The sense that the subject matter of the fine arts, their systems of circulation and value, belong to a privileged, male, white, conservative arena has led feminist and post-colonial perspectives on art to develop new and distinctly non-universal theories and practices: in the distinctions that I tentatively mapped in the Introduction, they tend to reject aesthetics as a discipline and initiate their own specific aesthetic-as-language, attuned to presenting that which traditional fine art obscured in a way that communicates with those it tended to ignore.

For Janet Wolff, however, the critique of aesthetics and its values has become 'kalliphobia',[22] an aversion to the beautiful, and a tendency towards ugliness in art. The recognition of the beautiful remains important to art criticism, even if its transcendence and absolute autonomy are no longer convincing; citing Lisa Tickner, she says:

> When we have done with the valuable work of demonstrating the various social factors in play in privileging certain work, determining which people have access to art, and producing particular ideological effects in the works themselves, we still have not answered the primary question of aesthetics: how good is it?[23]

In her proposal for an *aesthetics of uncertainty* she argues for a restoration of the importance of aesthetic judgements that puts questions of beauty into context, recognizing social production, exposing mechanisms of cultural domination and making criteria explicit. Elaine Scarry, similarly, regrets that the critique of beauty 'seeks to make the whole sensorium utilitarian',[24] even though the substance of her influential book *On Beauty and Being Just* is a theory of how beauty impels us towards creativity, caring for others, and caring for truth and justice. Isobel Armstrong takes up the challenge of Eagleton's *Ideology of the Aesthetic*, by re-framing the aesthetic for its radical potential to create a dialectical space to play with contradictions and paradoxes and to transform the structures of perception.

> [T]he components of aesthetic life are those that are already embedded in the processes and practices of consciousness – playing and dreaming, thinking and feeling. Or, put another way, ceaseless mediation endows language-making and symbol-making, thought, and the life of affect,

with creative and cognitive life. These processes – experiences that keep us alive – are common to everyone, common to what the early Marx called species being.[25]

Each of these writers returns the aesthetic to centre stage, but with considerable limits on its autonomy, insisting that art and its philosophy must pay attention to its contexts and its outcomes, but also that it is eminently suited to doing so. But in some senses, aesthetics never left this twentieth-century (and twenty-first-century) critical theory, which has always paid attention to art, and has always been concerned with the nature of subjectivity and subjective experiences. The 'species being' that Armstrong cites in Marx's is the beginning of a non-transcendental approach to the *sensus communis*, to what it is that people have in common.

From Kant onwards the importance of subjective experiences of these kinds to the understanding of experience and subjectivity in general has become increasingly clear. Much of this theory is very relevant, and familiar, to applied theatre dealing as it does with power relations and how they are hidden from view and perpetuated. The theories of ideology and hegemony are concerned with how subjectivity is constituted, as a felt experience of a place in a social order. They are also substantially grounded in theories of how the materials of art are the tools for constructing these subjectivities, especially writing and the visual arts. Language is the fundamental building block of a socialized, civilized and alienated sense of self, for Heidegger, Lacan and Derrida.[26] This is at its most imposing in the spoken language through which we learn to speak of ourselves, and find the grammar of subjectivity upon which to build our place in the world, but it is in response to the 'text' of written language where the critique is most sustained and stringent. The idea of the text, in which we read representations of ourselves and our relations to others, and which writes itself onto our bodies, is applied to other forms: other kinds of text, visual, aural and performative, with their varieties of grammar, impose themselves on us. Each (and other key figures such as Hans Georg Gadamer and Jean-Francois Lyotard) incorporates explicit theories of art, sometimes under the name of 'aesthetics', confirming its importance in the creation of subjectivity, and its importance to this tradition of philosophy, but aesthetics runs through this theory, as it interprets a vast range of phenomena as the interrelationships of texts and subjects. Aesthetics, viewed in this way, is concerned with ontology, phenomenology and quality for human subjects as such, having evolved from the question of how such subjects make judgements of taste, to how they are shaped in their sensuous encounters with the objective world.

The relationship of aesthetics to power has been tackled more directly, however, by Jacques Rancière. His critical approach to the historicism of the contemporary art world and its institutions – characterized as an 'aesthetic regime'[27] – involves a complex reading of autonomy and heteronomy, and culminates in a paradox. We must accept that both are true simultaneously, that art is intimately connected with the world while also remaining detached from it. In this way it legitimates itself as a distinct regime, while also having effects and being affected by its context. Disinterest is both an enabling fiction and a counter-intuitive requisite for political art; autonomy is ideologically conservative, but also potentially a vehicle for 'redistribution of the sensible'.

Rancière's theory of aesthetics has a number of threads, all of which depend on the 'lessons in inequality' that support and are taught by the current order of society. These lessons are found also in education, philosophy and political theory and action. The essence of the lesson in inequality is that there are authorities and experts who understand, and can communicate their understanding, and others who will always have to consult with, trust or learn from these authorities. The poor are consigned to this position of ignorance by a social order much like Plato's Republic, in which people are given and are destined to remain in positions appropriate to them. Artists are in danger of joining the ranks of these oppressive experts, particularly when they attempt to make art that is explicitly or instrumentally political. They are in danger of reinforcing a 'distribution of the sensible' in which the privilege of making, enjoying and speaking about art is unequally shared. It is

tempting to see the 'redistribution of the sensible' in work like applied theatre, which seeks to reconfigure relationships of subjugation
and subjectification, but Rancière is quite explicit, in books such as
The Emancipated Spectator,[28] that art or artists pursuing these ends
deliberately are to be equated with the pedagogues and philosophers
who try to emancipate others but only reproduce a self-serving
power dynamic. Though it is very instructive, and provocative, as an
analysis of the ideological power of art and the limits of interventionist
art, this theory is difficult to apply as a tool for the understanding of
interventionist theatre, so stringent is its criticism of intervening
artists.

Dewey's pragmatist aesthetics

Few major figures in the Anglo-American tradition of analytic
philosophy devote space to aesthetics in this way. It is instead generally
seen as a sub-discipline with its own esoteric questions that have little
to contribute beyond the discussion of art. John Dewey is a notable
exception, and his writing has undergone a renaissance at the hands of
some contemporary pragmatist philosophers who ally it to advances
in neuroscience and cognitive philosophy – I shall return to two of
these writers (Richard Shusterman and Mark Johnson) in the following
chapter. The principles of pragmatism, in general, are that philosophy is
directed at action as well as observation and analysis, and that the most
important meaning and knowledge is that on the basis of which people
are likely to act. Although pragmatists have respect for the principle
that truth is ultimately achievable through scientific and philosophical
enquiry (their approach is not relativist), they do not start by investigating
transcendent principles, but by looking for what is known and how it
can be put to work in a situation, whether in theoretical or practical
terms. Dewey's *Art as Experience* applies these principles by focussing
on the phenomenological involvement of the viewer and artist in the
moments of appreciation and production.[29] Continuity between art and

other aspects of life, experience and behaviour is central, as is the bodily engagement of the 'live creature'.[30] Although art experiences expose us to 'the immaterial', sensuous and physical involvement is fundamental to this encounter and its manifold pleasures are not set aside as merely 'agreeable' as they are by Kant. He distinguishes between experience in general and 'having an experience'[31] as something which stands out from the general flow. Art's capability to bring about such an elevated and individualized moment is called a 'consummation', and has its own qualitative unity which run-of-the-mill experience lacks:

> Experience in the degree in which it is experience is heightened vitality. Instead of signifying being shut up within one's own private feelings and sensations, it signifies active and alert commerce with the world; at its height it signifies complete interpenetration of self and the world of objects and events.[32]

This contrast with the 'inchoate' of humdrum experience preserves a special character for the aesthetic, but while remaining very open about what aspects of experience can be drawn together in this consummation.

Dewey was also very open-minded about popular art forms, and didn't restrict his view of the aesthetic to fine art. The work of the artist and 'the expressive object' remain important to him, but are subordinate to experience in its everyday sense, with its active and passive aspects. He refers to these as 'what is done and what is undergone', cumulatively building towards expressiveness, and subordinate to the experience of art:

> Art throws off the covers that hide the expressiveness of experienced things; it quickens us from the slackness of routine and enables us to forget ourselves by finding ourselves in the delight of experiencing the world about is in its various qualities and forms.[33]

Giving form to expression is the fundamental of the creative act, such that form and content are not distinguishable. Even more importantly, the distinctions of rationality and sensuality are meaningless to Dewey;

in this he is explicitly and adamantly opposed to Kant, as Armstrong puts it:

> By making experience central to his theory, Dewey deftly refuses to distribute the aesthetic across the conventionally accepted categories. He never splits up the aesthetic between producer, or artist, or artwork, and consumer or audience. Experience crosses the boundaries between maker, art object and response and reconfigures them . . . the potential for responding to and making the aesthetic is in everyone, possibilities held in common by the fact of being alive. Arousal is the cause and effect of experience and the aesthetic alike – and it occurs everywhere in our lives.[34]

So Dewey offers us a theory of art and the aesthetic that is founded on a theory of general experience first, and which prioritizes the continuity and heteronomy of art. It is especially relevant because of its pluralism; it suggests how art makes meanings in a way that puts very few boundaries around the idea of art, what it is, or who makes it.

Dewey's sense of the continuity of art with experience in general is echoed in the continuity between his aesthetic theory and his general epistemology, and its social and pedagogic extensions. Thomas Alexander summarizes the thesis of Dewey's *Experience and Nature*, published 7 years before *Art as Experience*, as a model for how:

> [M]embers of a community, rather than a single isolated organism, pursue through the use of symbol, expression and communication the ongoing project of directing experience towards intrinsically fulfilling ends which give human existence its depth of value and meaning. . . . [Experience] signifies the shared social activity of symbolically mediated behaviour which seeks to discover the possibilities of our objective situation in the natural world for meaningful, intelligent and fulfilling ends. And the skill at doing this Dewey calls 'art'.[35]

Experience itself is the basis of human understanding, rather than differentiated faculties of cognition, and it is mediated and facilitated both by our social interactions and the symbolic languages that they are based on. Far from needing to defend the autonomy of 'Art', Dewey's 'esthetics' places 'art' at the centre of human life, and its possibilities for fulfilment and change.

The aesthetics of participation

What are the aesthetics of *participation*? For me they form a longer and broader project that overlaps with applied theatre aesthetics. It includes audience participation in other kinds of theatre, people's participation in theatre as performers and makers, whether professional or amateur, and eventually theatre and performance attendance generally along with other kinds of cultural participation in and beyond the performing arts. It seems to me a worthwhile project to bring together and examine all the participatory aspects of performance through the same set of critical lenses, and under the various rubrics of 'aesthetics' as I begin to frame them here, but it is a project for other times and other books. It is relevant to the project of this book, as applied theatre in all of its forms engages questions of participation, whether directly in seeking to understand the effects of people's involvement in making theatre themselves, or in the potential of theatre to inspire participation in other forms of life beyond itself. But the two don't map entirely onto each other. Applied theatre asks questions about efficacy and politics, about beauty and quality, and about the nature of art, in distinctive ways. And insofar as all theatre forms can be deployed in 'applied settings', whatever their participatory elements, all theatre forms can be interrogated with these questions; but not all forms of participation in theatre need to be interrogated through the lens of applied theatre. Nevertheless, outlining the dimensions of the aesthetics of participation here will be of use in indicating some of the specific problems of the aesthetics of applied theatre.

Aesthetics is one sense a synonym for 'the theory of art', so in an important sense all thinking about art can be described as aesthetics, so all thinking about participatory art is part of an aesthetics of participation.

But what is distinctive is thinking about participation as art. That is, about an *ontology* of art that includes all sorts of activity that is usually treated as separate from art's objects and interactions, a *phenomenology* of art that has room for all dimensions of the participants' experiences, and a theory of *judgement,* or *value* that places these experiences at its centre. This requires interrogation, if not resolution, of heteronomy and autonomy, and of the distinction between the 'artwork' (i.e. the object made and perceived), the art 'work' (i.e. activity, labour) and the participatory 'artwork' (i.e. integrated, process-based, and created activity).

Participation in applied theatre is most often, or most characteristically, a matter of projects spanning days, weeks or months rather than involvement of audiences in performances themselves – though interactions of this kind are employed in some important forms, most notably perhaps in work drawing on Theatre of the Oppressed techniques. Aesthetics in applied theatre must encompass these processes, as well as the theatrical products they often lead to. The language of aesthetics is attuned to the fully consummated experiences that viewers, readers and spectators have of completed works, not to the difficulties and conflicts of extended engagement with non-professional participants. There will be moments of beauty, and other typically aesthetic experiences in these processes, but the difficulties and conflicts are important too, often being when the most significant learning or personal change happens. An aesthetics of participation should attend to all of these elements of process.

The idea that the process of making audiences into participants is an artistic process in itself, rather than just a means to create these new relationships, is one way of developing an aesthetic approach to applied theatre. That is, the process of being invited to join in, take a role, take the initiative, has meaning in a way that can be understood in the same way that performances themselves (and other works of art) are understood. But an aesthetics of participation for applied theatre would define longer-term, process-based activities that may or may not lead to performances for other audiences as artworks of this kind. Thus, it would recognize that the differences are incremental between the work of the facilitator greeting a new group and directing a scene with that group; between joining the group as a participant and acting that scene for an audience; between feeling oneself acting out a theatrical scene without an audience and the feeling of involvement as an audience member; and between sitting in a seat to watch a scene on a stage, and walking around an art gallery or a creatively transformed railway arch, factory or council estate, as is often the case in other forms of participatory performance.

In each of these cases there are practices which engage people and encourage them to participate constructively, and there are ways in which the activity of the participant is valued, and in which that value is communicated. What an aesthetics of participation must show is how the practices of participation and the experiences of participation should be valued as art works, accepting that some of these practices and experiences will involve working on people's emotional states and interpersonal dynamics. In other words, the material that is shaped in participatory performance includes the activity of the participant, and this shaping includes what might be called the manipulation of those participants so that they achieve interesting and important things. The idea of manipulation is troublesome, when applied to people it implies an unethical aspect, and connotations of deceit, control or coercion, which it would not when applied to the inert materials that artists work with in other circumstances. I will not discuss at any length how participatory action and its interpersonal strategies amount to the manipulation of aesthetic material, in these terms. This is an idea which I have examined elsewhere,[36] but not in detail in relation to applied theatre; a fuller development of an aesthetics of participation, for applied theatre, would consider it in more depth.

Though there may not be a coherent applied theatre aesthetic, there are nevertheless things that tend to be in common across the aesthetic languages observed in applied theatre. The orientation towards participation rather than presentation for the benefit of others is, of course, often framed in terms of the relative importance of process and product; Augusto Boal, in *Aesthetics of the Oppressed*, indicates a balance struck between the two in his practice:

> It is important to note the distinction which I make here between the making, that is, the Artistic Process, and the thing once it is already finished, or the Artistic Product. Process and Product – for the latter to exist, the former is necessary; though the Aesthetic Process does not necessarily have to result in an Artistic Product – it can be inconclusive. This will, however, be where we aim.[37]

An aesthetics of process suggests the value of working through, motivated by an end point of some kind, but not necessarily arriving conclusively at that end point, and that this working through is an aesthetic experience in its own right. Performance skill is not always important, or not important in the same ways it is in other kinds of theatre. Landy and Montgomerie describe the priorities of one of the pioneers of classroom drama:

> [Dorothy] Heathcote was not interested in the quality of acting or the theatrical skills demonstrated by the student with whom she played the scene. . . . When guiding sessions, she consistently drew students into her thought process, moving in and out of various status roles and making decisions along the way about optimal activities to serve the students and provoke their thinking.[38]

The technique described here is aimed at deepening the involvement of the students, rather than creating polished performances for the benefits of others, obviously. But it is still aimed at a high-quality experience that can be achieved only through such artistic methods; it is an aesthetic experience stimulated by the artistic skill of the facilitating teacher-in-role, who manipulates her own role-play, but also the relationships she has with the students and their involvement in the dramatic action. This manipulation of persona and relationship and structuring of participatory involvement is the artistry of the facilitator; it is in common, although in very different forms, in most kinds of applied theatre, and is a key dimension of the aesthetics of participation.

Chrissie Poulter says that this artistry is partly a matter of 'guardianship',[39] protecting people into activity not only via the choice of facilitation strategy, but also through the facilitator's presence in the work, via personality and felt judgement. Boal, in his books, gives some suggestions about how to use some exercises, but:

> He doesn't say what he does, how he reads a group, and who he is in the workshop. I'm wondering – can we as drama practitioners take more responsibility for consciously inscribing what we understand of our role as facilitator, without saying this is the only way of doing it? Can we enable someone else to take the work, make it their own, and be a good guardian?[40]

'Taking the work, making it our own' – this is the phrasing of an artist, and in this case expresses a need in the training of facilitators for the development of sensitivity and artistry. We might consider, by extension, that the thing shaped by this artistry is participation itself, the actual experiences of participants but also the potential participation that is latent in the scheme of work, the workshop plan, or the structure of a participatory performance; all of these things can be considered art works, and thus as proper objects of study for aesthetics.

Both Thompson and Shaughnessy indicate the importance of seeing participation as an aesthetic experience. Thompson, for example, seeing it explicitly for its potential for realizing beauty, which he characterizes as 'that moment of pleasurable, world-stopping sensation created through observing and, more particularly, participating in artistic activity.'[41] Conventional aesthetics, however, is guilty of 'beholder bias', a 'failure to take the perspective of the maker seriously',[42] and Thompson proposes a shift of focus towards the potential for beauty in the experience of the maker, and of the participant in performance particularly, and towards people and processes as aesthetic objects. Similarly, Shaughnessy pursues a participatory aesthetic, looking to academic writing about fine art and its move towards social or 'relational' practices for ideas of the 'decentring' of the art work, and for ideas of how the performer's body is an aesthetic object to the performer him/herself.[43]

Looking towards the following chapter, this discussion suggests that an aesthetics of participation needs to be:

- Open, widely applicable and plural, attending to a wide range of different people's experience; and
- To a plurality of different experiences, allowing that both the heightened and rare Aesthetic and experiences of art making that are more mundane, inconclusive or difficult are important to participatory art forms.

Consciously turning from a 'beholder bias' to a participant perspective, I suggest it is necessary to explore how we can more precisely define in what ways the participant may be an aesthetic object, functioning simultaneously as artist, audience and art work, and that an aesthetics of participation should attend to:

- How participants experience themselves (bodies, voices, and social selves) as part of a work of art as they perform, rehearse, take part in other related activity and reflect;
- How some of these experiences compare to the intense experiences that can occur in response to the very best art work;
- How these experiences are shaped by practitioners, and by participants themselves.

Interlude: *Eye Queue Hear*

Access All Areas is a theatre company that works with people with learning disabilities, based in Shoreditch in London's East End.[1] They run programmes that develop communication skills and reduce isolation, and which challenge negative public perceptions of learning disability. But alongside this interventionist and effects-based agenda, they insist that they produce performances for their own sake, and develop their participants as performers and theatre artists. Several regular group members have acted professionally, and in 2014 the company began to deliver a formal diploma in theatre making in collaboration with Central School of Speech and Drama. Like many other organizations that do what the academy calls applied theatre, and are aware of and articulate in its discourse, the group's permanent staff and facilitators intend that the work they make inhabits the theatre and performance world as much as it does the world of social intervention and community politics. Artistic Director Nick Llewellyn says: 'We believe in the power of art to change things, but we also believe in art for art's sake.'[2] It is fundamental to the company's ethos that they are a group that has the right to make their own art in their own way.

Some of the groups are very political: aware of the prejudice they face and its effect on their opportunities, and aware of what they would like to change and how they want to express themselves. They want to make ambitious and challenging performance, and their recent work demonstrates that their ability to critically reflect on their experience can become, with direction and facilitation, the basis of a subtle and substantial work of art. A piece of work that straddles these worlds is *Eye Queue Hear*, a performative audio walk that was devised through the summer of 2013 and performed in September of that year.[3] The performing company of seven worked with directors Nick Llewellyn and Ciara Brennan creating responses to the history and form of IQ tests, and

Figure 1 *Eye Queue Hear.* (Photograph: Caroline Moore).

to the streets of the locality around their rehearsal space in Hoxton and the performers' relationships to them. Its audience wore headphones and followed the performers, while hearing a multi-layered soundscape of recordings made by the group in rehearsals and on the streets where the performance took place. *Eye Queue Hear* was funded by Arts Council England, as a piece of contemporary theatre and on the basis of the training opportunities it offered, and did not draw substantially on funds directed at the support for learning disabled communities.

It had two audiences: those who bought tickets and followed the whole piece, listening to the soundtrack, and those passersby and residents who came upon it by accident, stumbling upon the group of young people. 'The Seven' (as they were called in the programme) were doing peculiar things; at different points in the 1-hour performance walking in slow motion through busy shopping streets, miming breaking shop windows, or dancing to Jimmy Cliff's 'You Can Get It If You Really Want' outside a nineteenth-century laundry building. Llewellyn says that this was the audience that excited him the most, and that seeing them following the procession of performers and headphone-wearing audience members confirmed that the piece had many layers of effect, and that there were many ways of accessing it. Post-performance surveys showed that many of the official audience were new to the company and to 'disability arts', not regular supporters of the company or people with interests or investment in this community. Those who were drawn into the piece while going about their daily business – who may or may not be aware of the issues faced by young learning disabled people – did not have an experience informed by the mission of Access All Areas, or by *Eye Queue Hear's* publicity. They may or may not have identified the performers as people with learning disabilities; they may or may not have been aware of the 'audio walk' as a form. Their experience of the performance was inevitably shorter and less detailed than the main audience – they couldn't hear the sound track that the official audience heard throughout the performance – but it was potentially fresher and more surprising and there may have been more potential for uncanny or unnerving effects.

For the main audience, the experience was both very personal and individual – the headphones discouraging interaction between audience members – and potentially intimate in the connection it could suggest with the performers. The recording evoked a kind of stream of consciousness, made up of fragments of speech and recorded sound: IQ test questions, snatches of conversation, memories being re-told, and noises that could have been coming from the life of the street as we walked but which seemed to be traces of other days on the same streets. As an audience member myself I found the soundscape disorienting, at the same time as having the effect of orienting me in the interior life of the performers we were walking with. While there was little direct communication from the performers, there was the potential to identify the recording with their thoughts or thought processes, and to enjoy something of a composite world view, in an impressionistic, non-linear fashion.

It also struck me as a beautiful work of art, in a variety of ways. The performance I saw (and participated in) took place on a sunny September afternoon, and the cumulative effect of music and layered voices over the course of nearly an hour's walking and watching made the climactic sequence – in which the performers separated from each other and with their arms open and heads raised to the sky spiralled through the circular grounds of Shoreditch's Boundary Gardens, until each stood still under a tall tree – very powerful. Other beautiful moments were more fleeting, such as the delight when a sound effect of breaking glass matched the gestures of the performers, or more spontaneous, as when I caught the eye of the passersby, and sensed their confusion at the action unfolding before them.

For Llewellyn the beauty of the piece derives from a kind of 'transcendence' inherent in the technique of using recordings and headphones in this way: the way they can simultaneously locate us even more firmly in everyday circumstance, and offer detachment from it. The constructed aural experience is interpenetrated by chance sounds, and the rehearsed performance also interacts with ordinary goings-on, creating a kind of composite or palimpsest; like the multiplicity of audiences, the performance itself is made up of layers. But he also sees beauty in the way the piece reveals the 'hidden voices' of the performing group, in hearing their playful and profound reflections and observations aired in such an unexpected and oblique way. The performers too found the work beautiful as they performed it. Paul Christian, for example, agreed with me that 'the end was beautiful, it drained me of energy, it was so emotional and beautiful', while Jolene Sampson found beauty in the music especially, which 'got you going, got the emotions going'. Dayo Koleosho's comment on the beauty of the performance is particularly striking: 'It was absolutely beautiful, like being taken on a journey. You can't wait to find out where it leads you. Looking up and seeing the light shining on you, is how you're feeling.' His understanding of the aesthetic quality of the performance is closely associated with its structure and its gestural vocabulary, and the specific affect of the performance on this particular day; but he re-casts these performance elements to describe what he understood, how he felt and what he imagines other people in the audience felt. Paul Christian, too, saw the piece as about 'self-discovery', while Lee Phillips described it to me as: 'Searching for an answer. You're on a journey looking for an answer. Like you feel inspired by people and want to follow them to see what you can achieve'.

It is clear that the piece has a particular aesthetic, in the sense of style or language that I have begun to explore. What is interesting and less straightforward is how the aesthetic of the audio walk, which the piece may share with other works using similar techniques, is enhanced in specific ways to become the aesthetic of this audio walk with young learning disabled performers, and then how this specific aesthetic evokes a variety of beauty that has something to do with the identity of the performers and how their experiences are shared. The aesthetic of the piece is based on a performance language that makes a strength out of the group's capabilities, which might be felt as limitations in other forms. The rigours of theatrical representation in most cases demands a precision and clarity which is not beyond this group, but which they will be less likely to manage consistently, such that it may be difficult even to play themselves 'convincingly' within the expectations of the form. That is, to realistically communicate the interior life and exterior attributes of someone with a learning disability in the dominant aesthetic of theatre – naturalistic or otherwise – demands that lines and moves are repeated accurately, inflections of speech have consistency and subtlety, and words and gestures are clear enough to reach everyone in the audience every time. This is a standard that is not unattainable for the performers of Access All Areas, but it is not, perhaps, an approach that gives them the best opportunity to easily and fluently communicate. An aesthetic that rewards the unpredictable and the imprecise, and makes a virtue of an audience's active listening and effortful assembly of meaning will suit the capabilities of this group much better. Aesthetics of these kinds are found in performance art, live art, and the theatre that draws from them. Llewellyn speaks of using 'the found space' as the aesthetic, along with the 'experience of being in the world' of The Seven. Directors often have their personal conceptualization of a work in progress which is not entirely possible to share with the rest of the artists involved, and this will be the case in applied theatre, despite the democratic aim that many practitioners will have to share as much as possible. But in this case, the group were aware of a spatial vocabulary of straight lines and circles, which derived from the space but then evolved in other elements such as movement, action and recorded speech, and in motifs of bubbles (speech bubbles, soap bubbles) and circles (a trail of coloured plastic circles left behind on buildings, the circle of Boundary Gardens park).

It may be that the beauty of this work is inflected with sentiment; that our strong feelings originate in a feeling of the injustice suffered by disabled people in their daily lives, a kind of interest which would make the aesthetic judgement in this case an 'interested' one, or a dependent beauty, in Kant's terms, as it depends on our impulse to make the world a more just place. In Chapter 2 I will consider how an interpretation of dependent beauty can be used to unpack this kind of response. Articulating the position of 'art for art's sake' in the company's work, Llewellyn says that 'Aesthetic art is something that you can be drawn into and you become one with. There's a feeling of transcendence sometimes, a reflection between it and the world that you might not understand till later.' And he is insistent that this is felt strongly by the members of the group as well as audiences, that they understand what they do in aesthetic terms, often more powerfully than they do in conceptual or instrumental terms. Llewellyn's notion of 'transcendence' here may not match a rigorous application of Kant's conceptless beauty, as he suggests that conceptual understanding follows after the experience; but there is a sense of the free play of the imagination, a groping after ideas suggested by strong impressions made by a deep experiential involvement.

This outline, however, has focussed on *Eye Queue Hear* as a performance. I have briefly noted what the experience of the performance meant to the performers themselves, but haven't begun to unpack the aesthetic dimensions of the process of its creation. To understand an *aesthetic of process* is the real challenge. This requires using the concepts of aesthetics to address the experience of the performers as they make as well as deliver the work, looking for what might be called beautiful moments, and other varieties of aesthetic experience, in the long and difficult journey from conception to delivery of a performance project.

The process of making *Eye Queue Hear* was led by Llewellyn and Brennan, with sound designer Philip Lee also playing an important role. It involved devising and writing exercises and long conversations with the group, sometimes around relevant subject matter such as the use of IQ testing or the 1886 'Idiots Act', sometimes about their daily lives, sometimes, as Christian puts it to me, about 'complete and utter nonsense'. These conversations were recorded and edited in collaboration with Lee to make up the soundtrack of the performance. Devising took place in the rehearsal room and outside, walking around and asking: what kind of feelings do these areas give us? Sound designer Lee followed the rehearsing group around with a boom microphone, making recordings. There were, then, several strategies for bringing ideas from the streets into the rehearsal room, and of drawing ideas from the group in a way that became different kinds of performance material.

The group spent lots of time looking at IQ tests, and coming to the conclusion that, in Llewellyn's words, 'it's the test itself that has got a problem'. This thesis was not very explicitly expressed in the performance, although it would be discernable to an audience member who was aware of it, in a sequence of obscure puzzles spoken at the beginning of the soundtrack. But it was explored in rehearsals in what we might consider an aesthetic as well as a conceptual way: trying the tests, talking about them, writing down feelings and ideas, and using these as the basis of performance exercises. This kind of 'aesthetic work', however, is very far from disinterested or purposeless; a Kantian account might consider this part of the craftsman-like manipulation of material that is necessary as the basis of art's ascension towards the Aesthetic, that the artists themselves are engaged in the free play of faculties during this work. But what is interesting here is not the transmutation of content into form – although that certainly is happening – but the manipulation of content in a meaningful but not rational way. Discussion and deliberation about the oppressive use of IQ tests may have taken place, but along with that work on feeling and emotion, and work that finds useful and potentially meaningful material by chance.

Discussing the creative process, the group recalled the challenges of remembering such an unusual set of performance sequences in preparation for the show, along with other practical problems such as dealing with a mobile audience. They recall challenge as a positive aspect of the work, associating it with the potential for personal growth that performance brings, and for proving to themselves and to others what they are capable of. For Jolene Sampson and Lee Phillips making a play can lead you to surprise yourself, and 'plays can change things, they can change you.' But along with this they remember the emotional effort of the work, as Paul Christian, another of The Seven, says, as a performer you have to: 'delve into yourself and talk about yourself'; and although the atmosphere and experience was generally easy going, there are times when 'you feel like packing up your tent and going home'.

One section of the performance seems to have provoked particularly strong feelings, by making use of extracts from the 1886 'Idiots Act' and the group's responses to it. This was staged outside a Victorian laundry, which was in a former incarnation a workhouse in which people with learning disabilities and mental illness were confined. For audiences this sequence, culminating in dancing to Jimmy Cliff, may have been relatively fleeting, but for the performers it was important. Another performer, Imogen Roberts, says she was 'passionate' about this section, and associated it with her dislike of hospitals and other institutions; for Christian it was about the difficulty of re-living these past horrors, and very powerful. Again, working through this in rehearsal was, for Phillips, about personal growth, about being strong and 'loving yourself'.

Summing up the process, Christian says the 'whole experience' was 'astonishing, beyond this world'; Sampson agrees, and that she found it 'quite beautiful when we worked together', because 'sometimes it's hard to trust people, and you can get to that stage where you can trust each other.' Her 'beautiful when . . .' runs against the conceptless and disinterested judgement of taste, but in fact seems consistent with the way this group recall most of their experiences of the performance and its process, as deeply felt and deeply thought, arising out of parts of the process that they value rather than something transcendent or ineffable.

In the following chapter, I will use this extended example to elucidate some dilemmas of an aesthetics of participation in applied theatre, and in some instances extend the discussion of particular moments of the performance and its process with the help of the ideas developed through the chapter.

Aesthetic Autonomy and Heteronomous Aesthetics

Aesthetic autonomy

*[T]he development of modern Western aesthetics can be characterised
as a declaration of independence for the aesthetic, emancipating it
from the grip of the moral, the conceptual and the practical.*[1]

How can this ever be accommodated in our thinking about interventionist art? Why shouldn't we simply accept in principle that to
understand effects, we need a theory that accepts heteronomy, and
should dispense with this 'declaration of independence'? First, to
simply sidestep autonomy would be to sidestep much of theoretical
aesthetics with its account of the practical understanding of art in
society. This paradox, that art gives value to society through separating
itself from social life, has a long and not entirely futile history; we
can borrow its insights while being alert for its misconceptions.
Secondly, as I have already observed, separation has a role in applied
practice: we create safe spaces, preserve the special character of
the rehearsal room and stage, and make claims for art's particular
powers. Thirdly, the notion that we do these things and observe
these powers because of a faculty that is difficult otherwise to access
deserves investigation. It may be that the history of 'the aesthetic'
is bound up with histories of privilege and domination, but it may
be that one of those very privileges is the aesthetic itself, denied to
all but a few, a privilege that we are actively seeking to share more
democratically.

The trend in commentary on applied theatre is to move towards an understanding of autonomy and the arguments around it that is serviceable and useful to a practice predicated on heteronomy. Such thinking can help us to articulate what is special about art practices in relation to other interventions; it can show how art activity can be both deeply connected with the practical concerns of life and also detached from them – that is, how a principle of autonomy helps to get things done. At the same time, there has been a recognizable effort to loosen 'the grip of the moral, conceptual and practical', in the specific sense of effect and outcome-driven evaluation of practice.

This chapter will show some areas where further progress of this kind might lie. The place of beauty in applied practice has been quite confidently and eloquently asserted, but it has not necessarily been articulated in relation to the experiential structures of applied practice. Using *Eye Queue Hear* as a source of some examples, and the questions that evolve from them, I shall explore how some ideas of the value of beauty might be claimed for the experiences that the participants in the project told me about, and for participatory aesthetics in general.

As noted in the previous chapter, theories of art as an institution have developed in relation to fine art innovations, and the arguments involved are often most easily captured in relation to fine art objects, events and controversies. They are also effective in accounting for theatre and performance, insomuch as there are clearly institutional forces at work in legitimating some kinds of behaviour as theatre or performance as such, along with interrelated social practices that support and facilitate those institutions, practices of reception being as important as practices of production. In recognizing performances of these special kinds, we allow them a kind of autonomy, in their special licensed realm. But it is a limited kind of autonomy, a set of practices marked off by other practices, which would otherwise be mundane or even meaningless. As Richard Shusterman points out, these may be the most powerful descriptive theories of the phenomena of art in our societies, but they do not offer a means of deepening or improving art as such a practice.[2] Beyond the legitimating effect of recognizing art practices of a broad character, and as such potentially undermining the high art and low art dichotomy, institutional and art-as-practice definitions offer no theory of value. They recognize how art values are historical and contingent, but do not guide us in engaging with our own history and contingency in exploring the values of what we would like to bring into our art practices.

In the second half of this chapter, I will move on to discuss those aspects that make use of the language of aesthetics much more broadly, to the extent of seeing it as a basis for all human understanding. But in this first section I will be concerned with the 'Aesthetic', in its special sense, particularly that which we experience as beauty. Yet there is a distinction within this version of the aesthetic as an exceptional experience too, that will not be so easy to maintain: the distinction between the aesthetic as it is encountered in experience of the natural world and as we make and find it in our art practices and experiences. For the aesthetic autonomy of the experience of the natural world is something elusive and beyond our control. It is autonomous because it comes to us unpredictably, and while we might seek it out, even shape our world to try to capture it, the experience itself is beyond our control. The aesthetic autonomy of Art however, while it has an experiential element that is similarly ephemeral, also exists as that set of social practices that are quite deliberately managed and observed. The exceptional aesthetic, within Art, appears to have its appropriate territory: in performances, paintings, books and so on; and it seems to belong in different ways to creative artists and their audiences. For applied theatre, however, different places, times and objects take priority, and the distinction between the artist and the non-artist is broken down. An aesthetics of participation, or a process-oriented aesthetics, has to find this consummation of experience in fleeting and unrepeated moments in workshops, rehearsals, discussions and other kinds of encounters, as well as in fully realized performances, and must show how it manifests for the semi-skilled and the tentative as well as for the confident fully-fledged artist. The aesthetic object that is important to most theories, even those focussed on art as experience,

is harder to define in these cases, as the object shaped is often the body
and voice of the participant; the distancing practices through which
theatre would tend to demarcate the aesthetic object (which might be
defined as the performance itself or perhaps the text that it reproduces)
for the audience do not apply, but the participant is nevertheless in the
role of the audience member, having an aesthetic experience in relation
to their own actions.

In this section, therefore, I shall return to ideas of how beauty, as
the prime example of the aesthetic in its exceptional form is viewed as
a social, progressive or even radical good, along with how we might
think of the act of participation or the experience of process in the same
terms as the aesthetic experience of the creative artist, and finally I will
look to Rancière's version of the conflict between the autonomous and
heteronomous in the aesthetic, and how it might apply to an aesthetics
of participation.

Genius, participation and *The Radical Aesthetic*

Isobel Armstrong in *The Radical Aesthetic*[3] elaborates how a broadly
Kantian free play of meaning-making is exercised through paradoxes,
contradictions and transformed structures of perception in the
interests of social change and the disruption of ideology. Similarly,
in both Wolff and Scarry we see different strategies for reclaiming
beauty for progressive ends. For Scarry, beauty is a provocation to
take greater care in our dealings with other people and the world in
general, because of the revitalized attention that beauty inspires in us,
while Wolff – taking a quite different tack to Scarry – notes how the
pleasures of the beautiful have not gone away, despite the kalliphobia
of two decades of criticism and art practice, and that we can conceive
of beauty in the light of social and ethical critique.[4] These are ways of
finding meaning and value, with a contemporary attention to power
relations, in the Aesthetic. But how far do they help to understand
participation? We can account for beautiful participatory experiences

in these ways, as Thompson, Winston and others have done; but a close examination of how people recognize the beautiful and the Aesthetic in participation is also possible. We can give credit to what people say to us about the beauty of their experiences, and to our own perceptions of experience too; but we need to look closer at the particular dimensions of participation – its plurality, and the potential for an experience of beauty that doesn't involve an external object – in order to know which people, and what experience is being referred to.

Continuing to follow the Kantian schema of the Aesthetic, there is a key role for the artist to play as the vehicle for the expression of the free play of the imagination, which can be explored in relation to the work done by participants in applied theatre. His word for this is 'genius', and our modern conception of the genius has largely evolved from the eighteenth-century idea that a work of Art is created by someone who can combine special insight and practical skill. But it is worth noting the differences between the contemporary idea of the genius, and Kant's: he excludes from his category scientists, or anyone else whose discoveries are arrived at through the exercise of the faculty of cognition, or the replication of a method that has been followed by others. Genius is specifically the capacity to produce beautiful objects, just as taste is the capacity to judge them. And Kant does say quite plainly that whereas a brilliant scientist differs only in degree from the less brilliant, there is a difference in kind between those 'whom Nature has gifted for beautiful Art', and those it has not.[5] We might, however, choose to disagree with Kant about the distribution of genius, but keep an open mind about the possibility of genius as a capacity, perhaps available to all people, situated less in the individual and more in the potential for this creative act. As Augusto Boal puts it:

> Although some people are given the title of Artist, the truth is that each and every human being is, substantively, an artist. We all possess, to some degree or other, the capacity to penetrate unicities [sic], whether by making art or making love. We are all capable of encounter with the Singular.[6]

Boal's 'unicities' have more in common with a Hegelian idea of the aesthetic as a revelation of the absolute, rather than a uniting of the divided faculties of reason and sensibility, but the aesthetic he is suggesting here is not a materialist dialectical process, realized through careful performative analysis of a social oppression, but a transcendental intuition. How can we unpack the idea of genius as Kant uses it, for more plural purposes? The important, original component of genius comes from 'spirit', which:

> in an aesthetical sense, is the name given to the animating principle of the mind. But· that whereby this principle animates the soul, the material which it applies to that [purpose,] is that which puts the mental powers purposively into swing, i.e. into such a play as maintains itself and strengthens the [mental] powers in their exercise.[7]

There is nothing in this that belongs to the extraordinary individual genius; it is a description of what brings each of us to life, although as Kant moves on from this it is clear that he intends that some 'spirits' animate the mind more effectively than others. But each of us has a spirit capable of animating the mind towards combining imagination and understanding in free play, as is evident in our capability for judgements of taste. What may be lost in granting genius to all and sundry is the ability of the genius to access the *sensus communis* and make works that appear beautiful to many other people. It seems fair, and not especially elitist, to acknowledge that some people are better at this than others, but this does not mean that the rest of us are not capable of creating a work of this kind, even if only once in our lives. Nor does it mean that as individuals we are not capable of producing work that might inspire such feelings in ourselves. Kant gives the name of the Aesthetic to a kind of experience, and then associates it with the (capitalized) Art that provokes it. A pluralistic 'genius' that potentially manifests in anyone making art, so that their work might on occasion rise to the status of Art remains true to some essential parts of the structure of Kant's model of Aesthetic experience, while undermining the importance of the capacity of judgements of taste to reveal beauty, and therefore the

sensus communis to us. But it makes a place for a plurality of people
as agents of the Aesthetic, one of the important components I have
suggested for an aesthetics of participation. It also moves us towards a
kind of plurality of outcome, as it places less emphasis on the aspect of
a work that is accessible to other people; but it is still the transcendent
Aesthetic, a rare manifestation of the free play of faculties.

This notion of a pluralistic genius demotes the importance of *sensus
communis* as the basis for a shared capacity for Aesthetic judgements,
and for the phenomenon of taste as far as it is shared between people.
This may be no problem at all however, as *sensus communi*s is one of
the more problematic elements of Kant's aesthetics. If a common sense
underpinning aesthetics is seen as a way to come to know other people,
or to know that in principle we have things in common with other people,
then it may be taken as giving a moral dimension to the Aesthetic. The
evidence of experience, however, is that taste is not shared so evenly as
to convince that we find the same things beautiful, and a theory of the
value of beauty that is based on commonality is in danger of falling into
this simplification and into the troubling conclusion that people ought
to agree about what is beautiful whatever their differences, or will agree
if they can only learn to appreciate things properly. This, as Andrew
Chignell puts it, is the problem of 'particularity' in Kant,[8] the resolution
of which does not entirely become clear in the *Critique of Judgement*:
the problem of whether beauty is particular to the object or the person
who has the judgement about the object, whether beauty is, in fact, 'in
the eye of the beholder'. This is a matter, really, of the definition of taste,
which, as I have said, is not especially of importance in this context; as
the Aesthetic moment we are looking for in participation is not generally
shareable with others, we need not be overly concerned with its universal
validity, and we can be satisfied with the idea of an Aesthetic that is
personal.

Nevertheless, the apparent incommensurability of a common
ground for taste with the subjectivity of aesthetic response is one
of the core questions of the *Critique of Judgement*, and the cause of
some of Kant's most complex arguments. It gives rise to the idea of

'subjective universal validity', which exposes something more relevant and potentially troublesome. The subjective judgements that arise out of the free play of mental faculties (of reason and imagination) do not come out of nowhere: they call upon an intuition of the 'supersensible as a substrate of nature', as the principle that inspires the purposiveness we find in beautiful objects – that is, the structures that are in common between the phenomenal world and our minds, when we apprehend it in a moment of the Aesthetic.[9]

What this means, and why it is potentially troubling, is revealed in the idea that Kant opposes to it: 'the contingently similar organisation of the different subjects',[10] where judgements arise out of the way that we as individuals happen to be put together. This contingency is a much more modern-sounding idea, but for Kant it is an unsatisfying recourse to 'psychology', and thus undermines the ambition of his systematic approach. If we allow a 'supersensible' structure, then we have the common sense that binds us together, not necessarily leading us all to agree on the beauty of every object, but as a grounding for the impulse we have to claim beauty where we find it, not only therefore to have some theoretical grounds for judgements of taste, but for the Aesthetic as a shared experience. But for the supersensible to be manifest in art works seems to require that the inspired individual genius makes it available to all. The contingently organized subject as the source of judgements is more plural, but it is a vision of the aesthetic that is more atomized, and therefore more limited in potential.

Nevertheless, it opens up the range of manifestations of beauty in the process and the performance of projects like *Eye Queue Hear*. Audiences share in the beauty of the performance, because it draws on shared understandings and common sensibilities, and has the artistry – the genius – to bring them to mind for a group of relatively diverse strangers. Moreover, the participants themselves, working in collaboration with directors, facilitators and other professionals, have personal experiences of beautiful moments throughout the creative process, benefitting from the individual genius that is sufficient to create and activate these moments. When Dayo Koleosho remembers 'looking up and seeing the light', as his personal image of beauty, it may bring to mind for others a gesture from the concluding sequence of the performance, but it cannot give us access to the experience that he constructed and enjoyed for himself.

Dependent beauty

The issue of the disinterestedness of the Aesthetic and its relationship to concepts, in the context of participatory performance, can be explored further, and the nuances of 'free' and 'dependent' beauty provide some scope for this development. Although initially proposing that a properly Aesthetic experience is disinterested, Kant has to admit that the experience of beauty is not straightforward: there are many instances in which we might mistakenly call something beautiful when we should say that we find it agreeable or good, and that we may even believe that we are experiencing something as beautiful while being unaware that our judgement is contaminated by either the agreeable or the good. Furthermore, he says that although a 'bare reflection on a given intuition'[11] is at the basis of a pure judgement, rather than its being attributable to a concept, a pure judgement can be made about things that have ends, provided the judgement itself *doesn't depend on a concept* of the end.[12] Happily, for a broader sense of what might be encompassed by the Aesthetic, the purposes that undoubtedly can be detected in virtually any object, and the concepts that we are bound to entertain in relation to it, do not preclude our having an experience of 'free beauty' in response to it; Aesthetic judgements can happen, are bound to happen, in defiance of the presence of concepts and interests. For James Kirwan:

> the freedom of free beauty, then, depends, I would suggest, not on that beauty's being undetermined by a concept, but rather upon that beauty's being cognised, at the moment of judgement, as being undetermined by a concept.[13]

The principle of the purity of the Aesthetic shifts away from the object itself and its relationship to concepts and interests, and further towards what comes to mind in the moment of judgements.

In addition to these misapprehensions, overlaps and cognitive overrides, there is a further development where genuine judgements of beauty do in fact involve concepts, such that they become 'aesthetic ideas'. In this case the judgement is *dependent* upon the concept but without being fully determined by it: the idea is uncertain, ungraspable, out of reach. It is an idea that 'no language fully attains or can make intelligible.'[14] The judgement, being handled by the freely playing and combined faculties of reason and imagination, rather than by reason alone, responds to more than just the concepts under question, so that it has 'an effect greater than the sum of the parts.'[15] For Kirwan, there seems, in fact, to be a dependent element in virtually all experiences of the Aesthetic; it seems that judgement based on *dependent* beauty, involving 'aesthetic ideas', is more prevalent than pure judgement.

Like the logic that supports the 'subjective universal validity' of Aesthetic judgements, the elaboration of free and dependent beauty can feel like the tortuous shoring up of a theory of taste, with all its troublesome antinomy and paradox. And yet, once again there is the germ of something more flexible and plural, in the variety of ways in which we can experience a pure judgement, and in the possibility of a dependent judgement which brings concepts – and therefore interests – under the influence of the Aesthetic. This may allow us to use Kantian terms for the varied kinds of beauty found in 'applied' situations. The model of dependent beauty certainly fits Nick Llewellyn's reflection about ideas that don't make sense until later, and it also allows us more purchase on the kind of 'free play' and opening up of new ways of thinking that Scarry and Armstrong talk about. Where a working process is beautiful *because of* growing trust, as described by Jolene Sampson, her judgement is clearly dependent on a concept in some way. Is she actually describing an experience of the agreeable or the good, rather than of the beautiful? It is hard to know, but trusting her intuition that this is a thing of beauty, it might be that her initially apprehensive relationship to the others in the group, when it begins to turn to trust, is ungraspable as a concept and combines with the imaginative play of sensations around creative collaborative work.

Heteronomous aesthetics

There may be a place for a pure, or non-dependent aesthetic in participatory performance. However, the previous discussion of an autonomous aesthetic(s) reveals how much it would not encompass. For a start, there is all that would be counted in art that is *directly* meaningful: what we see in the work and perceive clearly according to concepts. Along with this the aspects of art that are directed at having effects, as so often evidently exist, intimately connected and engaged with the world around them. Moreover, there are the other emotions, affects and feelings that arise around the art experience, which cannot be subsumed within the definitive aesthetic experience.

All art has these heteronomies, but participatory performance is particularly prone to them and produces them in its own ways. It is most often created to be effective, or to connect directly with people's lives. As it involves its participants physically and actively, it is replete with meaning, overflowing with concepts. And finally the processes of participation depend on and provoke many layers of feeling apart from the occasional purely 'aesthetic' response. When non-professional performers get involved in making and performing, or take part in theatre practices that reach a crescendo of effect and affect before or without public performance, heteronomy takes precedence over autonomy in the main. So art is always more than 'the aesthetic', always more than 'Art' in a pure sense, and applied theatre celebrates and encourages this heteronomy more than most other art practices. In this section, I will outline some contemporary approaches to aesthetics that have room for this heteronomy, and in some cases for a return to the aesthetic in its pre-Kantian meaning, as the study of sensation and sensibility rather than Art as something special.

Yuriko Saito, in her *Everyday Aesthetics,* insists that better design –
in household objects, buildings and in our approach to food, drink and
the natural environment – contribute to better quality of life at a deep
rather than superficial level. She quotes Yrjö Sepänmaa, on aesthetic
welfare: 'He points out that true welfare states should guarantee not only
"health care, education, and housing" but also "an experiential aspect
of welfare. An aesthetic welfare state should offer a beautiful living
environment and a rich cultural and art life."'[16] The previous chapter
has indicated how beautiful experiences might be seen, alongside
beautiful objects as an essential component of a full and rich life. For
Saito and Sepänmaa, the penetration of aesthetics into the everyday is
through the extension of the territory of beauty, to fully conceive of
that which is pleasing to the eyes and ears, to touch, taste and smell, as
properly beautiful rather than trivial matters of subjective preference.
In this way there is a recognition of the consummation of experience
in ordinary, unexceptional circumstances. There is an alternative way
of looking for the aesthetic in the everyday, however, which returns to
Baumgarten's aesthetic as a study of the faculty of sensation. This is to
allow that *aesthesis* is the category of all sensual experience, and of the
meaning of that experience. Changing tack at this point to look at the
unexceptional aesthetics of the everyday may show how art practice
can have effects and affects without needing to approach the rarefied
consummatory fulfilment of experiences of beauty.

Thomas Docherty, like Woolf and Armstrong, notes how critical
theory has rejected the aesthetic, and along with it some fundamental
aspects of the art experience. His response, although concerned with
art rather than everyday aesthetics, draws attention to the importance
of the personal and ephemeral in art experiences, and perhaps in
experience in general.

> Aesthetic experience – that feeling that provokes me to say 'I like
> this' in my encounter with art – has been rather disreputable in
> sophisticated or in institutional modes of critical reading. On one
> hand, it has been seen as the trivia of subjectivity, a local irrelevance

in the face of the abstract general truths about art that can be derived from a reasoned response. . . . On the other hand, however, experience is making a return, exemplified by the recent autobiographical turn in criticism. . . . My point here differs from both these tendencies and derives from the fundamental question: 'why are we so wary of the particularity of a specific aesthetic experience?' Such wariness is odd if we see culture precisely as something experienced, lived, by specific individuals and their societies, rather than as something detached from human being and from 'human becoming' as such.[17]

This particularity, especially in connection to 'human becoming', reminds us that although there may be an aspect of the aesthetic that belongs to *sensus communis* such that the individual's life experience and personality fade into the background, there is much more to it that can only belong to them and to no-one else: it is peculiar to the history that arrives at this particular moment, and reveals itself only to this particular subjectivity. Docherty's reference to 'human becoming' acknowledges that this subjectivity is not a fixed entity, but the constantly evolving interface between the individual human being and the world around them. If a subject is always 'becoming', always changing, then 'the aesthetic' will play a part in that, and perhaps a significant part.

Berleant and *The Aesthetic Field*

Arnold Berleant is a leading figure in environmental aesthetics and the expansion of the field to apply to landscape and urban design and other phenomena at the borders of art practice. His work has been an evolution of the idea of an 'aesthetic field', which was originally formulated to address what he saw as distortions in aesthetics as the theory of art, that derived from prejudices and preconceptions rather than from artistic and aesthetic phenomena themselves. In his 1970 book *The Aesthetic Field*, he stakes a claim against supernatural and transcendental definitions of the aesthetic (including Kant's) because they evade the task of fully understanding art, and place artificial limits on knowledge. We should not begin from principles but from experience itself, he says: 'Abstract a priori principles have been notoriously unsuccessful in settling issues that concern matters of fact and experience.'[18] His method is to begin initially with the phenomenology of art, that is, its experiential dimensions examined without preconceptions, and to move on to 'aesthetic facts', about situational contexts, objects, judgements and the practices of judgement, and data from other disciplines, as well as experience itself treated as a body of 'experiential facts'. Only after gathering these empirical data is he ready to move on to an aesthetic theory.

In contrast to this empirical approach, Berleant says that what has come before has tended to amount to a set of 'surrogate' theories of art, that is, theories that draw from other agendas, rather than from an open-minded attention to the phenomena themselves. Thus he criticizes Clive Bell and Roger Fry's formalism[19] as it supports the value of some kinds of art, while providing no useful terms with which to understand others. It is a critical position that is ultimately self-serving, rather than an attempt to account for the broad phenomenon of art. Kant's aesthetics could be seen as a surrogate in another way, as his assumptions appear to be drawn from his motivation to integrate his overall philosophical project, rather than to investigate art in the circumstances in which it is actually found.

The aesthetic field is understood by 'making reference to the total situation in which the objects, activities and experiences of art occur', rather than excluding elements that do not conform to a preconceived idea of what is relevant or valuable in art. This inclusive approach leads logically to the continuity of art experiences with 'the full spectrum of human activities', as what he calls the 'invariants' of aesthetic experience are shared with these other activities rather than sharply separated from them.[20] There are four significant elements of the aesthetic field: the object, the artist, the perceiver, and the performer. Whereas in other theories the emphasis is often on the object, or the artist's relationship to the object, Berleant gives equal weight to the role of the perceiver in the moment of artistic experience. The performer, too, has an equal place in the aesthetic field, even in non-performing arts, because of the temporal element that they draw attention to. Where there is no actual performer, their role is 'collapsed', or 'telescoped',[21] into that of the perceiver, who in effect performs the work by actively engaging with it in the experiential moment of perception.

Berleant emphasizes the continuity of aesthetic experience with that which surrounds it. He lists factors that condition the aesthetic field: biological, psychological, historical, social and cultural influences which provide the context and the content for these elements. Aesthetic experience is a transaction among these factors and elements, with the transaction between a perceiver and an object as typically the crucial thing; but in the flexibility to see that perceivers and objects can telescope into other roles we have an opportunity to understand process and participation.

Berleant's notion of 'telescoping' can be useful for dealing with participatory arts, as it is a strategy for observing the different functions that are at work in an aesthetic experience, while allowing that the locus of the functions is variable, rather than belonging to a typically linear artist-object-performer-perceiver structure, where each is a separate physical entity. In participatory performance practice there will often be many individuals with functions telescoped into each other; although they will engage with the performances of others around them as perceivers of objects, or performances produced by other artists, they will also engage with their own performances, either in the moment they give them or afterwards in retrospect.

To be schematic about it, a participant may be a performer-perceiver when acting out something scripted or directed by another, or artist-performer-perceiver when acting out something they have created (or are in the moment of creating) for themselves. We might find this latter kind of aesthetic field in *Eye Queue Hear* both in the performances when the group experienced their self-devised script enhanced by the presence of an audience, and in their work devising the text and movement. In Berleant's theory, the text and movement in performing arts is the artistic object, and does not collapse into the element of the performer. This makes sense in the context of collaborative creation, as well as in the treatment of the performance of pre-written scores. When the Access All Areas group undertake exercises based on IQ tests or the 'Idiots Act', and create script as a result, or when they wander the streets of Bethnal Green and return to their studio to develop movement, they are working with this material. Although it occurs as gesture and speech in their own bodies, in Berleant's theory their relationship can be seen as both subject and object. This is significant when considering how performance material that is strange, troublesome or even traumatic is worked with: in, for example, the quotation of sections of legislation that had been explicitly oppressive to people with disabilities. Although the telescoped roles of artist-performer-perceiver may have each been present in devising, rehearsal and performance, they each suggest different relationships to the object (a textual object in this instance), as an object of exploration and experiment, as something to gain mastery over, and as something to present and share with others. In each case the object is both brought close to hand and kept at a distance, and the distance can be manipulated in different ways.

Shusterman: Updating pragmatism

Berleant was influenced by pragmatist aesthetics in Dewey's mould, although he does not explicitly identify with it until his later writing. Overt development of Dewey's theory has become increasingly influential, partly for its capacity to overlap disciplinary boundaries and thus become useful in articulating the insights of critical theory (in one direction) and cognitive science (in another). Dewey articulates the continuity of 'esthetic' experience with the everyday, but still holds that this 'esthetic' is something special, a consummated version of the meaning-making of the everyday. Mark Johnson and Richard Shusterman, however, endeavour to extend this view of experience beyond art and to use it as the basis of nuanced understandings of everyday meaning-making (Johnson) and body practices (Shusterman).

These more radical versions of heteronomy, even though explicitly moving beyond art, provide useful perspectives on activist art, and suggest approaches to some of the conceptual problems unresolved by the previous two sections.

Shusterman opposes pragmatism to the analytic tradition in aesthetics, which had been dominant in Anglo-American academia throughout the twentieth century, giving it preference because of its avoidance of the analytic's dependence on disinterest, a-historicism and the isolation of aesthetic objects. He tackles the institution- and tradition-based theories (of Arthur Danto and George Dickie, as briefly discussed in Chapter 1), which he finds to be the most convincing definitions of the ontology of Art as we find it in contemporary society, but which are contentless in and of themselves. These theories, he states, are 'transparently present, contain and conserve their object – our understanding of art', but do not enhance or modify it.[22] He shows how a fixation on interpretation on the part of academic aesthetics obscures the varied and diverse responses to works that ordinary people might have, while privileging the professional critical responses of specialists; this is despite the democratizing impulse in the origins of these theories of 'reading', based on an impulse to deny authoritative and correct interpretations of works. Conversely, he sees in Dewey a number of connected positive attributes: 'holism, historicism and organicism',[23] that is, attention to all aspects of the phenomenon, interest in its specific social and historical context, and integration of the meaning of aesthetic experience for the 'natural needs, constitution and activities of the human organism'.[24] He is also deeply influenced by Dewey's 'meliorative' tendency, that is, the belief that rather than merely reflecting on social phenomena, philosophy has a role to play in improving them, so that his theory becomes an intervention in itself, playing a part in the evolution of art and aesthetic practice.

Shusterman chooses to situate pragmatism as a meaningful mediator between the Anglo-American analytic tradition and continental deconstruction when dealing with the subject of 'organic unity'. Unity, from Greek philosophy onwards, is often considered an important element of the ontology of the art work. In G. E. Moore's formulation,

the unity of the art work is like that of the living organism, where each
component part may be able to exist apart from the whole thing, but is
transformed by being part of the whole. Deconstruction, in the mode
of Jacques Derrida,[25] would hold that the 'whole thing' is dependent
for its meaningful being upon its difference from other things, rather
than upon its own essential make up, such that it is never fully present
as a thing in itself but only as traces of its difference from other things.
Pragmatism, however, conceives things as being 'interpretations, but
interpretations so inextricably entrenched in our actual thinking that
they take the status of fact or reality.'[26] In other words, pragmatism does
not need to reject the epistemological scepticism of deconstruction in
order to engage with the logical structures that we apply to things as
we find them in experience or portray them to ourselves. Pragmatism
is less interested in revealing the ontology of things in either essences
or endless play of *différance*, than it is in the force or coerciveness of a
perceived reality and its usefulness for practical life.

What is the use of this to participatory performance? It suggests a
theory of unity, and therefore of the sense of an art work as a distinct
thing, based on use rather than essence. A participatory process
is difficult to define as a 'work of art' because of its extension over
a (potentially) long time, the different kinds of engagement and
involvement of participants (changing over time as well as varying
between individuals), and its varying and often conflicting outputs and
effects. In looking for what is important to a participant, we might want
to consider a single workshop or rehearsal, or even a discrete exercise
from an aesthetic point of view. These shorter events might have a part
to play in the organic unity of a whole process, but we might think
of them in themselves as having the potential for unity, for bringing
something to experiential consummation for the participants. The
pragmatist approach allows us to frame these incidents or occurrences
as art works, as far as they function as such within their own terms.

Shusterman doesn't rest there, but proposes a significant departure
into a more heteronomous aesthetics, in the inauguration of a
practical-theoretical field of 'somaesthetics', predicated on a unity of
body and mind, and directed mainly towards facilitating a healthy

and meaningful life through bodily practices. He draws on the ideas of creative self-fashioning put forward by Richard Rorty, which sees the aesthetic potential in everyday life and our choices of how to present ourselves – to others and ourselves – within it.[27] Shusterman allies this to the potential of 'the beautiful experience of one's own body from within',[28] the excitements and affects of exercise and activity, the full appreciation of life as it is lived, and a practical awareness that will help us to live better and healthier lives. This is where the 'meliorative' aspect of his approach comes to the fore, in a proposal for a discipline that has a pragmatic and practical dimension as well as an analytic one. We might, for example, see the challenging physical work of the rehearsal period of *Eye Queue Hear* as a 'somaesthetic' practice, stretching the capabilities of the participants and connecting physical exploration work with focus on feeling and thinking, in a process that several of the group identified with personal growth. Although the well-being of the individual is an explicit aim in some kinds of applied arts, and an undercurrent in others, social change is at least as important and so somaesthetics does not map across entirely comfortably. Nevertheless, it does offer the useful perspective on the aesthetic experience of oneself, in this case the experience of the body and the body-mind, but with awareness of the social aspect of the self, too. Participatory performance is partly work on the self, and it depends on the aesthetic perception of the self in the physical aspect – as we move and interact in performance, but also in the social and interpersonal aspect – as we represent ourselves and adapt our representations of ourselves.

Johnson and aesthetic understanding

In Mark Johnson's hands, the aesthetic is intimately involved with the idea of embodiment, leading to a model of aesthetic understanding. In *The Meaning of the Body*, he shows how any rational, conscious understanding – the kind of understanding that is important to more conventional philosophies of mind, truth and logic – occurs out of a foundation that is bodily, emotional and situational.[29] Johnson's evidence is wide ranging: brain imaging of structures that share situational data in a non-discriminating blend (as described by Thomas Metzinger); the key role of emotion in effective decision making (as famously shown by Antonio Damasio); the body-based schemas that underlie language (in the cognitive linguistics of George Lakoff); the affordances to objects and environments that shape action prior to thought (as with James Gibson); and the phenomenology of embodiment (as in Maurice Merleau-Ponty).[30]

Johnson's approach is rooted in an enactivist theory of mind, based on the understanding that mind *happens* to us, in action, and it happens not in a disembodied way, but as a set of highly integrated processes across the brain and the rest of the body. In the enactivist model '[m]eaning is embodied. It arises through embodied organism-environment interactions in which significant patterns are marked within the flow of experience'; mind is the phenomenon of the meaning being presented as if to a coherent monitoring subjectivity.[31]

This experiential meaning is also emotional: we respond to situations in unthought ways, with emotions that often stimulate action and response even before they give background and colour to conscious thought; emotions are thus an important part of the quality of an experience. Experiential meaning is both grounded in our bodily interactions and always social;[32] it is relational and instrumental, in the sense that arises when our attention falls on things and other people, or when we direct our attention to them.[33] This is a deeply anti-Kantian conception of how the faculty of understanding works, bringing together in a constant interaction of sensation and rationality which he could only reconcile in the very particular free play or imagination and cognition in the pure aesthetic. For Johnson:

> Meaning involves the blending of the structural, formal, and conceptual dimensions on the one hand and the preconceptual, nonformal, felt dimensions on the other. Meaning resides in neither of these dimensions of experience alone, but only in their ongoing connectedness and interanimation.[34]

Calling this an 'aesthetic' process has, then, expanded the territory of the term radically, but not without basis. It makes very explicit what cognitive science and philosophy claims to have demonstrated empirically, that although we may be able to abstract rules and principles for rational thought, this faculty is fundamentally based not on the manipulation of mental representations of the world, given to us by our senses, but on the continuous enactment of our embodied and emotional being in the world, which partly manifests as a rational perspective and a connected rational aspect (no more) to our decision making.[35]

Johnson, like Shusterman, is deeply influenced by Dewey, even though the scope he gives to the aesthetic is much wider. Dewey, he notes, does not give this name to run-of-the-mill experiences:

> Dewey describes these only partially developed experiences as 'inchoate', and he contrasts them with 'consummated experiences' that we more properly call aesthetic, in order to mark those cases where experience develops and acquires meaning and direction as it reaches a certain fulfilment marked by its unifying quality.[36]

But Johnson goes against this distinction:

> We need a philosophy that sees aesthetics as not just about art, beauty and taste, but rather as about how human beings experience and make meaning. Aesthetics concerns all of the things that go into meaning – form, expression, communication, qualities, emotions, feeling, value, purpose, and more.[37]

Johnson's is a massive project, to re-figure *all* forms of understanding in this way, including, of course, the understanding of art and art practices themselves, but as a subset of aesthetics rather than its main object, and in continuity with the rest of experience. Despite Dewey's generally more conservative categorization of aesthetic experience, he sees this broader aim as an unrealized tendency, and calls it 'Dewey's big idea for aesthetics'.[38]

A key, and troublesome, part of the big idea is what Dewey calls the 'pervasive unifying quality' of the consummated experiences that we have in relation to art works and other experiences. For Dewey and Johnson, the knitting together of the many dimensions of phenomenal experience into a whole means that experience, and the understanding of it, is a qualitative matter above all, and one that does not make itself explicitly available to consciousness.[39] And the quality is singular, even though it may be broken down into different elements by consciousness. This is not uncontroversial: pervasive qualities of experience are discernable, but to insist that the distinction of one sense mode from another, (or thought from feeling, or action from thought), is only ever a retrospective cognitive intervention, is to deny the veracity of some powerful aspects of phenomenal being.

What this might have to offer is an aesthetic theory of identity. In Johnson's list of 'all of the things that go into meaning' we find form, expression, communication, qualities, emotions, feeling, value, purpose. This could be seen as a set of factors that are important to our sense of self, things about which we make choices and judgements; the basis on which we react to and have opinions about the world; these are the ways in which we know ourselves. This is of interest to performance studies, and to participatory theatre in particular because we are interested in the ways performance works with and sometimes changes people's sense of self; and sometimes we are interested in making the work that instigates that change. This theory puts the limits of the reach of aesthetics around every aspect of the person, with scope for performance's multi-modality, and for participatory performance's engagement of the whole person. There is some empirical evidence for qualitative unity in experience. Johnson is cautious, but has done a lot of work with the kind of ideas and evidence in play in the sciences of mind. The evidence is based on how different parts of the brain handle information, and the kinds of response to situational data that the mind is engaged in while making the data available to conscious understanding.[40]

To take a step further into this aesthetics of identity, which I'm framing as an aesthetics of self-understanding in a very basic sense, and to explore the problematics of 'pervasive qualitative unity', it is worth turning to another enactivist, whose work deals with how identity comes upon us, as an impression of a singular continuous self. In *The Ego Tunnel*, Thomas Metzinger portrays our sense of being as a selective construction out of the many other things that the mind and body undertakes simultaneously but without drawing them together into a unity. We have a 'self' because of the drawing together of relevant visual, aural, tactile, kinaesthetic, somatic information, and uniting them temporally. The quality of this tunnel changes because it articulates itself in relation to a changing world. In essence, this is aesthetic, in Johnson and Dewey's terms. We feel ourselves. But it is very difficult to get a full picture of this qualitative dimension, as Metzinger says, much of what makes up the mind is inaccessible to the ego, it is ineffable:

> The Ineffability Problem arises for the simplest forms of sensory awareness, for the finest nuances of sight and touch, of smell and taste, and for those nuances of conscious hearing that underlie the magic and beauty of a musical experience. But it may also appear for empathy, for emotional and intrinsically embodied forms of communication. Once again these empirical findings are philosophically relevant, because they redirect our attention to something we've known all along.[41]

What have we known all along? That quality is hard to observe and articulate. The cognitive biases of the conscious mind, and especially of language, are more selective and reductive, and lead us to overlook this qualitative aspect of meaning. This presents real difficulties for the analysis of experience because when we reflect on experiences that we itemize and separate, we find it very hard to think about unity, and to a lesser degree, we find it hard to speak precisely about quality. Nevertheless, although it describes a meaning-making process that is largely ineffable, it might allow us to reframe aesthetic work as the bringing-to-consummation of this everyday aesthetic. What Paul Christian describes as the 'astonishing' experience of devising and performing with 'Access All Areas' could be framed in these terms as a consummation of otherwise inchoate understanding of his experience. He is astonished, as we all are, by the intensity of understandings that are given to him as a pervasive qualitative unity, and which resist capturing in language. The aesthetic material that he has worked with has been synthesized from the same phenomena that his everyday enactive understanding emerges out of; yet in this situation it has become, in Dewey's terms, 'an experience', something recognizably whole and distinct, and substantially meaningful, memorable and personal.

Conclusion

In this chapter, I have considered how we might look for a Kantian Aesthetic where it does not easily belong – in participatory performance practice. I have found room for *plurality* in a more liberal attitude to 'genius', in which any person involved in creative activity might evoke an experience of the Aesthetic in themselves. I have discussed a view of 'dependent beauty' which involves concepts and interests in productive play, while preserving the autonomy of the Aesthetic judgement itself. I have also looked at three theories which broaden the remit of the aesthetic, and assist in theorizing how participants experience themselves in aesthetic terms. I have adopted Berleant's aesthetic field, for its helpful telescoping of the artist-performer-perceiver, along with Shusterman's sense of organic unities of a variety of shapes and sizes, and of an aesthetics that extends well beyond the realm of art – a theme that is taken further by Johnson, particularly, in his theory of understanding as body and affect based, and enactive. This fusing of sensibility and cognition, where the interplay of faculties is not an exceptional phenomenon, but a daily and largely unconscious one, means that a convenient distinction between the *Aesthetic*, as Kant proposes it, and the *aesthetic* for Johnson is not viable. To separate the autonomous Aesthetic, recognized through the apprehension of beauty, from an ongoing aesthetic aspect of daily life, might be the basis of a schema for the pluralist aesthetics that participatory practice requires, recognizing both the potential to achieve that which is highly valued in Art, and the many other valuable things that happen when we apply ourselves to making art. But at the basis of Kant's epistemology are the faculties of pure reason and practical judgement, and their potential union in the Aesthetic; to bring this together in a single theory that has separate strata for the 'Artistic Aesthetic' and the 'everyday aesthetic' would be self-contradictory – if the everyday element is based on a union of faculties that actually precedes, and gives the foundation for reasoned thought. Contemporary cognitive philosophy, especially of the enactivist school, considers Kant's model of the mind to be fundamentally wrong.

Nevertheless, the exploration of what theories of aesthetics have to offer at least provides some options for the articulation of participatory performance practice. Unresolved epistemological issues aside, we find that the value of beauty, in one of its most challenging manifestations, can be read in relation to the creative work of participants, and in the plurality of their perceptions of their experience. And we have seen that there is an alternative potential for the aesthetic that gives space for the full connectedness of participatory practices with and within the people who undertake them as part of their ongoing meaning-making. It seems that the theoretical underpinning of the Aesthetic in its autonomous form, pursued through Kant's formulation, still demands this autonomy; and to make a theoretical space for all that happens in applied theatre demands a theory that has considerably more scope for heteronomy.

In relation to the elements of an aesthetics of participation, both of these ontological options address the plurality of people taking part and having creative initiative, but an ontology based in the more recent sense of a heterogenous aesthetic can better address the plurality of experiences that happen in applied theatre participation. In one sense this does serve to clarify the core issue of applied theatre aesthetics: there is art in participation that invites people to experience themselves differently, reflexively and self-consciously, and that is shaped both by facilitating artists and by participants themselves. The artistry and art work involved is substantial and highly valued in the specialist fields of applied theatre, but within its diverse activities there may occur instances of consummatory experience, where something worth calling Art in a different sense appears, something unpredictable and extraordinarily difficult to measure (and even to define in theoretical terms), but with potentially life-changing and life-affirming effects, as well as affects. It is likely that it is only as applied theatre artists and participants that we can observe these moments of intensity, with theoretical speculation as a reminder to value them and defend their place.

Part Two

Dancing With Difference: Moving Towards a New Aesthetics

Nicola Shaughnessy

A descriptive-structural analysis and an evaluative-affective analysis of the aesthetic will always be in tension. The one is always the problem to be explained by the other. We will always be at this broken middle, unless the terms can be changed by working from the broken middle itself.[1]

It seems to me that the dilemmas of a post critical aesthetics are exactly those of a post critical ethics. . . . In the twenty-first century it is clear that there are no longer solid and stable criteria of evaluation. If, in the case of politics and morality we can make the case for the discursive production of values, emerging from specific social groups in specific social contexts, then I suggest the same is possible in the field of aesthetics'. . . . If aesthetics can be rethought as the debate about value after the loss of certainty, a groundless aesthetics, then the relation to beauty has a different look.[2]

The multiple layers of subjectivity – self/other/society – are picked up by the kaleidoscopic interplay which theatre enables between self and other, subjective and objective, empathy and distance. And these are particularly appropriate ways of approaching the issue of ageing.[3]

Beauty reflected, recollected and reconceived

I remember the moment when I first began to question the meaning of beauty and aesthetic values in socially engaged theatre. Sian Stevenson, a practitioner and colleague, was sharing with me some photos of a

dance-based performance, *Ballroominating*[4] – featuring participants
in their seventies and eighties and which she described as 'beautiful'.
I endorsed her description wholeheartedly; the pictures of the
performers dancing, the pleasure evident in their shared smiles, the
fragility and elegance of their bodies interacting and hands touching,
were extremely moving and uplifting. Although my response to the
photographs was informed by my experience and memories of this
community performance, the photos were powerful beyond this context
and functioned as more than illustrative documentation of a live event.
The photos had an affective quality that was part of their aesthetic value,
functioning as one of several layers of performance art. In her critique
of Roger Scruton's 'photographobia', which excludes photography from
the category of the aesthetic, Isobel Armstrong challenges Scruton's
distinctions between painting (creative, affective and philosophical)
and photography (empirical, factual and devoid of emotion) with a
passionate defence of photography's time-based aesthetics:

> Photographs are celebrations of the uniqueness of every moment of
> being, every configuration of shadow and substance, and an elegy
> upon them. The permanent structures guaranteed by the physics of
> light, and the impermanent moment when the light never again falls
> in exactly the same way, are its dialectic. Photographs are as heavily
> mediated as paintings, depending on light, camera angle, the grain
> of paper, the mood of the artist. Photographs of the same object by
> different people are always different, utterances about the play of light,
> universes exposed in a single lens, epiphanies of transience.[5]

In the photography of the tea dances (documenting *Ballroominating*),
the rich and affective textures involved interplay between the physical
representation of the elderly subjects, the performance context in
which they were situated (imbuing emotion, grace and glamour)
and the broader social and cultural framework within which ageing
is conceptualized. The images countered the dominant media
representations of ageing, offering alternatives to the variously comic,
sentimental and largely negative stereotypes that Mike Featherstone

and Mike Hepworth refer to as the dualistic 'heroes of ageing/bodily decline'.[6] By contrast, *Ballroominating* staged the complexities and pluralities of what has been referred to as a 'storied process',[7] the multiple layers of consciousness and subjectivity, analysed by gerontologists and articulated by Michael Mangan in his study of Theatre and Ageing:

> Ontological subjectivity can embrace the 'I' that I am now. But the 'I' that I am now is older than the 'I' that I once was. Can my experience of that younger self be the same as my experience of my present self? Perhaps it depends on the detail: how much younger? A minute ago? Yes, surely. Yesterday? Maybe. Last week? Last year? Ten years ago? Thirty? Fifty? At what point does that 'I' start to feel like the [older] other? And how much like the other does it feel ... even more radically, to contemplate the older person is also to imagine myself as older, to imagine a subjectivity that I have not yet experienced but which I will or might experience.[8]

In his introduction, Mangan problematizes the oft-cited mirror-up-to-nature metaphor, distinguishing between biological and social ageing in an argument which complements Armstrong's discussion of the time-based complexities of photography's aesthetics. He cites Simone de Beauvoir's mirror moment where she looked at her reflection and registered the disconnection between her perception of self and the fact of being aged 40 (the ageing 'other' is a biological reality but is not embodied). This has been identified by social psychologists as a common perception of ageing, and is a recurrent theme in the case studies discussed here as indicated in the programme note to Fevered Sleep's *On Ageing*: 'In the many conversations we've had with people about ageing over the last two years, one theme has surfaced again and again: the idea of being one age, but feeling another.'[9] Performance, as a time-based medium operates in a liminal temporal space appropriate for the articulation of these complexities as it can explore the gaps Mangan refers to 'between how one feels oneself to be, and how one may be perceived.'[10] The linearity of the social narrative of decline (as exemplified in Shakespeare's oft cited seven ages of man speech in

As You Like It) in which ageing is set against youth and associated with loss (physical, social, economic), is being challenged as increased life expectancy and changing social conditions contribute to new understanding and perceptions of ageing as evident in the research underpinning the practices discussed here.[11] This is a key theme of Mangan's study, which draws upon Kathleen Woodward's seminal work on ageing:

> In recent years, social gerontologists have been quick to insist that age cannot be taken for granted as a biologically grounded 'given': rather it should be understood as one of the key bases for the production of social identity. And, like any kind of identity construction, it does not operate in a vacuum, but as part of the complex web of beliefs, assumptions and power relations that make up the ideological formations of a culture . . . what I have termed 'gerontideology' is like [Woodward's] mirror stage of old age, 'inherently triangular, involving the gaze of others as well as two images of oneself.'[12]

Gerontologists explore the changing relations and interactions between generations as behaviours and expectations shift. The active/passive dichotomies, which previously characterized youth in terms of agency as creators of the future and older generations as dependent and disempowered recipients of care, are no longer relevant. Grandparents are a source of childcare, enabling parents to work, while the 'silver surfers' remain socially connected as the internet offers new ways of communication and new forms of community to include on online courses, clubs and dating websites for the over fifties. The changing perceptions and images of ageing through increasing longevity are evidenced in the 'Mass Observation Project', which informed Fevered Sleep's *On Ageing* production. Started in 1981 at the University of Sussex, participants of all ages were invited to write about their experiences and perceptions of getting older. The responses cited by the company demythologize ageing through positive images and counter stories to the traditional narrative of decline. The production understands identity as 'complex', 'multiple' and 'accumulative', while the citation from Anais

Nin's diary in the 'On Ageing' programme note is equally relevant to the palimpsestic structures and aesthetics of *Ballroominating*[13]:

> We do not grow absolutely, chronologically. We grow sometimes in one dimension, and not in another, unevenly. We grow partially. We are relative. We are mature in one realm, childish in another. The past, present and future mingle and pull us backward, forward, or fix us in the present. We are made of layers, cells, constellations.[14]

Past, present and future interacted spatially and thematically in the multiple layers of Stevenson's mixed media production. The past of the rehearsals, the interviews that contributed to the process and the personal and social histories of participants were featured in an installation, situated above the dance hall while the performance took place on the floor below. Large windows enabled audience members to witness the dancing while visiting the installation, connecting the two modes of performance. The event engaged audience members on a number of levels, involving a wide mix of academics, families and children in participatory art, which, like Welfare *State's Barn Dances*, 'created community'. Tea and cake was served, while audience and performers also conjoined as visitors to the installation could join the dancing below to become part of the community creating the performance event (and vice versa). Documentation of the elderly performers sharing reminiscences of dances in their pasts were experienced by the performers themselves, as they visited the installation, thereby engaging in a performative and mediatized version of Woodward's mirroring triangle, interacting between the multiple subjectivities of remembered, present and future selves and others. The material in the installation offered a window into history through the accounts of the participants and their recollections of the teenager's first dance, first love, the experience of war and the communities of their past. There was beauty in the dancing and beauty in the documentation contained in the installation.

In my use of the term 'beauty' to discuss the aesthetic qualities of a community performance project with the over sixties, I draw upon critical defences of the term, particularly Isobel Armstrong's argument that to neglect the concept of beauty as bourgeois, elitist and associated with cultural hegemony is 'to fail to address the democratic and radical potential of aesthetic discourse'.[15] Beauty is being reconfigured in the twenty-first century and applied theatre scholars are new players in the field of aesthetics. Joe Winston's profound provocation in *Beauty and Education*, articulates beauty as a pedagogical concept with attention to its cognitive, affective and ethical importance, challenging educators to re-evaluate the curriculum.[16] James Thompson's pioneering work also complements Armstrong's radical aesthetic and her attention to affect. Citing Elaine Scarry's seminal discussions of beauty and pain, Thompson finds beauty in the context of war zones, writing about the 'performance of pain [and] performance of beauty' that he experienced through a drama intervention in a Sri Lankan refugee camp: 'The sheer physical enjoyment and energy that these projects can elicit, make them potential examples of the enactment of beauty – *a performance of beauty*, moments that make the heart beat faster, and people start searching for "something of the same scale".[17] The beauty I have attributed to *Ballroominating* had similar qualities: while some of the material in the installation contained references to war, pain, grief and sorrow as part of its autoethnographic fabric, this was part of the rich texture of the performance, contributing to its poignancy. The ageing bodies of the performers signified the passage of time, physically conveying the lives lived, the journeys taken and the injuries suffered but the performers moved beyond this (literally), using their bodies as instruments of expression and experience. I describe the 'affect' as 'uplifting', with reference to Thompson's terms: 'making the heart beat faster', as we responded to its affective aesthetic.[18]

I have continued to reflect on the categorization and quality of beauty and questions of value in participatory performance through my encounters with the 'extra ordinary' in a range of contexts wherein beauty is located in the everyday.[19] A girl on a beach, repeatedly dipping her toe in the water, interacting with the ripples and rhythms of the waves, unaware of being watched, is an image which Jayne Thompson remembers as a trigger for her interest in the aesthetics of the untrained body and the beauty of the everyday.[20]

Reflecting on Stevenson's photos when reading Janet Wolff's account of 'uncertain aesthetics' and her distinction between 'the *pleasure* involved in viewing' from 'the *beauty* perceived in the image', raises further questions concerning changing conceptualizations of beauty and pleasure as I discuss below.[21] As Wolff indicates, 'we can find pleasure in the unbeautiful and observe the beautiful without pleasure – with distaste, or even with admiration.'[22] John Lutterbie's work on cognition and aesthetics has also informed my thinking. Lutterbie debates similar issues to Thompson and Armstrong through his discussion of spectatorship and affect in his response to Romeo Castellucci's *Concept of the Face: Regarding the Son of God* and its disturbing images:

> Moving away from the idea of aesthetics as 'positive affect' or the pleasure of beauty, I argue that the experience of art is most powerful when meaning is deferred, perhaps long after the experience with the art object, and that fluency and disfluency are useful metaphors for understanding the processes that give rise to feelings of the aesthetic.[23]

Lutterbie looks at Brecht's concept of *verfremdungseffekt* in conjunction with dynamic systems theory as 'a partial model for understanding how time based aesthetics operate'. In Lutterbie's analysis, the derivation of meaning arises over time because of the ambiguity and disruptions of the unexpected, such as the shock factor of the incidents staged in Castellucci's production (to include an incontinent father repeatedly and spectacularly soiling himself, an image of Jesus crying dark, tainted tears and a subtle but definite smell created by what John O'Mahoney describes in a review as 'synthetic prop shit').[24] Informed by discussions of aesthetics and neuroscience and with particular reference to Vilayanur Ramachandran's conceptualization of the 'Aha' moment in terms of mirror neuron theory,[25] Lutterbie suggests that aesthetic experience, located in affect, is rather more complex than the neuroscience suggests. For Ramachandran, there are nine universals in art which constitute the aesthetic experience and give rise to the 'Aha' moment when areas of the brain such as the mirror neuron system are activated (the process whereby the same sets of neurons are activated in an observer watching an action as the individual actually engaged in an action). Ramachandran's analysis, however (like most scientific studies of creativity), is based on traditional art forms and this is the basis of Lutterbie's critique: 'Ignoring conceptual art, minimalism and those where the making of the work does not readily reveal the process of creation is not sufficient for understanding the aesthetic experience.'[26] Lutterbie's graphic description of his response to the sensual assaults of Castellucci's staging, identifies the heart of the aesthetic experience in a liminal space, a shifting between the familiar and unfamiliar in a processing of contrasting states of being:

> My aesthetic experience . . . is located in the movement between attraction and repulsion, between emotional engagement with the narrative and the 'alienation' of the incontinence episodes. Integral to the dramaturgy of the piece, each occurrence was repellent, taking me out of the story, only to be drawn back in as the old man was carefully cleansed [by his son], and I once again became aware of the father's growing shame and his son's love and increasing frustration.[27]

Although very different in content to the case studies discussed here, the Castalluci piece, and the 'cognitive dissonance' Lutterbie describes, worked through an aesthetics of accumulation, common to contemporary performance practices. Its various parts created different sensory experiences and rhythms in a non-linear iterative sequence, whereby the last two sections disrupted the 'dialectical movement' of the first. The stoning of the image of Jesus by a group of seven teenagers, the oscillations between the auditory, visual and olfactory and between realism and abstraction in the imagery and staging, contributed to what Lutterbie conceives as an 'on-going "aaaaaahhhhhhaaaaaa. . ."' in his concluding speculation:

> Through the shifting of proximities this, too, became a time-based experience. Aesthetics may result in an 'Aha' moment, but it is because of the dynamic interaction with the work of art, the shifting perspectives,

and not the firing of neurons in the pleasure centres of the brain that the emergence of meaning is possible.[28]

Although the Castalluci production is not 'applied' theatre, the aesthetic experience Lutterbie conceptualizes has synergies with the case studies featured in this chapter and the work of numerous scholars and practitioners in social, educational and community contexts, producing participatory process-based modes of performance which are both practice and research, pure and applied, challenging the dualisms of the 'aesthetic' and 'non aesthetic' as defined, for example by Erika Fischer-Lichte. In *The Transformative Power of Performance*, Fischer-Lichte seeks the meaning or purpose of performance in what she calls its 'specific aestheticity', and which she defines in relation to 'autopoiesis', a term used to define and explain dynamic living systems which are self-perpetuating and interactive. This conceptualizes the feedback loop between actors and spectators, producers and products, collapsing the binaries between subject and object in the shift from 'art' to 'event' whereby 'perception turns into an entirely emergent process'.[29]

While this process is as pertinent to the transformational aesthetics of the Castalluci production as it is to the case studies, which follow, Fischer-Lichte's categories might be seen to exclude applied theatre from the category of the aesthetic:

> While I defined aesthetic experience as liminal experience and simultaneously asserted that all genres and performance open up the possibility for liminal experience, this does not necessarily imply that all types of liminal experience can be subsumed under the category of aesthetic experience. While I will label those liminal experiences aesthetic which make the journey the goal, the liminal experiences which use the journey to reach another goal are non aesthetic. Such goals consist of a socially recognised change of status, the creation of winners and losers of communities, the legitimisation of claims to power; the creation of a social bond; entertainment.[30]

Such categorizations raise questions about the status of practices referred to as 'applied theatre' if the purposes involve social transformation and the creation of social bonds, both of which are readily identified as objectives when working in social and community contexts. The need for new evaluative criteria to recognize aesthetics *and* ethics within applied performance practice is recognized by the companies discussed here and is a topical theme in professional contexts: As Jane Willis has articulated:

> It seems that the arts and health sector is caught between two masters. While we strive to deliver artistic excellence, we also have to demonstrate clinical effectiveness. I believe that the path to excellence lies not in choosing which master to serve – the either/or dilemma – but in creating a shared set of values and a framework for assessing quality. . . . Perhaps it is in recognising and reconciling tensions that arts and health practice is at its most powerful and transformative.[31]

The participatory practices discussed in this chapter, collapse the binaries Fischer-Lichte identifies, to include her own distinction between the aesthetic and non-aesthetic. Spectators are 'partakers' and producers in work that is both art and event, exemplifying the complexities of the perceptual process she describes:

> The more frequent the perceptual shift between the arbitrary order of presence and the purposeful order of representation the more unpredictable the entire process and the more focused the subject becomes on perception itself. In the process, the spectators become increasingly aware that meaning is not transmitted to but brought forth by them.[32]

The interplay between binaries is fundamental to the aesthetic experience of the pieces discussed here. What we also see in the Castalucci piece and which is also shared with the practices I feature is an interaction between youth and age; past and future (via the performed present); and father and son, through the shifting of roles and values that so frequently occurs with the passage of time. This is also an unstable aesthetics beyond the traditional prototypes of beauty, in keeping with Janet Wolff's theorization of a 'groundless aesthetics' where 'the relation to beauty has a different look'.[33] Lutterbie's analysis has strong synergies with the new aesthetics proposed by Armstrong, whereby 'the aesthetic is important partly because it is a way of holding play and disintegration together'.[34] The various modes of engagement in the case studies that follow also explore 'the many ways in which experience is art-work, as well as furnishing the raw material for works of art'.[35] Steven Connor's commentary on Armstrong's work, reflecting on the timeliness of her call for a new aesthetics, appropriate to the twenty-first century, evokes the context for the performance practices I discuss.

> Scientific thinking about the nature of life, matter and form has become unignorable, even by literary critics and . . . the relations between the mental and the material have become so much jumpier and more interesting. . . . A physics, and an aesthetics formed in its terms, which is based upon work, one-way transformation and determinate output (heat, light, poetry) is giving way to a physics of interfaces, ecologies, probabilities, reciprocities, probabilities and the turbulent circulation of energies. Following the curious temporality of science, from now on, for the time being, this will have been the way it always was.[36]

What is described here might be conceptualized as relational and socially situated aesthetics, 'grounded in community', anti-individualist and without 'a foundation in certainties and universals', to use Wolff's terms.[37] The rest of this chapter explores these aesthetic formations through case studies involving inter-generational performance processes in work we can describe as socially engaged, but which is somewhat uneasily situated in relation to categorizations of 'applied' theatre. As Sian Stevenson emphasizes, participatory practices involve a working with, rather than an 'applying to', challenging production hierarchies.[38] Both the companies featured, moreover, are developing evaluative models with criteria which are recognizable in the context of applied theatre *and* performance in terms of impact on participants (and audiences), well-being and inter-generational and community engagement. Both companies are also committed to evaluating the work as art and to developing a new aesthetics of performance.[39] The first example features the development of Stevenson's work through a series of projects created with her collaborator, Jayne Thompson and their contemporary dance theatre company. The focus is their most recent piece, *More Please* (2013) in which the story of the emergence of the company's distinctive aesthetics of community is the basis of the choreography.[40] This is discussed in conjunction with the work of Fevered Sleep and their productions of *On Ageing* (seven child performers delivering a verbatim script made from conversations with people of all ages) as well as *Men and Girls Dance*, involving prepubescent girls and professional male contemporary dancers who are starting to experience the challenges of an ageing body. As Armstrong advocates, 'Evolving another poetics means challenging the politics of the anti-aesthetic', but does not mean 'returning to a pre-theoretical innocence . . . to give new content to the concept of the aesthetic means broadening the scope of what we think of as art.'[41] My analysis draws upon Armstrong's account and the aesthetic components she identifies as 'embedded in the practices of consciousness, playing and dreaming, thinking and feeling or put another way, ceaseless *mediation* endows language making and symbol making, thought and the life of affect,

Figure 2 *Men and Girls Dance*. (Photograph Benedict Johnson).

with creative and cognitive life. These processes . . . can become the basis from which to develop a democratic aesthetic.'[42] Drawing upon the work of Terry Eagleton and Gillian Rose, Armstrong describes the aesthetic cognitively and affectively, emphasizing the importance of play, 'the drive to experiment' and the process of mediation theorized by Rose, where the movement between opposites creates breakdown, contradiction and a restructuring of relationships:

> Rose's new understanding of mediation releases discussion from the experiencing consciousness of the subject and moves to what consciousness does, not a self-struggling but the nature of struggle itself; not a representation of the subject, but the subject of a representation, which is not a self, not an object, or a thematics, but the structuring movement of thought and feeling. . . . I argue that the broken middle is the constitutive moment of the aesthetic.[43]

This notion of the in between space of the broken middle, and the bridging of affect and thought, emotion and cognition as well as the recognition of the need for 'an adequate *analytical* language for affect'[44] anticipates the turn to cognition in performance scholarship. Lutterbie's reading of the Castaluccio production (and his experience of the broken middle) can be seen to exemplify how, to use Armstrong's terms 'a cognitive account of the emotions as mutually inclusive is the core of a remade aesthetic.' My account brings cognitive theory into dialogue with conceptualizations of relational, community and socially situated aesthetics with particular reference to Evelyn Tribble and John Sutton's definition of cognitive ecologies, as a means of exploring the interplay and connections between cognition and affect:

> Cognitive ecologies are the multidimensional contexts in which we remember, feel, think, sense, communicate, imagine, and act, often collaboratively, on the fly, and in rich ongoing interaction with our environments. . . . These models share an anti-individualist approach to cognition. In all these views, mental activities spread or smear across the boundaries of skull and skin to include parts of the social and

material world. In remembering, decision making, and acting, whether individually or in small groups, our complex and structured activities involve many distinctive dimensions: neural, affective, kinesthetic, sensory, interpersonal, historical, political, cultural, technological. . . . Many cognitive states and processes are hybrids, unevenly distributed across the physical, social, and cultural environments as well as bodies and brains, hooking up in both temporary and more enduring ways with other people and with certain things – artefacts, media, technologies, or institutions – each with its own history and tendencies. In other words, this is a systems-level mode of analysis.[45]

What is described here is the complex process through which we embody cognition and make meaning; the dynamic, relational and iterative interplay between neural, social and affective domains that produces language, emotion, memory, perception and action, creating our sense of 'being'.[46] A cognitive systems approach challenges the dualisms between the intrinsic and extrinsic, creating the possibility for synergies between the 'social' and 'artistic' and the tensions identified by Jane Willis.[47] The rest of this chapter explores a series of questions concerning how the work featured is valued, analysis of its affect and the qualities of a new aesthetics emerging from the tensions within the 'broken middle' to create interactions between pasts, presents and futures and between physical, social and cultural environments.

Moving beyond moving: StevensonThompson

The collaboration between Sian Stevenson and Jayne Thompson, conjoins shared interests in feminism, autobiographical modes of performance, movement-based theatre and the expressive potential of the untrained body. Stevenson's commitment to working in community contexts and with disability stems from her background in anthropology and social work prior to her professional theatre career.[48] Thompson's engagement with community performance draws upon her work on verbatim and the use of multimedia to explore stories and perform ethnographies, complementing Stevenson's body-based approach.[49] The work engages with and emerges from the social, material and physical environments that have shaped participants' experiences. All the work (as the titles of productions indicate) explores and embodies memory – personal and cultural. Seeking to 'create quality work which frames peoples experiences in a public forum', the company creates art from the everyday, performing lives as part of a developing aesthetic that aims 'to find the extraordinary in the ordinary'.[50]

The company's evolution is itself something of an *autopoiesis* (to use Fischer-Lichte's analogy), developing as a self-perpetuating and interactive system through an iterative feedback loop, whereby relations between producers and products are reconceived, challenging the dualisms and hierarchies of traditional theatre structures. The legacy of the first production, *Moving Memory* was the formation of the Moving Memory Company as the participants wanted to continue working together. *Moving Memory* emerged as a follow on from Stevenson's previous work with older people in *Ballroominating*. In partnership with Thompson the collaborators secured funding to create new modes of performance which would challenge perceptions of age and the older body, questioning how audiences perceive older people and exploring relations between women and women as well as men and women. The work involved a layering process, an aesthetics of accumulation as material was located (in a variety of contexts), transposed from its originating source and transformed into art based on experience to use Armstrong's terms. Indeed, Armstrong's aesthetic categories can be mapped onto the company's methods: 'playing and the drive to experiment'; community being central to 'cultural dreaming'; the dynamic relation between the cognitive and the affective ('thinking and feeling'), as meaning is embodied. Also pertinent to Armstrong's aesthetic is the 'transverse' politics of the company's structure as community participants develop into co-performers, contributing increasingly to the devising and choreographing process and eventually forming a company of their own, as a self-sustaining legacy from a production process.

The first project developed from workshops in a residential care home for people with dementia whose stories were subsequently transposed by able-bodied performers. The context presented some challenges as the home had a varied population of people from diverse socio-economic backgrounds with differing staff perceptions of residents' capabilities and limited resources for running workshops. However, some staff were willing to participate in workshops which were run in a small garden room and as the work progressed and confidence developed, the stories began to emerge that would be the basis for *Moving Memory* (2010) and its sequels: *Moving on* (2011) *Moving on Moving* (2012) and *More Please* (2013). The experience of working with John and Winifred had particular significance for the development of the work.[51] Winifred was in late-stage dementia, and spent most of her time curled up in a ball on the floor. Her husband, John, visited her every day and through the workshop process, discovered new ways of being with her as he recounted memories of his courtship and dancing. The Veleta waltz that was John and Winifred's favourite and was core to their generation became central to the company's work.[52] Their daughter also contributed during one of her visits, recounting the story of her mother's red ball gown getting wet in the toilet. It was John's desire to physically dance but not having sufficient mobility to do so which stimulated the company's later experiments with digital forms, dancing with avatars as a digital self or partner.[53] *Moving Memory* tells the stories of people who couldn't move beyond the physical confines of their residential space through the bodies of a disparate group of 50–80 year old women. Source material from the original workshops was developed through a series of ballroom dancing workshops; the John and Winifred story provided a loose narrative structure underpinning the movement-based devising process that is central to Stevenson Thompson's methods. The process of transposition, involved a layering process as the narratives from the people in the care home interacted with the experiences of the participants. Performing the lives of others involved an ethical responsibility that participants were very aware of and which contributes to the company's aesthetics as they question, explore and transform the relations between the selves who dance and the others whose stories are the basis for the performance. The elderly women developed new understandings of their bodies as expressive vehicles to develop and convey new meanings. 'Questioning is play', Stevenson explains in discussing the company's methods in terms which directly connect with Armstrong's conceptualization of a new aesthetic.[54] Drawing upon Winnicott's theory of transitional objects in conjunction with Vygotsky's discussion of play and pedagogy, Armstrong suggests that the term 'transitional object', 'gives room for the process of being able to accept difference and similarity. It is not me and part of me.'[55] For the elderly participants in *Moving Memory*, the interplay between ethics and aesthetics involved an understanding of the identity performed being both self and other, or 'me' and 'not me', moving in between subject and object. The play-based processes of the workshops were a site of transition in precisely the way Armstrong describes whereby 'play is and creates a shared cultural reality' as part of an intersubjective aesthetics of community.[56] Citing Winnicott, Armstrong describes a relational interplay that maps onto the processes of participatory performance and its becomings: 'The place where cultural experience is located is the *potential space* between the individual and the environment (originally the object). The same can be said of playing.'[57] Through the deep play involved in the participatory processes Stevenson and Thompson describe, a group of disparate women became an ensemble and the material gathered through workshops was transposed into performance. The women danced with each other and with elegant ball gowned mannequins, representing the absent others whose stories were being danced. The stagings were in outdoor community spaces – a plaza and a labyrinth on a university campus adding a further layer to the composition process through choreography that emerged from and responded to the performance environment. The stories appeared to 'spiral out of the landscape' to adapt Doreen Massey's terms with the women drawing the paths of others, transforming a community space as part of the transitive aesthetics.[58] Stevenson's reference to choreographing 'with', rather than 'on', describes the company's relations to people and place as sources for performance and the company's approach to participatory practice, which they articulate as 'the ethics of not applying to'. This, then is a version of Armstrong's democratic aesthetic and her reference to John Dewey's *Art as Experience* uses terms which engage in dialogue with the company's description of their methods:

> Often travestied, Dewey's account of experience and of artwork is always hyphenated in the sense that for him both always work on and with the world. His is not an individualist but an intersubjective theory, which he saw as severely exacting because it demanded arousal of the faculties. . . . Dewey's commitment to ideas of community is the impetus for a return to the politics of cultural dreaming.[59]

In StevensonThompson, these transitive aesthetics involve 'working with' people through participatory processes and 'working on' audiences through arousal in what we conceive as 'affective performance'.[60] Dewey's remapping of the aesthetic anticipates the anti-individualist 'cognitive ecologies' Tribble and Sutton refer to as meaning is made through interactions that 'spread or smear across the boundaries of skull and skin to include parts of the social and material world'.[61] Moving is at the heart of the company's work thematically and conceptually, as their 'transportations', to use Helen Nicholson's term, move audiences to new understandings and perceptions of aesthetics, ageing and themselves.[62] This is the transformative potential of performance as described by Fischer-Lichte, which, however, is effected through a transitive aesthetics that embraces the social bonding of socially engaged theatre.

The performance of *Moving Memory* wasn't an ending but a context for the next stage of Stevenson and Thompson's work in moving towards a new aesthetics. 'Another layer' was needed, they explain, and this involved the personal and the digital. The introduction of younger performers, aged 18 to 22, added a further dimension to their intersubjective explorations. These 'Mini Me's' as they were known explored their emerging identities, on the cusp of adulthood in dialogue with their elder counterparts. Multimedia contributed to the company's performance vocabularies to include filmed footage, photography, verbatim recording, digital projection, motion capture technologies and avatars. Identity, embodiment and ageing continued to be core to the company's practice. The physicality and materiality of the performance process moves beyond the metaphors of object relations and psychoanalytic paradigms. Armstrong, brings mind and body together, articulating the importance of the cognitive *and* the affective in aesthetic experience and arguing that 'emotion should be included in a definition of the rational'.[63]

Bodily sensations and experiences are the basis for developing the personal choreographies of what has become the *Moving Memory* company as the women have continued to work together, developing their movement-based vocabularies through weekly workshops and a series of productions under Stevenson and Thompson's directorship. The intergenerational work uses body states to bring the experiences of the younger and older performers into dialogue. 'Where has this body carried me?' the company of elders were asked, responding through writing and/or physical expression. A related exercise with the 'Mini Me's' involved them focussing on parts of the body that hold a memory, verbalizing it and then moving. Subsequent productions by the *Moving Memory* company under the direction of Stevenson and Thompson, built upon the translational processes of the previous work; stories gathered through movement workshops in dementia care homes were the basis for developing auto/biographical choreographies. The Veleta waltz became a 'key inspiration' for the dance-based theatre emerging from the process and the trilogy of productions devised and revised over the next 3 years as the 'Moving Memory' company developed the multimodal performance vocabularies and ethnographies which distinguish the work. In both *Moving On* and *Moving on Moving*, filmed footage and verbatim recording contributed to the staging which fully exploited the production technologies of building-based theatre. Young and old dancers interacted playfully with washing lines and brooms as props of domestic lives; salt was poured slowly and gracefully to create delicate white spirals in an intertextual reference to the previous performance on the labyrinth. The addition of young men and women to the choreography created juxtapositions of age which were profoundly moving as elder women danced elegantly and tenderly with younger men: 'bucking conventional images of age' to use the title of the post-show platform.

The diverse outputs from the StevensonThompson collaboration (to include Flash Mobs, place responsive performance, public engagement events and a training DVD) are conjoined by the commitment to 'celebrating difference, community and communication'. Their next piece *More Please* developed the self-referential meta-textures of previous work by making the story of the *Moving Memory* company the basis for the performance. Its members now meet weekly and are paid; confident in their abilities to contribute, they are able to analyse and articulate shared values of accessibility and authenticity, hence the importance of working with their own material to define form. The collaboration with Butch Auntie[64] enabled the performers to work with avatars as well as movement sensors. This generated a perceptual shift by working as a distancing tool through which the women could see themselves as other, viewing their bodies and patterns of their movement through an abstract form of mirroring.

Figure 3 *More Please.* (Photograph: Matt Wilson).

Watching rehearsals for *More Please* provided further insights into the ways in which the company's methods challenge traditional dualisms through interactions between process and performance, past, present and futures, art and science. The rehearsal space itself exemplifies this with the dancers positioned in a creative in-between space as projections create a scenic backdrop behind them while a line of cameras, computers and individuals observe them as an audience of producers and technicians contributing to the performance making. The phrase 'engineers of the imagination' springs to mind as the technology engages in dialogue with the choreography;[65] images of previous rehearsals and performances interact with the dancing of the here and now, the liminal no/where of performance temporality. The piece fuses the pasts of previous rehearsals and performances with the physical real and the virtual as body sensors, avatars and projection create what Amelia Jones has described as 'the shifting, pulsating, writing, dancing, expressive action of bodies in space over time'.[66]

What moves me? What is moving them to move? I think of Helen Nicholson's reflections on the concept of transportation: 'If the motive is individual or personal transformation is this something done *to* the participants, *with* them or *by them*? Whose values and interests does the transformation serve?'[67] The participants are also producers; the work is for them and by them but is also for others; the 'gift of theatre', to use Nicholson's terms. These women are deeply engaged in modes of self-expression, while also aware of and contributing to the collective dynamics of devising. The piece is about themselves and their creative others; a story of collaboration, mapping the individual and collective process of the company's transformative journey. A single white feather floats and dances on the screen, introducing the swans and Swan Lake, an accompanying story of becomings. Stevenson is both inside and out as she watches and participates, leading the choreographic process and working from within, weaving in and out, interacting with individuals, sometimes modelling and sculpting movements, counting time, conducting and orchestrating this ensemble. The dancers touch each other, stroking backs, supporting and carrying, exchanging energies, creating and releasing tensions, in time and in tune. This is entrainment (defined as 'the process that activates or provides a timing cue for a biological rhythm'),[68] a being together through kinaesthetic empathy. I am part of this process, a participant spectator, dancing with them in my imagination. 'Body bits' is about each dancer's relationship with her body; they are touching the bits they want to hide, some twitching and jerking to convey their experiences of disembodiment, bodies as objects, habits and behaviours becoming performed actions as the sequence moves from the personal to the inter-personal and they share with each other. I feel the pain in these movements, empathizing with the dancer pulling at her stomach and another touching her neck and throat. There are no words for this, but the physical vocabularies powerfully articulate and explore feelings, emotion made conscious and body-based memories. The textures here are 'shifting, pulsating', actions speak louder than words as the dancers gesture towards pain, self-harm, abuse, anger and sadness. As the sequence progresses, the tension relaxes and the movements convey care, compassion and tenderness. I am drawn in, thinking of bellies that have carried babies, boobs that have breast-fed, the silver stretch marks, scars and wrinkles where life and living is drawn upon the skin. Neuroscience challenges the mind/ body dualism, helping us to understand concepts of embodiment which are at the heart of this work and that how we think and feel is in part shaped by perception of activity in the body.

'Get your tits out – show us what you're showing' Stevenson encourages towards the end of a run. Laughter and play are also at work here as the dancers fight over chairs and act out grandmother's footsteps with a biscuit, exploring the hierarchies and power struggles of group dynamics and the process of ensemble formation. Teasing becomes taunting and envy as the dancers eye each other up, form partnerships and groups, rejecting each other and casting out the weak and the vulnerable. 'What is she wearing', Sian interjects as Thompson's high-heeled elegance sweeps the stage acting out her original entry to the company's performance process as an artistic director who began working from within the ensemble during the *Moving Memory* production. Thompson describes her role as an intermediary between the performers and directors, feeding confidence or acting as a saboteur to support the performers as they contribute to the devising process.

More Please explores the complexities of the company's journey towards ensemble performance and community aesthetics. The politics of the company's changing hierarchies are staged with simplicity, poignancy and humour. Performers enter in the order of their arrival in the company and find their place on the row of chairs, centre stage. As more performers enter, the others change positions; one sits on top of another and shortly after Thompson's entry, one of the dancers loses her place and stands at the side of the stage – isolated, head lowered, body cowering, before the music changes and the body lifts, confidence is recovered and this dancer takes the lead, the stage is hers to dance her story. The solo is also the company's story as it discovered its performance vocabularies: 'It's about building connections', Stevenson explains, 'really enjoying dancing together, building relations and discovering a new language.'[69] Relational aesthetics, defined by Bourriaud as 'artistic practices which take as their theoretical and practical point of departure the whole of human relations and their social context, rather than an independent and private space' can be seen as part of the fabric of the performance and its choreography as well as being a context from which the work has developed.[70]

The interaction between the ethical and the aesthetic in the work of StevensonThompson is evident in their evaluation methodologies and criteria, as articulated by Thompson in discussion of the company's collaboration with the Sydney de Haan Centre for research in arts and health:

I think it is fair to say that the project, in this particular case, probably differed significantly from others involving older participants in relation to the arts and health. In the first instance, the project involved a group of females aged 50-82 for whom the outcome would be a public performance. Alongside the artistic directors' ambitions to develop a new performance aesthetic privileging the older female body was an attempt to explore and exploit the integration of digital technology in both the creative process and performance. It is worth noting that earlier experimental workshops had demonstrated a number of potential beneficial effects (physical) that had emerged in, and as a result of, participant engagement with digital projections. Key to the ongoing development of this latest performance was the development of new creative approaches and an anticipated increase in creativity, as well as mobility, on the part of the participants. To this end, the work was being evaluated in terms of the need for sustainable cost-effective interventions that have the capacity to support physical, mental and cognitive wellbeing and subsequent prolonged independence. There were further ambitions to assess the feasibility of transferring such initiatives using digital technology from the open community to continuing-care residential environments for older people.

In terms of the evaluation of impact, what was being measured in this project again differed significantly from other conventional research projects and one of the key aims for the De Haan team was to develop an evaluation tool to enable the assessment of levels and intensity of involvement in creative activities among people with and without memory impairment. It was important for the researchers that any methods for measuring these factors should be transferable to residential care settings and to people with disabilities, particularly those associated with dementia.[71]

The company's concerns with both the artistic quality of the work produced as well as its affect on participants involved the development of new modes of evaluation, using a range of qualitative and quantitative measures to assess efficacy and affect. This can be seen then as both a 'principled' and relational aesthetic, to adapt Wolff's terms, whereby the grounds for judgement are 'made transparent' and which is 'the reasoned outcome of dialogue and communication on the basis of community.'[72] Aesthetic evaluation, as Wolff contends, is always situational and a product of its contemporary culture and values. The concept of social capital has offered new ways of thinking about the function and value of the arts in the twenty-first century, and its ideologies inform and sustain what is now referred to as 'socially engaged art'. If the core thesis of anti-individualist social capital theory is that relationships matter, this must serve as one of the most important criteria for value in the work of StevensonThompson and other companies (such as Fevered Sleep below) whose work blends participatory practice, 'social' *and* 'aesthetic' theatre.[73]

Relational aesthetics (conceiving of contemporary art as an encounter in the context of social relations) in conjunction with cognitive perspectives have important and 'co-operative' roles to play in conceptualizing and evaluating the dynamic interplay of these elements in a 'systems-level mode of analysis', to use Tribble and Sutton's model. For Gregory Minissale (with reference to Rancière), 'What is remarkable about relational aesthetics . . . is that it is inherently social *and* metacognitive, an emancipation of seeing and doing in aesthetic exploration with others.'[74] In *The Psychology of Contemporary Art* he argues:

> The only comprehensive way to do justice to [its] dynamic complexity is to integrate not only different disciplines but also different theories such as situated and extended cognition, analogy, embodied approaches, conceptual blending and relational knowledge. . . . Against the customary cynicism with which contemporary art is often met, even within its ranks, it still offers the opportunity to create an emancipated imagination consisting of aesthetic *and* ethical possibilities. Such an imagination maybe antagonist yet also participatory, consisting of social involvements where agency is both assured and shared.[75]

In the work discussed in this chapter, *newness* is found in the *old*, in making the familiar strange, in finding the extraordinary in the ordinary and in value systems which challenge or differ from the individualist and materialist, in favour of community and in which co-operation and awareness of others is part of the performance experience or encounter. As contemporary forms of aesthetic and socially engaged practice, the work offers what Minissale refers to as 'chances to experiment with different kinds of connections between concepts, whilst requiring us to become more aware of the everyday'[76] and, I would add, its beauty. Minissale's commentary on participatory art and relational aesthetics is pertinent to both case studies as modes of participatory theatre, involving community engagement with 'new' (i.e. untrained) performers in professional contexts and in pursuit of artistic goals (articulated in terms of a new aesthetics) and within which 'immersion in the social exchange in and around the art work becomes the theme of the art work.'[77]

Fevered Sleep and 'Social Works': *On Ageing* and *Men and Girls Dance*

In the work of Fevered Sleep, my final case study, the aesthetic experience is located in exchanges and interplay between elders and children in *On Ageing* and the different ages and genders in *Men and Girls Dance*. Both productions involved the 'chances to experiment with different kinds of connections' and 'immersion in social exchange' as part of the process and performance. Performed by children for an audience of adults, the textures of *On Ageing* involved a series of juxtapositions whereby the space in-between is the 'broken middle', the in-between space where meaning is made and the site of our affective response. The gap between the expressive language of the words spoken and the audience's receptive understanding and interpretation as children speak the words of others draws attention to the difference between the script and the speaker, particularly when children deliver grown up lines. When a young girl refers to 'being twenty-nine and not liking it', we are aware that the words she is speaking are not owned by her; as one of the children comments, 'It's more for grown-ups than it is for actual children because it's grown-up jokes.'[78] The evaluation report refers to audience members commenting on the effect of having older people's words spoken by children: '[They] were conscious of the way it helped them to see beyond the physiology of ageing',[79] Rebecca Johnson reports and quotes the dramaturg's perception that 'it was not just children talking, [rather] it [was] children talking as if they know what ageing is.'[80] In her conclusion to *Social Works*, Shannon Jackson discusses the disruptive and paradoxical role of the child in her conceptualization of 'interdependent performance': 'The child is riveting because of the potential to destroy the aesthetic frame; in their phenomenological presence and their social unpredictability she is a walking threat to the divide between art and life.'[81] In her revisionary account of relational art, Jackson builds upon the critical response to Bourriaud, pointing to the significance of the social structures supporting and producing artistic practice, interrogating questions of agency and autonomy and, in contradiction to Bourriaud, foregrounds the importance of responsibility: 'The resonance of this relational work' she argues, 'lies in the fact that it both requir[es] and index[es] a supporting system- one that [is] material, spatial, temporal, and too formally intriguing to dismiss as "servile".'[82] Thus her account explores performance sites where 'aesthetic and social provocations coincide' prompting 'shift[s] in perception' and drawing attention to 'the social stakes of that perceptual shift.'[83] Children, she suggests, 'are to some extent the ultimate figure of interdependence', although I would argue that the elderly are similarly configured and in *On Ageing* it is the interplay between these social groups that creates perceptual shifts. *On Ageing* plays with the dynamics Jackson refers to whereby the child 'is both a welcome refreshment and an annoying pain . . . both a welcome distraction and a figure who demands new kinds of care and attention',[84] such as the performer who requires the audience to break convention, acknowledge her real life identity and sing happy birthday. For some audience members this is perceived as disruptive and precocious, for others it is charming: 'What a pleasure, what a pain', to use Jackson's terms.

The spaces between past, present and future are also part of an affective interplay between differences and connections, as indicated in the programme notes:

> These performers are not people who dwell on the future or the past, they all live so completely in the present. That's the place where people of their age live. . . . In the show, there is a lot of playing in the moment,

of discovering objects and what an object can do, or what it can be, because that is what children do. But for us watching it, *with our experience*, an object isn't just an object. It resonates with a history and evokes some sense of memory or a person, or a potential future and we realise that all this playfulness and living in the present is not a state of being that we can stay in forever (my emphases).[85]

Objects of emotion are the media interacting between the different temporal and perceptual realities of child performers and adult audiences. This temporality is a contributory factor to the landscape of performance art as discussed by Adrian Kear: 'The time of the present replaces representational time as the currency of performance; performance becomes less an art of narrative presentation than an art of being *in* the present.'[86] This sense of a continuous present, being in the moment and its intensity is a characteristic of the contemporary performance vocabularies used by Fevered Sleep. Connected to these production values is the concept of 'not acting' in order to be 'present' in the moment and in the room with the audience – the space of performance. The company selected children who could play and 'didn't have the desire to act'.[87] A strategy that contributes to the qualities of authenticity and integrity that are also part of the production values for all the companies I have discussed. Jayne Thompson refers to the importance of authenticity in StevensonThompson's aesthetics as they foreground the processes involved in making performance and the real lives generating the material. Authenticity is located in the spaces between art and life, the social and the aesthetic. The term is used when Thompson refers to their experiments with verbatim recordings of children's voices that reflect on ageing, using similar strategies to Fevered Sleep. Rather than being 'seen but not heard' Thompson's interviews with children foreground their voices as they convey their perceptions of ageing at the opening of *Moving on Moving*. Asked what they think about growing old the children's recorded conversations progress from wrinkles to memories of grandparents and then to the stories surrounding the grandmother who was a professional ballerina and whose influence is felt as a continuing presence by the child who talks about her and who wants to be a dancer when she grows up. This sequence frames the intergenerational (and interdependent) dance theatre which ensues, creating a social and contextual backdrop for the work, fusing the ethical and the aesthetic in an acknowledgement of the familial and cultural structures from which the work has emerged and the responsibility towards those whose stories are being danced. This is where authenticity and integrity is located. Thompson's work on verbatim in the context of naturalism informs the company's approach.[88] This self-reflexive style of performance, doesn't depend on pretence but draws attention to the 'here and now' of the theatre space, drawing upon and referring to the spontaneity of improvisation, acknowledging the audience and letting us hear the pauses, laughter and interruptions of children's conversations. In both companies, authenticity is understood as something that is produced, emerging from the spaces between the aesthetic and the social.

In *On Ageing,* authenticity is derived from the quality of child's play. On one level we are an audience for a play on play as pretending to be grown up is part of children's every day activities and what is enacted might be seen in a playground. It feels as if the children are and are not acting, a meta-theatre which is both simple and sophisticated, innocent and experienced. This 'doubleness' which 'blur[s] the lines between grown-up art and childhood play' is commented on by Jackson as a feature of productions for adults where:

> children are not only the content dramatised but the medium by which it is performed. . . . On the one hand, such performing children exude the kind of naturalised authenticity that make audiences feel they are in the midst of the real. On the other, the odd attraction of the child performer comes from her ability to overcome the chaos of childhood with precocious performances of virtuosic poise.[89]

In addition to creating authenticity, this 'doubleness' also functions, somewhat paradoxically, as a distancing device, making us aware of our perspectives as adults watching children in a theatre and responding to grown up lines 'from the mouths of babes'. *On Ageing* moreover involves modes of direct address which remind us of our presence and temporality as an audience; as in the final stages where one of the child performers remarks to the audience: 'At the end of the show, you'll all disappear, but that's ok, because we'll still be here tomorrow.'[90] Lines such as these refer to the performance environment as part of a series of connections and disconnections, making us aware of our relations to the material and our roles and responsibilities as audience members watching a show performed by children. The aesthetic response is also ethical, as evident in Jackson's discussion of the structures of care and interdependence in performance work with children. The risks of aesthetic and ethical compromise are critical: 'Child performance risks obfuscating sentimentality. The "aaawww" that comes reflexively from the audience is evidence enough that the affect of the child onstage is over-determined, set in advance before he arrives.'[91] Our awareness of the 'aaawww' factor, however, resonates with Lutterbie's discussion of the 'Aha' moment, as we remain conscious of our affective and aesthetic response being located within our cultural, material and physical environments within and beyond the theatre.

Men and Girls Dance develops this interplay through a piece that is more radical in its exploration of inter-generational relations and the use of children in performances for adults. Exploring interactions between different sexes and ages, *Men and Girls Dance* creates challenges for audiences in how to respond to the work. The piece is situated precariously between what is and isn't socially acceptable and taboo. The playing here is deeper and arguably more dangerous in terms of ethical and aesthetic risks. Indeed, Harradine's original proposal involved collaborating with a neuroscientist to explore the effect of the work on audiences through the kinaesthetic empathy invoked when watching dance.[92] The initial impetus for *Men and Girls Dance* came from an audition process and the image of a group of girls and men improvising together. A pilot project involved 6- to 14-year-old girls interacting with the older male professional dancers. Both age groups were in transition as the girls moved towards puberty, experiencing their changing body states, while the male dancers were also adjusting to changes in their bodily capacities, requiring them to move differently.

In her introduction to *Social Works,* Jackson cites the cultural critic Vivian Sobchack, who coins the term 'echo focus' in reflecting on her leg amputation 'to describe this back grounded awareness of the tools and body rhythms one uses to move through the world.'[93] This is a central metaphor for Jackson's theory of interdependency between performing art and its 'supportive publics' in what she defines as 'social works', a definition appropriate to all the work featured in this chapter as it blurs the lines between art and event, aesthetic and social theatre:

> The social world is in fact a large systemic prosthesis for the normative bodies its structures support. If, however, this social prosthesis 'is subordinate to our focus and goals' [Sobchack] then it requires a break or deviation for us to remember that it is there. For the 'differently abled' writes Sobchack, it means realizing 'whether suddenly or routinely – that the world is not your dance floor.'[94]

This is pertinent literally and metaphorically to the structures of *Men and Girls Dance* as the deviation from the norms of dance affects performers and audience, making us aware of the social structures that support and constrain the production of art.

In a 2013 pilot project[95] Harradine's performance experiment focussed on the politics of the body through non-sexual encounters and the difficulties of exploring this in terms of physical relations between men and girls. The mixed responses to the proposal can be attributed to a constraining 'echo' in the wake of the Jimmy Savile controversy and the cultural discourse lurking behind the project.[96] Harradine refers to those who were 'troubled by the idea, suspicious of its intentions, unable to get past the negative connotations of bringing men and girls together. This reaction made it clear to us that there is something political at stake in this project, something to do with the politics of interaction, of relationships, of empathy and of love.'[97] Given the hyper-sexualization of relationships that are currently prevalent in the media, Harradine's project aimed to explore alternative scenarios of paternity, tenderness, care and play between men and girls. Improvisatory processes sought to find out more about how social contexts, preconditioning and social taboos impact on how dancers move together (across age and gender), as well as how an observing audience interprets those movements, and the bases of these assumptions and responses:

> We imagined a performance in which a group of adult male contemporary dancers performed alongside a group of young girls who study ballet, who dance for fun. At this stage, we were interested in difference: male and female, adult and child, professional and amateur, contemporary and classical.[98]

Working with three male dancers and four groups of girls, the devising process involved a series of movement exchanges and sequences, a dynamics of 'call and response' as the dancers took turns to lead, copying or developing the movements of each other. The start of the process involved the girls in large and small groups exploring interactions with the male dancers. Their choreography reflected movement vocabularies acquired through dancing socially and 'for fun' rather than through dance training, while the male dancers drew upon a professional training to create exploratory choreographies that were responsive to the girls as they danced around, between and with them. For many mainstream dance practitioners, the code of practice excludes touch but Fevered Sleep's experiment started with contact improvisation, exploring the politics of touch and anxieties around touch, coded behaviour. Harradine explains how the work moved beyond image and the contrasts between bodies to explore a 'body politics', investigating and challenging the infrastructures within which the work has struggled to find expression, the pain and pleasure of working within and against constraint, to use Jackson's terms: 'Its politics will not be in its content', Harradine explains, 'its politics is inherent in its form: a physical performance performed by men and girls. Adult bodies. Children's bodies. Men's bodies. Girl's bodies. Dancing together. Being together. The politics of that.'[99] As the workshops developed, the process explored the relations between men and girls to generate understand-ings physically, emotionally, intellectually.

The questions and issues, Harradine articulates as part of the project's aesthetic and ethical inquiry resonates with Jackson's study. There are strong synergies between *Men and Girls Dance* and Jackson's concluding discussion of Joe Goode's reworking of *Deeply There*, a piece of dance theatre 'about AIDS, sex, death. Hope and kinship'. Jackson describes the moving choreography between Frank (whose partner Ben is dying) and his son from a previous relationship as they dance together using lifts and exchanges of weight to 'question the division between the independently grown and dependently young.'[100] In *Men and Girls Dance*, Harradine refers to being surprised by reversals of care relations emerging through improvisations:

> The strong sense of tenderness and support and care that has emerged has not been the tenderness, support and care of adults for children but of children for adults. This has led us to be interested in working with men who are well into their careers, whose physicality might be changing; men for whom keeping dancing might be more difficult than it used to be. The contrast between a vulnerable strength (men) and a strong vitality (girls) has become important, along with exploring ideas around emotional vulnerability, playfulness and risk.[101]

As a 'social work' the piece, like the others discussed here, challenges the supports and constraints of the structures of theatre. Like StevensonThompson's work this is both theatre and dance, professional and community work where people and places are its form and content. *Men and Girls Dance* invites audiences to think differently about dance and what it is, Harradine explains. He is interested in making work which comments on dance and which makes direct connection with the people who live in the places where the work will be performed.[102] The company's decision to locate the work in community venues is articulated by Harradine as an aesthetic choice. The touring model he has developed involves the company of men on tour with the girls being recruited locally through a series of residencies in the local venues for the work. Presented in partnership with arts venues, performances will be in community spaces – the church or village halls where girls might dance for fun. Aware of the difficulties of developing relational work in community contexts, the touring model involves residencies being preceded by a 6-month programme of regular visits to work with the children participating as performers. The company is seeking to explore the different aesthetics of the places in which the work is located and the fluidity of devising in a place. Thus in *Men and Girls Dance*, Fevered Sleep is also seeking to explore the 'relationships between arts spaces and community',[103] articulating an understanding of and engagement with Jackson's concept of interdependence in social practice: 'A term that combines aesthetics and politics as a term for arts events that are inter-relational, embodied and durational.'[104]

Jackson's terminologies connect to the cognitive perspectives articulated by Lutterbie in his 'time-based' aesthetics as well as the cognitive ecologies model evoked by Tribble and Sutton all of which conceptualize performance as 'distributed, co-constructed, system-level activities',[105] in which the aesthetic experience is associated with 'thinking or remembering in action'. In all the work discussed we see the interplay and interdependence between cognitive and affective mechanisms, the social and material environment, ethics and aesthetics. Indeed, in seeking to understand the relations between men and girls and the audience response, Fevered Sleep turned to neuroscience, as Harradine explains:

> In talking about and exploring empathy, we've started some initial research into neuroscientific ideas around the function of mirror neurons in the brain: the mechanism through which one can have a physical or emotional response to the physical and emotional experience of another. To be able to feel another's pain, to experience another's emotions, to physically understand something that someone else is experiencing physically.[106]

As we have seen, however, and as Lutterbie has concluded '[Our] pleasures [and pain] are not those of Ramachandran's neuroscience and our mirroring responses may give rise to different states of empathy than those envisioned by the neuroscientists.'[107] In all the work discussed here, it is a shift of perspective (variations on the 'aha' moment), where the familiar becomes strange that aesthetic experience is located as we become aware of the action of perception and reconception, and of our interdependent positioning as producers of meaning in the context of our social, cultural and physical environments. For Jackson, interdependence in theatre making involves a three-part process: 'To work in performance is to remember and then to forget and to remember again.'[108] It is this dynamic interaction 'which can yield forms that are both aesthetically and socially innovative. And it means acknowledging the degree to which art worlds and social worlds are not self-governing.' This approach is consistent with cognitive perspectives; interdependency involves the understanding that develops from 'the multidimensional environmental contexts in which we remember, feel, think, sense, communicate', to adapt Tribble and Sutton's formulation. As we have seen in the examples discussed, these relationships can be variously reactive (responding to), interactive (responding with) and proactive through new forms of authorship and collaboration, thinking and action to produce new meanings and new audiences.

Conclusion

Aesthetic values change over time as the social and cultural contexts in which we are situated change. Aesthetics in the twenty-first century have broadened to include the everyday as part of the various turns to affect and to the relational through differently inflected configurations of community, situated and social aesthetics. This is evident in reappraisals of relational aesthetics, as we have seen in the work of Armstrong, Wolff, Minissale, Bishop and Jackson. Performance is a medium that is in between states of being and representation as a form that is both real (as experienced) and not real (as fictive/pretence/constructed and performed). The contemporary vogue for immersive and participatory art as well as verbatim forms might be regarded as a new aesthetics emerging from mediatized societies seeking experiential modes of art and a valuing of qualities of authenticity, affect and emotion to complement the technical artistry, plasticity and artifice of contemporary culture's virtual realities. In all the work discussed we see an interest and inquiry into the everyday and the potential for making the ordinary extraordinary. Contemporary cultural policies similarly conjoin aesthetic and social priorities as evident in Arts Council England's slogan 'Great Art for Everyone'.

All the work featured in this chapter can be seen as 'social practices' as aesthetic and ethical, professional and community modes of art. Above all, however, it is the awareness of the relations between the past (the contexts remembered) the forgetting or forgoing of ourselves in the presence of the performance moment and the realization of our new positioning in past and present environmental contexts which create the shifts of perception, the felt 'ahahaaa' of embodied cognition that transforms and transports us into an awareness that what we are experiencing is difference.

Revolutionary Beauty out of Homophobic Hate: A Reflection on the Performance *I Stand Corrected*

Mojisola Adebayo

Beauty, no doubt, does not make revolutions.
But a time will come when revolutions have need of beauty

Albert Camus[1]

Our quest is for Beauty, like any other artist

Augusto Boal[2]

I cannot find the words. Beautiful

anonymous audience member[3]

Part one

Applied *politricks*

When I was invited to write a chapter for this book, I must admit, I hesitated. I am not an academic writer. I am a playwright, performer, facilitator, devisor, director and like many theatre practitioners, I have a problem with the term 'Applied Theatre.'[4] The name omits its politics and this omission is very politically tricky, hence the name for this introductory section, *politricks*.[5] Other names for practices under the applied theatre 'umbrella' suggest leftist socio political objectives, even for someone who has not encountered the work before.[6] For example, Theatre for Social Change suggests theatre that is doing something to actively address a problem in society, it is the antithesis of conservative by definition (as in conserving things as they are) and is inherently revolutionary (in that it is seeking change). When I worked in Burma through Pan Intercultural Arts with support from the British Embassy immediately after Cyclone Nargis in 2008, the military regime allowed us to run our theatre training course for workers from Non-Governmental Organizations working in response to the catastrophe but that the only word we were not allowed to use, whether verbally or in writing was 'change'. The Burmese authorities understood nothing of what we were doing (otherwise I am sure we would not have been allowed in). They no doubt assumed we would be training people to be entertainers as a distraction from the disaster and their inept and corrupt response to it. However the words 'social change' clearly worried them. We dropped the title of the workshop altogether and shared the same material we would have done anyway. I am certain the regime were not aware that these (Theatre of the Oppressed) techniques grew out of resistance to fascist military dictatorships in Latin America in the 1960s and 1970s. There are now over 20 Theatre for Social Change Forum Theatre companies across Burma, led by facilitators who came to this training.[7]

Another term placed under the applied theatre umbrella, Theatre for Development, signposts the layperson towards a dramatic, dynamic mechanism for growth in a place of depravation, probably in a 'developing' country, that is, a location in recovery from crisis such as colonization, occupation or war.[8] Alternative Theatre implies that there is a mainstream and this kind of theatre is offering another way in representing marginalized groups and forms of expression. Community Theatre is likely to be made by or for any group of people in a specific location, or with a shared experience or interest, who are possibly from a group whose voices are not often heard in public, having come together to express something that affects them. Participatory or Engaged Theatre tells me people are going to be interested and are welcome to join in. Theatre of the Oppressed is the most politically explicit of all. It is theatre first of all – not Oppressed Theatre but Theatre *of* the Oppressed. It therefore belongs to those who have had power used against them to stop them doing what they want to do, or make them do something they do not want to do, or be on a social and individual level. All of these different theatre forms have something in common. They all point towards differences in power and or access for certain groups of people and the possibility of theatre to radically challenge the status quo. Delving deeper into the words alternative, community, engaged, participatory and oppressed inevitably leads us to thinking about social hierarchies. Applied Theatre however suggests that someone is doing something to someone else by implementing theatre. The applier is the one who is in action, the recipient, the applied to, comes second. It sounds like an instrument used to fix somebody or something through theatre. There is an inherent hierarchy embedded in the phraseology and the thinking. The means to do is separated from the done to, the power to do is in the hands of the few, the done to are the other, lower and probably of another class.

Applied Theatre has been defined by the drama academy in the West, where the discourse is re/generated by scholars teaching on degree programmes. Those who cannot afford to access the increasingly capitalist domain of higher education in countries such as England and those who do not have the PhDs to get a job in academia, stand outside the umbrella in the rain. I have friends who have run workshops in communities for three decades, who themselves grew from being members of youth theatres and community arts groups, that when I have mentioned the term have said, 'Applied theatre, what's that?' I used to be Convenor of a Masters in applied theatre at Goldsmiths, University of London. I saw it as my role to encourage students to problematize the term 'applied' and reinvent and reclaim the subject. Though the problem was that very few black, disabled or working class people ever came onto the course, they did not have the means to access it. I have black friends and colleagues in their 40s and 50s who have said to me that they would love to do a Masters, but cannot afford to do so. This is a problem that stems from increasing economic and educational inequalities in Britain. As a result, it is now harder and harder for people without a qualification in applied theatre to ever get work in the field, let alone teach in the academy. And so the field is regressing. It is becoming whiter and more middle-class.

There are also very few men applying for Applied Theatre MA courses, certainly across the University of London, in comparison with programmes such as Writing for Performance or Performance Making. Some of the reasons may be connected to the very terminology. In a feminist analysis, women are seen as those there to service, help, fix and attend to need. Men are there to innovate, envision, create and take the artistic lead. It may be that men are not being attracted to MAs in applied theatre because it is seen as a vocation, like nursing, rather than an artistic subject in a creative setting. The mostly young able-bodied middle-class white women with MAs in applied theatre who go out to work in community centres, pupil referral units, prisons and inner city schools will often be 'applying' their drama to black boys, people who are working-class, people from minority cultures and people with disabilities. Many of these young white women graduate and then describe themselves 'applied theatre practitioners', which denotes that it is seen no longer as an umbrella term but a methodology in itself, a method of correcting the other. The terminology is shaping the field and is troubling many of us including Judith Ackroyd who has written 'applied theatre has created its own discourse to articulate itself and now masquerades as something neutral and democratic. Yet it emerges as a restricted, even an exclusive, theatre form'.[9] I agree with Ackroyd that things need to change.

Last year I worked with a group of ten young emerging actors and a young writer on Talawa's TYPT: 2013 (Talawa Young People's Theatre) where we created a production called *Sweet Taboo* which explored and debunked taboos in sex and gender. While working on that project I was taught the phrase 'check your privilege'. It means, in every social situation, pay attention to the hierarchies that affect your interactions and place in the world and the fluctuating levels of discrimination. For example, a young white woman who uses a wheelchair was not able to fully participate in TYPT: 2013 because Talawa's space is not accessible. Thankfully as she is principally a writer she was able to stay engaged online and Talawa arranged for one rehearsal session a week to be held in an accessible space at Goldsmiths. However, the issue highlighted in no uncertain terms that all of us black and Asian able-bodied participants and leaders on TYPT: 13 had been privilege checked by a young white woman who uses a wheelchair. As people from minority ethnic backgrounds, we all had some experience of racism and social disadvantage due to the colour of our skins but we also need to check (think about) the privilege afforded to us as non-disabled people and take this learning into action. Talawa is now addressing its lack of access. Applied Theatre people – let us check the privilege this phrase constructs and know when we have been privilege checked!

Applied *lackaesthetics*

The other problem I have with applied theatre brings me directly to the subject of this book. The term to me is not only politically tricky but lacks a sense of aesthetics. This is why I am actually happy to be part of this timely edition. I have also been excited by reading the recent work of scholars such as James Thompson (2008); Joe Winston (2011); Nicola Shaughnessy (2012) and here Gareth White who have all brought much closer attention to aesthetics in the discourse of applied theatre recently. Jan Cohen-Cruz (2010) opted for the term 'engaged performance' but does not recommend dropping the term 'Applied Theatre' as it is such an established term on university courses.[10] This takes me back to my point about the commodification of our work in the big business that has become Higher Education. Are we really in favour of allowing the market-place to dictate pedagogical terminology? Marketability and convenience is no reason to stick with words that don't work and are, as Ackroyd (2007) has discussed, exclusionary. Language makes meaning. I humbly urge my colleagues to lose 'Applied' altogether as it is not only politically dubious and ideologically dodgy it is, perhaps even worse, un-artistic.

To my ear, the ear of an old 1980s street rapper, 'applied' has no style, no energy, no flavour, no colour, no rhythm, no artistry, imagination or play; it is only a functional, mundane instrument with no musicality at all. Alternative makes me think that the work might be eccentric, wacky, unusual, on the edge, something I would not see at a commercial theatre. Community is probably going to be cheap and cheerful, down to earth, maybe celebratory and unifying, possibly worthy. Engaged, Participatory, for Development or Social Change is no doubt going to be very active. I wonder how all these phrases sound to you. To me, Theatre of the Oppressed (TO) sounds very serious. Whenever I facilitate a workshop in TO I ask participants how the phrase sounds. They often say it sounds 'heavy'. I also think TO is a problematic term for this reason because the games, exercises and techniques such as Forum Theatre are much more fun, fluid, laughter inducing, sweat releasing, playful and dynamic than 'Theatre of the Oppressed' suggests. This is why many TO practitioners have ditched it preferring titles such as 'Power Plays'.[11] Yet at least 'Theatre of the Oppressed' has an identity, a colour. I think the term applied theatre does a disservice to so much of the beautiful, eclectic and experimental work in communities that does happen. It implies that the purpose of the work is more important than the art. Art does something that nursing, social work and teaching cannot do. Moreover we must be competent and confident theatre artists if our work is to be ethical. Competence, says Stella Barnes, is a crucial factor in measuring the ethics of a participatory project.[12] If we are not artists we should not be using art with groups. Which is why the study of applied theatre needs to emphasize artistic excellence and an engagement with aesthetics as much as all the other questions of community, education, intervention and participation that concern us.

The term 'Applied' is also weirdly in the past tense. It assumes the very purpose has already been fulfilled. The success of the work is assured. There is no negotiation in the past tense. Where is the dialogue in applied? It is like saying theatre is cooked. Where is the gathering of the ingredients together, chopping and seasoning, simmering, sharing, feeding our one another? Applied is a done deal, confident, certain of itself and self-satisfied. As Ackroyd has pointed out, there is an inherent assumption that 'applied' theatre work is for the good. She goes on, 'a discourse is being created that enshrines applied theatre as, ironically, *pure*.[13] The moralistic tone of applied is deeply problematic. Having either no indication of its politics aside from the assumed direction of the privileged to do good by improving the other and having no implication of its aesthetic aside from its function to correct, the term feels inappropriate for me as a politically activated and animated theatre artist who does not recognize the division between the doer and the done to, the professional and the community. Dialogue through creativity is at the heart of the art. In this thinking I am following the teaching of Paulo Freire (1996) and Augusto Boal (1978), as well as all the women including women-of-colour and women with disabilities who have taught me so much about theatre for social change who are hardly ever mentioned in the history books and or do not write as many books about theatre as their male counterparts, probably because they are just too busy doing it. So let me take this opportunity to big up Sue Mayo, Manisha Mehta, Chrissie Poulter, Sandra Vacciana, Jenny Sealey, Stella Barnes, Terry O'Leary, Anna Wallbank, Deni Francis, Barbara Santos, Adwoa Shanti-Dickson, Antonia Kemi Coker, Mita Banerjee, Susan Quick in the mix to name just a few.

Like many of the women I have named, sometimes I make work with people who are paid, sometimes I make work with people who are unpaid, sometimes I work in secure children's homes and sometimes I work on stages. It is all theatre. I have made work with the Royal Shakespeare Company in England and I have made work with VIDYA[14] slum dwellers touring theatre in India. The work with VIDYA was much more memorable, life changing and significant and given the choice I would rather make theatre in an Ahmedabad slum than Stratford-Upon-Avon, though I would not want a world without Shakespeare. Theatre is the art of human relationships. All we need to make theatre is human beings, time and space. I make theatre with and for anyone to raise debate and challenge abuses of power.

Having made theatre for two decades, I resent the idea that some of my work and the work of practitioners I respect falls outside the umbrella of applied theatre as defined by Thompson (2003); Taylor (2003); Nicholson

(2005) and Prentki and Preston (2009). Reading these key text books in the subject, one could not say that a professional theatre company where people buy tickets to go and see both classic and new plays created and staged by paid playwrights, actors and directors, is applied theatre. Therefore Graeae theatre company are not applied theatre and nor do they define themselves as such.[15] Yet Graeae, being led and made up of trained and professional artists who have physical disabilities and or sensory impairments, are certainly an alternative to the mainstream, political in demanding social change and development, engaging people who are excluded and oppressed, making shows that are inclusive and celebratory, representing communities and challenging inequalities in our society. If Graeae were run by 'able bodied' people and the disabled members were unpaid would they be classified 'applied', like Mind the. . . . Gap or Heart and Soul theatre companies? If Graeae are not applied theatre there is something wrong with the phrase Applied Theatre. And why do we need such a phrase anyway? What is wrong with just using the phrase, *theatre*? Who loses power from dropping that prefix? Who gains status from keeping it? Who is excluded from owning it? I agree with Victor Ukaegbu (2004) who discusses that all theatre in Africa has historically had a social purpose.[16] This being so, the applied label in this context is meaningless. It is interesting that Cohen-Cruz borrows from an African performance tradition of call and response singing and storytelling to define engaged performance. Yet still academics hold on to the Eurocentric term 'applied'. My performance heritage is of the African Diaspora and this may be partly why I do not relate at all to the notion of 'applied'.

Unapplied and uncorrected

In my contribution to *Applied Theatre: Aesthetics* I want to tell you about the performance *I Stand Corrected* (*ISC*), a collaboration between myself and South African dancer and choreographer, Mamela Nyamza. *ISC* is a piece of African Diasporic queer interdisciplinary dance and theatre performance that is not applied theatre, by any text-book definition. Yet *ISC* could prove a useful example for why the applied is an ill-fitting word and the aesthetic pursuit of beauty is important in the process of making theatre for change. *ISC* addresses the rise in so-called corrective rape, which is the hate rape of black lesbians and trans-men in South Africa to make them (us) straight. Although the South African constitution guarantees full equality for Lesbian, Gay, Bisexual, Trans, Queer and Intersex (LGBTQI) people, rates of hate crime are still very high. Statistics are difficult to provide as so many crimes go unreported but colleagues from The Triangle Project for LGBT people say they receive around ten calls per week from lesbians and trans-men who say they have been raped.[17] The victims are often also murdered by the perpetrator, so ironically, they have no chance to become 'corrected'. Mamela and I wanted to raise the subject of homophobic hate rape alongside exposing the inherent violence of the homophobic anti-gay marriage lobby in Europe. It is a subject that affects us both as lesbians and black women from South Africa and Britain. *ISC* was developed in Cape Town, South Africa where it premiered at the Arena Theatre as part of the annual Women's Festival in July 2012. It was commissioned by Marlene LeRoux of Artscape, supported by Jean September of British Council and Deborah Williams of Arts Council England – all of whom are politically identified black women occupying rare positions of power in the arts with considerable access to resources, without whom this show would have never been possible. *ISC* has since been performed at Ovalhouse Theatre in London and Soweto Theatre, Johannesburg. At the time of writing we are about to play at the Singapore International Festival of Arts and will go on touring to wherever we are welcome, whether it be a theatre festival or a township community hall, either live or digitally. Our ambition is to present the work worldwide and use it to raise the debate about homophobia, particularly in post-colonial countries that have been left with European homophobic laws, and are seeing a startling rise in homophobic attitudes and actions, such as increased criminalization and violence as a result of the rise of fundamentalist religions, principally Christianity and Islam.

Mamela and I began our process by questioning another term we both dislike: corrective rape. The term started to be used by Non Governmental Organizations (NGOs) in the early 2000s though the precise origin is not clear. Both Mamela and I resist the term as it ironically seems to be reinforcing the idea that to rape a woman for being a lesbian is correct. So we decided to delve deeper into this word 'corrective'. I then wrote a short story based on the question, what if we accept the twisted logic of corrective rape and ask well, what if it worked? What if you could actually take a woman, rape her, kill her and then she was corrected into being an ideal feminine figure. What if this corrected woman then came back from the dead to seek out her perpetrator? And what might be the worst moment in your life to die and to lose the love of your life? Perhaps, I thought, on the night before your wedding. This lead me to the question of equal marriage. And so the short story on which the performance is based is about a South African lesbian woman named Zodwa, played by Mamela, who is raped and murdered on the night before her wedding and her partner black British partner Charlie, played by myself.

We began the devising process based on the short story I had written. As Mamela is a dancer and I am an actor, we used the shared language of physical games through which to find material. The games lead to improvisations that lead to action, text and choreography. For example, we played hide and seek and this lead us to a flash back scene of where the two central characters, Charlie and Zodwa first meet and have a playful sexual *double entendre* dialogue around looking for each other and coming. Hide and seek eventually became a movement, musical and textual motif for the play. We played Augusto Boal's Colombian Hypnosis but sprayed perfume on our hands and followed the scent with our eyes closed (instead of following the hand visually as in the original game).[18] This exercise led to the dramatic moment where Zodwa leads Charlie with perfume (more on this below). We played Lois Weaver's Butch and Fem game (e.g. 'smoking is butch . . . no smoking is fem. . .') taught to me by Joey Hately, where you take one action and make it masculine or feminine. This lead to a choreographic sequence with Mamela dancing between butch and fem on top of the bin. Mamela's role is mainly expressed in movement and mine in words. Aesthetically then, the performance is a dynamic conversation between dance and drama. Mamela's movement is informed by her training in ballet, contemporary and Xhosa dances and my text is poetic, polemic and playful. We both also enjoy interaction with the audience in our use of dialogue and the gaze.

As part of our process we held two theatre workshops with other black lesbian women in Cape Town who are not theatre professionals but are also activists and many of them survivors of rape. The women were invited to come to Artscape, in the city centre. Artscape is a huge theatre complex very far away from the townships where the women live. It was important to Mamela and I that the women felt welcomed into the space, a place that was during the apartheid era only for white people only. The workshops were enabled through the support of Zanele Muholi, a photographer and film-maker who is also a black lesbian and has almost single-handedly documented black lesbian lives since the fall of apartheid, including shooting every single funeral of a black lesbian victim. Zanele put the women in touch with us and subsequently some of their photography, along with Muholi's work, has toured in an exhibition with the show. The women's voices are also recorded in the show in the opening activist song and they came to watch the performance. *ISC* was also made and seen by many others who are not black lesbians such as the designer Rajha Shakiry, the lighting designer Mannie Manim, the music supervisors Mix 'n' Sync and the stage and production managers Jerome Chapman, Crin Claxton and Alfred Rietmann. It is a piece of theatre created by we, women and trans people who, like me, are survivors of rape; by people whose mothers, like Mamela's mother, have died in rape and men, who abhor rape. It is created by a group of people who are united in a desire for full equality and equal treatment under the law for all LGBTQI people everywhere. It is just theatre and theatre for justice and despite its confronting, disturbing and repulsive subject matter there is one word that has recurred in feedback from Cape Town to London and that is, 'beauty'. I am struck that we seem to have made a beautiful art work out of an abhorrent topic of homophobic violence. In this chapter, I am going to investigate the reasons why audience members considered the work to be beautiful and what beauty might do.

First of all I would like to give you a brief insight into the production.[19] As the audience enter they are given programmes that are like a wedding order of service. In the theatre, through a soft haze a long silky white wedding dress and embroidered jacket appears to be suspended from a huge bunch of gold and white helium balloons, set against the back wall: a long stretch of burnt blackened wood, reminiscent of an alley way of township shacks. Along the floor close to the wall is a long pathway of ash. To the stage right there is in a corner an old metal dustbin surrounded by black rubbish bags covered in ash. As the lights dim and the audience settle, the dress begins to flutter in the breeze with the sound of the women singing an uplifting South African protest song, acapella. The women's singing is drowned out by the sound of heavy rain on corrugated iron, building to a clamouring crescendo. Out of the darkness is a sudden flash of lighting hitting the rubbish bin. At first we see the bin is empty. Then suddenly in another flash there are two upturned legs seen in apparent rigour mortis, standing straight up from the rubbish bin, feet up. The lights go to black again and the body in the bin is now on the floor. We can only see the body from the pelvis down. The torso remains moving inside the bin for a long time. The body is of a black woman, who we later discover is Zodwa, played by Mamela. A physical sequence ensues where she appears to be coming back to life. Her movement suggests fragments of a physical memory of violence but it is quite staccato and abstracted. Slowly she comes out of the bin. The woman starts to discover how to move, like a creature that has just come to life. She explores her body and her surroundings, starting with the rubbish bags. Inside the rubbish bags she finds an old magazine and starts to copy the images of women that she sees. She discovers an old radio dumped in the rubbish bin, turns it on and starts figuring out how to dance. Once the sequence is finished, she rests and another woman begins to walk incredibly slowly through the haze in soft pink light along the illuminated aisle of ash at the back to the sound of Louis Armstrong singing, *We Have All the Time in the World.* The woman, who we later discover is Charlie, played by myself, is wearing silky white trousers, an embroidered corset, a necklace of South African beads and a high white African headdress. She carries a bunch of red and white roses. She is apparently a bride to be. She stands and waits downstage facing the audience at what appears to be a wedding. There is slight house light on the audience so she can see their faces as they see hers. She waits for an uncomfortably long time. Zodwa does not arrive. She hands the flowers to an audience member and dashes out to make a phone call. The story continues as Charlie's quest to find out what has happened to her partner, Zodwa. We discover through the play that Charlie is from England and came to Cape Town to teach cricket to girls in the townships. She met Zodwa who was watching her while she was teaching cricket. They have a love affair and we see fragments of their life up to the wedding. Charlie's narrative is conveyed through storytelling in direct communication with the audience who are effectively cast in the role as wedding guests. She goes out to a police station to try and report her missing partner and through her encounter with a homophobic police officer the debate is raised around homophobia in South Africa, the legacies of apartheid and colonialism, Christianity and how all this connects with British history, through Charlie, a black British woman, adopted into a white family and the daughter of an Anglican Vicar. Meanwhile Zodwa's narrative is of a woman who is trying to figure out why she has been left in a rubbish bin. She is looking for clues, trying to understand who and what she is, who Charlie is to her, why she is drawn to smoking a cigarette and why a single balloon reminds her of the head of a mysterious man who haunts her body memory. Zodwa eventually discovers that she has been attacked by a man who asked her for a light for his cigarette, she has been raped, choked to death, her body has been stubbed with cigarettes, placed in a rubbish bin in a township alley way and she has been set on fire. A heavy rain came and put the fire out. Eventually Zodwa leads Charlie to her through the scent of her perfume. They dance together and kiss but Zodwa must return to the dead. There is a memorial service

Figure 4 *I Stand Corrected*. (Photograph: Taryn Burger).

at which Charlie speaks and burns her wedding speech. This transforms into the ancestral wedding of Charlie and Zodwa, a Xhosa marriage of the dead and the living. The protest song we heard at the beginning plays out their wedding march and they dance off stage together at the end. *ISC* is both visual and verbal, a dance of theatre, words, music and lights. At every performance there was a standing ovation, many sang along with us, many cried, there we moments of laughter, people talked and talked after.

In Cape Town and London we invited people to fill in feedback slips to enable us to develop the work and we also listened to people's responses in conversations with us. Of all the productions I have created or have been involved in, I have never read or heard the word 'beauty' used more often to describe a performance. Out of the 148 people who filled in the overwhelmingly positive feedback forms, 28 described the show as beautiful. Critics too have described the production as a work of beauty. I would say the production is beautiful. The second word people most frequently used to describe the show was 'powerful'. People from all backgrounds said their feelings about homophobia had changed. One man, a black South African man who had never seen a piece of theatre before said to us that he did not know anything about lesbians before the show, that he is a Christian and this issue would not normally be something he would approve of. Yet he said he watched the show and was so moved, he found the show so beautiful and moving and kept thinking, 'what if this happened to one of my daughters?. . .' This man was able to enter into this discussion because he was drawn into the story through the aesthetics of the piece.

The last book my teacher Augusto Boal wrote before he died, returned to the discussion of aesthetics. Quoting Dostoyevsky 'Only Beauty will save the world', Boal wrote that this is 'a phrase which we could translate to: "Only Aesthetics can enable us to attain the truest and most profound comprehension of the world and society"'.[20] Furthermore, James Thompson writes that 'beauty's power to disturb is crucial and has important, rarely acknowledged, political power'.[21] In the rest of this chapter, I will use *ISC* to illustrate how the aesthetic beauty of *ISC* exemplifies the political potential of beauty. I will ask, what do people mean when they say *ISC* is beautiful, what, if anything, might beauty move people to do and what are its limitations? In my analysis, I will draw on theories of beauty offered by philosophers such as Roger Scruton, Elaine Scarry, Umberto Eco, Achille Mbembe, Sianne Ngai, Daniel Herwitz and theatre practitioner/theorists such as James Thompson and Joe Winston. In using the likes of conservative thinkers such as Roger Scruton, I am, like Gareth White's use of Kant earlier in this book, deliberately reclaiming aesthetics from the hands of reactionary thinkers and using them to argue the case of the radicalism in aesthetics. Finally in this chapter I will return to the question of applied theatre. I shall use the example of *ISC* to argue that if anything must be 'applied' in theatre it is beauty itself. This critical reflection stands as an argument for dismantling the corrective phrasing and thinking in the academic discourse of 'applied' theatre. As theatre, *I Stand Corrected*, stands as an argument against 'corrective' rape.

Part two

Beauty and the senses

From the feel of Zodwa's dress blowing in the breeze to the sound women of singing through the rain, to the taste of fruit from the platter passed around for the spectator as they wait for a bride who never comes, to the scent of Zodwa's perfume that leads a trail to her body, to the heat of the burning wedding speech that Charlie lights in the fire at the end, *I Stand Corrected* gives the audience a series of sensations within the structure of a sexually charged love story. Roger Scruton says, 'There is an ancient view that beauty is the object of a sensory rather than an intellectual delight, and that the senses must be involved when appreciating it.'[22] He points out that the eighteenth-century philosophy of art called itself aesthetics following the Greek *aisthesis*, translated as sensation.[23] One of the reasons so many people described *ISC* as a work of beauty may be because it affects every sense.

The one section of the performance that people refer to again and again as being beautiful and moving is a scene where all the characters' senses are stimulated. For most of the play the performers come close but do not touch. Their stories, in words and dance, weave in and out of each other. Charlie and Zodwa try to find each other across a mortal divide. Towards the end, the invisible ghost Zodwa sprays her perfume to guide Charlie to herself. Charlie follows the smell with her eyes closed. At last their fingers touch each other. They hold hands, then play a sexy game of thumb wars where one is trying to press down on the other's thumb and when their thumbs touch as equals they simultaneously open their eyes. The women embrace, they kiss and taste and caress each other. Zodwa eventually pulls away and returns to her grave as Charlie breaks down in tears. There is a love song playing loudly over the scene while the lighting dances with their movement. This is the moment where many people said that they were moved to tears and we could hear people crying as we wept. It is beautiful because it is sensual and romantic though there is a danger that this glosses over the tragedy. It is true that beauty takes the edge off the pain of this piece, certainly even for me performing it. To be honest, emotionally, I am not sure how I would cope with performing the piece if it were not beautiful. For myself as a survivor of male sexual violence and for Mamela having lost her mother in this brutal way, it is important to us that rape is transformed into hope. In this way, beauty can be therapeutic in recovering from trauma not just for us and hopefully for people in our audience.

ISC touches every sense in the body and has the potential to touch anybody in the audience because it is at the centre – is a story of love and loss. It appeals to all the senses and it appeals to *common sense* as it is based on this simple premise: women love each other, make love, experience loss and grieve just like anybody else. Therefore, we are human. Therefore, perpetuating crimes against us are just as wrong as if they were happening to anyone else. The audience members are not asked to agree, morally, with homosexuality but to accept our humanity. What is at stake in universalizing a social issue is that the specificities can become too generalized to be useful. However, the very first step in any challenge to discrimination is humanization of the other.

Aesthetics has the power to humanize the other in the eyes of the hater. Albert Namatjira (1902–59) was an aboriginal impressionist artist who was the first indigenous artist in Australia to work with oil paints in a European tradition. He was so successful and respected as an artist that his work sold widely in galleries and some of his work was bought by Queen Elizabeth. He was the first aboriginal person to be given citizenship so that he could travel with his work and meet the Queen. He led the way for aboriginal people to be considered human beings in Australia. Up until Namatjira, aboriginal people were classified not as human beings or citizens but as flora and fauna, equivalent to kangaroos, flowers and rocks. His beautiful art was part of what made Australian white supremacists change their thinking and change the law (though there is still a long way to go there in terms of racism).[24] We hope to do the same with *ISC* with homophobia as Namatjira did with racism. It is horrific to think that black people, whether they be in Australia, apartheid South Africa or in antebellum America were at points in history not considered to be fully human. In many senses there is nothing radical in the argument that black people and LGBTQI people are equal human beings. It is the bottom line. It *is* very general and it is absurd that we should even have to engage in such a question, but it is the only basis on which to begin to make change. I have gone some way to illustrating how *ISC* employs beauty through the senses to appeal to the sense in audience members. I will now go on to discuss another important element in what makes *ISC* beautiful: the sacred.

Beauty and the sacred

The beautiful and the sacred are part of every civilization and we often place the two concepts side by side (Scruton 2009; Eco 2010). Indeed, one of the most common phrases one hears after a wedding or a funeral are, 'it was a beautiful service', 'the bride looked beautiful', 'the eulogy was beautiful'. Perhaps we are almost obliged to consider a sacred ceremony beautiful and beauty itself serves a sacred function. Who leaves a Church wedding or funeral service and openly says, 'well that was ugly!'? That would probably border on the profane. *ISC* is perceived and described as beautiful because it is framed within the chronological and formal structure of a wedding, a sacred service, from the walk down the aisle, to performative vows sealed with a kiss. Just like at any wedding, there are balloons, flowers, food, wedding outfits, a dress, a dodgy DJ (the stage manager) playing inappropriate music, jokes, speeches and playful interaction with the guests. Even our playfulness in the show is also, according to Joe Winston, an essential element in developing a sense of beauty.[25] The wedding guests are even given the chance to leave: 'go home' says Charlie, 'I think everybody should just go home' because like most weddings, something has gone wrong. Only here, the wedding goes dreadfully wrong. The wedding transforms into a memorial service for the dead bride. Finally, with the reappearance of Zodwa, it concludes as a traditional Xhosa ancestral wedding, a supernatural marriage of the dead and the living, where eternal vows are taken before God. But before the ritual commences Charlie asks the audience 'If you will be our witness?' and pauses. By saying nothing, the guests give their consent. They are now participants in a binding social and spiritual contract. For without a witness, a marriage does not exist. This is a crucial difference between civil partnership where there is no witness and equal marriage where there is. The ritual ends with a kiss under falling confetti and the two women throw the bouquet of flowers that is caught by one of the guests: black out. The circle is thus complete. We came for a wedding, we get one in the end: the end.

Perhaps the danger with the configuration of *ISC* as a ritual is in that very sense of completeness. Complete means the work is done. Beauty, in Western philosophy has since Plato been related to the idea of things being fitting, just enough. Beauty is aligned with that which John Carey and others have referred to as the 'golden mean' theory of beauty: 'Not too little, not too much.'[26] If *ISC* is a complete, fitting, beautiful work that is just enough, what is there left for the audience to do? My own critique of the work is that we have not left the audience with anything they must do in order to complete that circle. They may feel it is over when they applaud. By playing on the cliché of weddings and funerals, maybe, that ritualized beauty is a seduction, a manipulation, rather than a provocation to action. Furthermore, we may be reinforcing the value of the inherently conservative and heteronormative construct of religious marriage through the use of this framework. We made the work while legislated equal marriage was still in doubt in Britain. On 28 March 2014 it came into law. So before we perform in Singapore (where it is also still illegal to be gay, thanks again to laws left by the British colonisers) I am going to go back to the script and question the whole idea of marriage with this reflection in mind because I think the seductive context of a wedding may be politically de-activating if it goes unquestioned.

What *is* politically significant about the function of beauty as sacred in *ISC* is that unless people walk out before the show is over (which few have ever done), whatever their beliefs about homosexuality or marriage, they have participated in a lesbian wedding and have sat respectfully at a lesbian memorial service, albeit fictional. One of them has even caught the flowers that we throw at the very end. The one who catches the flowers at a wedding is traditionally considered to be the next. In *ISC* the idea of 'the next' is even more significant. The question is implied, is this guest the next to be married or the next to be murdered? By participating in *ISC* we are all implicated in the issue, no matter what our sexuality or beliefs or nationality. Furthermore, most people who attend a wedding or a funeral are family or friends. By attending the show and remaining in their seats, the audience become our relatives and when they stand and clap as so many did, they stand in solidarity with us not just appreciation of us. The flowers passed on, the protest song plays us out and the audience clap along in rhythm. The two brides rise from the ashes, dancing into their future, fists to the air. Perhaps *ISC* is not an incitement to radical action but, like a wedding or funeral, the sacred narrative circle provides a space for all people, whatever their political persuasion in relation to queer politics, to take part. Although the use of the sacred has its political limitations, it serves an important function in enrolling the audiences as participants in the first step in a rite of passage that is the process of change, if not change itself.

Beautiful women, ugly feelings

ISC not only utilizes beauty but offers a critique of the heterosexist ideal of feminine beauty. Our poster features a self-portrait by Zanele Muholi entitled *Ms Amsterdam* where she stands dressed as a beauty queen, in a red white and blue bikini and tiara that is reminiscent of the American TV show, *Wonder Woman*.[27] At a distance the image looks just like any stereotype of a beautiful woman. However, on closer inspection it can be seen that the model has hairy legs and full bushy pubic hair. The poster provoked such strong reactions. Mamela told me she walked past two men who were stroking the pubic hair on the poster and discussing it. Many people raised the subject with me and some would not believe the model was actually female, determined that she must be a man in drag. Transport for London even insisted Oval House Theatre air-brush out the hair sticking out from the bikini for the tube poster in London! The image was effectively 'corrected' to the right kind of image of female beauty. We inadvertently were able then to use Muholi's poster image to engage in debate about what it means to be the right kind of beautiful woman.

In the show itself, one of the responses to the work is that people have said that we, the performers, are beautiful. This feels somewhat ironic and uncomfortable as we are actually trying to question the idea in the show and I want to discuss it as I think it reveals a problem with the piece. As one of those performers, it is difficult to discuss perceptions of my looks with any objectivity and it feels weird to attempt to do so. So I shall refer mainly to my co-performer, Mamela.

Mamela is beautiful. What do I mean by this? Her symmetrical bone structure, her proportionate fine features, her unblemished skin, smile, wide eyes, bow shaped lips, her even white teeth, figure, her use of the gaze, are all signs of what we might conventionally consider to be female beauty, certainly in the West. Umberto Eco, discusses the body as one of the most common signifiers of beauty in Western art.[28] Mamela is a contemporary dancer with training in ballet and her body is beautiful, slim, athletic and elegant. Mamela is also costumed to look conventionally beautiful, in her long silk white dress and red corset. Mamela's beauty is no doubt a contributing factor in a feeling in the audience that the entire piece of work is beautiful.

What is problematic is that we may be reinforcing what the feminist theorist Naomi Wolf has termed 'the beauty myth'. This is the observation that Western society is based on the idea that 'the female body is always in need of completion, of man-made ways to perfect it' – make up, heels, hair styling, weight loss.[29] These become sticks with which to beat women. Therefore, we see the increase in eating disorders, self-harm and cosmetic surgery. Wolf's thesis is that women's status in a sexist capitalist society is dependent on the successful achievement of beauty: 'The contemporary economy depends right now on the representation of women within the beauty myth.'[30] So Mamela and I may be inadvertently promoting this sexist position by presenting ourselves within a conformist paradigm.

One area in which the production is lacking is that I think we have neglected to directly address the key factor that it is actually mainly butch lesbian women and trans-men who are being raped and murdered in South Africa. The majority of people who are victims do not conform to the beauty myth. Their butchness is what makes lesbians and trans-men so easily identifiable by the perpetrators. Although we refer to Zodwa's butchness (when she was alive) through physical flashbacks to her former self, because we never articulate this in words, the significance might easily be lost. Also the point of the play is that Zodwa in coming back from the dead and is in the process of being corrected. Therefore, the narrative follows her physical transition to heterosexist femininity rather than focussing on her own female masculinity.

Although the play is certainly lacking in a precise and complex exploration of butchness, what we do well is to disturb the idea of feminine attractiveness by placing it in an ugly context. A key scene in this subversion is when Zodwa finds a magazine in the bag of rubbish that has been displaced by her dead body. She teaches herself how to be corrected by copying the poses in the magazine. Wolf highlights that magazines are the transmitters of the beauty myth 'as the gospel of a new religion.'[31] Through the narrative *ISC* turns the popular faith in femininity into horror. Like Frankenstein's monster, Zodwa is constructed into the image the perpetrator wanted. And when she eventually realizes what has happened to her and addresses him (using the balloon with a face drawn on to signify his head), she says to him: 'I stand corrected. Is this what you wanted? *(In Xhosa)* You fucking bastard.' The speech ends with Zodwa bursting the balloon/head, which is a symbolic destruction of him and his belief system. With the loud bang the stage is suddenly consumed by bright white light washing the entire space. The nastiness is bleached out and the sensual scene of perfumed lovers commences.

What is perhaps more memorable and significant than the performer's individual beauty is the tragedy of the story as whole. Achille
Mbembe, in his analysis of the beautiful in Congolese music, states:
'Because this society, so accustomed to atrocity, is playing with death,
its music is born out of tragedy and is nurtured by it. So is beauty.'[32]
ISC is also born out of tragedy: the tragedy of apartheid, the tragedy
of British colonialism, the tragedy of hate crime in South Africa. It is a
dance of death. We feel its beauty and life all the more acutely because of
this juxtaposition. As an audience member put it: 'Sometimes beautiful
things come from the ugliest of experiences. Thank you for telling our
story and especially for those that stand corrected in their . . . places. We
shall not be silenced. *Enkosi.*'[33]

James Thompson has highlighted that beauty can be an important
observation and critique of that which is most ugly in our society.
'The poppy in a vase is certainly somewhat beautiful, but in the fields
of Flanders, at the end of a brutal war, it was beautiful in a startling
way because it is compared critically with the terror of battles that were
fought there.'[34] Like that poppy in a Flemish field, Zodwa, stands up high
on the bin that we found her body in. She is brightly illuminated and
dressed in white. She looks all the more beautiful to us precisely because
we remember the darkness of the rubbish bin she was found in. She
shines like an angel, like a saint, a Christ-like figure, who has endured
the most terrible torture, but who is now transcendent, arisen from the
ashes of her burnt body. We embrace the symbolic connection between
light, God, goodness and beauty that Umberto Eco has observed.[35]

However, if we apply Eco's observations on beauty further still,
it is possible that this juxtaposition of the ugly story and Mamela's
transcendent beauty serves to make the ugliness of corrective rape
easier for the audience to bear, even making it more acceptable. Eco
states:

Various aesthetic theories, from Antiquity to the Middle Ages, see
Ugliness as the antithesis of Beauty, a discordance that breaks the rules
of proportion on which both physical and moral Beauty is based, or a

lack of something that a creature should by nature possess. In any case a principle is admitted that is observed almost uniformly: although ugly creatures exist, art has the power to portray them in a beautiful way, and the Beauty of this imitation makes Ugliness acceptable. There is no lack of evidence regarding this concept, from Aristotle to Kant. If we go no further than these reflections, the question is simple: the Ugliness that repels us in nature exists, but it becomes acceptable even pleasurable in the art that expresses and shows 'beautifully' the ugliness of Ugliness.[36]

Have we made the ugliness of rape and murder somehow even pleasurable by presenting it in juxtaposition with beautiful? Eco goes on to discuss that ugliness is sometimes even a 'Requirement for Beauty'.[37] He illustrates, there is a romantic connection between beauty and death.[38] Are we exploiting dead lesbians to make a beautiful show, like some kind of high-end pornographers? Could we be nullifying the debate by matching the ugly subject matter with conventional female beauty? I cannot bear to contemplate that could be what we are playing to but we must consider that there might be a price to pay for making beautiful from brutal.

Sianne Ngai, however, argues that feelings of beauty and disgust cannot coexist in exactly the same moment. She theorizes the 'aesthetics of minor affects' in literature and concludes that disgust lies at the outer limit of ugly feelings.[39] Disgust she says, is juxtaposed with desire and she draws on Kant to illustrate that disgust is the only kind of ugly feeling that destroys all aesthetic pleasure.[40] So perhaps by this rationale when *ISC* is ugly it is ugly and when it is beautiful it is beautiful and we do not feel the two things at the same time. At certain points, such as Charlie and Zodwa playing their sexy game of hide and seek, we feel pleasure and at other points, such as the conversation with the rapist with the balloon head, we feel disgust – importantly towards him, the rapist. The audience can then critically reflect on these dichotomous experiences and feelings. Homophobia is in part the expression of disgust towards lesbian and gay people. Presenting lesbian women in a beautiful artwork is therefore set up as an adversary to the ugly homophobic feeling of disgust, not a costume to cover it and indulge in it. Ngai goes further in saying 'disgust is never ambivalent about its object. . . . Even if disgust is boiled down to its kernel of repulsion, repulsion itself tends to be a definite response. . .'. She goes on 'Disgust is urgent and specific'. In South Africa this definite, urgent and specific response to homosexuality has included rape and murder. In *ISC* we take those who have been considered disgusting and set ourselves in the context of beauty. Beauty and desire go together, it attracts, it draws us close to it. As Ngai says, desire presents a much more fluid response than disgust. Desire she writes 'seems capable of being vague, amorphous, and even idiosyncratic in ways disgust cannot'.[41] Therefore, beauty, attraction, desire in challenging homophobia or any discrimination is not just an aesthetic cover up but has the potential to be a dialogic free thinking strategy for engagement. Ugliness makes for distant enemies and beauty creates closer allies. Indeed, not one person, in London, Cape Town or Soweto said that they were disgusted by *ISC* on the contrary, only two people ever walked out and every night, people rose to their feet. Like an intervention in a Forum Theatre play, this stand for beauty could be a rehearsal for the time when all people of reason must stand up for human rights that include the rights of LGBTQI people in every country on the planet. I need to believe this otherwise I would never want to perform the piece again.

So far I have gone some way to exploring three reasons why audiences may feel *ISC* is beautiful: because of the stimulation of the senses, the sacred structure and the performer's beauty signifiers. I have also indicated some of the potential limitations and dangers of beauty in theatre that aims to raise debate and make change. I have concluded that beauty could be a revolutionary force for change that galvanizes allies in the struggle for sexual liberation, I certainly hope so. I now want to use *ISC* to dig a little deeper into investigating how beauty can be used to make people think and what, if anything, it might encourage them to do.

Thinking beauty

Umberto Eco has observed that beauty has historically been characterized by that which is proportionate,[42] 'nothing in excess' just the
right rations and therefore synonymous with that which is rational.[43]
Homophobia is an irrational fear, killing someone to make them
straight is not rational thinking. Murder does not make sense, ugliness
does not make sense, beauty makes sense and love makes sense. As
Boal said, 'love . . . is an aesthetic experience' . . . 'Loving is art, and art is
love'.[44] Love is not just feeling, love is the expression of a thought, art is
the expression of thought, beauty, therefore, might be part of a formula
to aid rational active thinking about love.

Yet maybe all this warm and fuzzy talk of beauty is not an aid to
thinking but a dangerous distraction from social consciousness. Elaine
Scarry's counter argument is beauty 'incites deliberation'; she maintains it provokes not just feeling but thought. 'Something beautiful fills
the mind yet invites the search for something beyond itself, something
larger or something of the same scale with which it needs to be brought
into relation.'[45] Scarry is saying that we make comparative meaning
following an experience of a beautiful thing. The third most common
phrase audience members used in their comments on *ISC* was that the
play was 'thought provoking'. Scarry asserts that this is a very active
kind of thinking:

> What is beautiful prompts the mind to move chronologically back in
> search for precedents and parallels, to move forward into new acts of
> creation, to move conceptually over, to bring things in relation, and
> does all this with a kind of urgency as though one's life depended on it.[46]

This movement of the mind, she says, compels us to move our position.
Beauty literally moves us. A beautiful song makes us want to hum the
tune. A beautiful scene makes us want to capture it in a photograph.
A beautiful painting makes us want to follow its line, perhaps even to
take up a brush and paint. Beauty makes us want to trace it, copy it,
follow it. As Scarry states: 'It seems to incite, even to require, the act of

replication. . . . Beauty brings copies of itself into being.'[47] Beauty makes us want to re-create and in so doing, create. Thus, beauty increases knowledge. Being moved by something beautiful is a way of knowing it, and re-creating is a way of making knowledge that never ends. Scarry says this impulse and process is the basis of all education. Joe Winston, author of *Beauty and Education*, would agree. *ISC* could be an important part of an educational process.

Beautifully black

So if beauty can make us think, what else in *ISC* are we made to think about? Sarah Nuttall points out, the concept of beauty in Africa has an ugly past. Africans have been presented as savage. Nuttall cites Kant's conclusion that the African is ugly, unfeeling and stupid. 'Racist accounts, widely accepted into the time of European colonization and beyond, present the African continent as the metaphor *par excellence* for physical ugliness and moral decay'.[48] *ISC* makes us think about beauty in different ways when it comes to race. *ISC* however presents black women not as metaphors for ugliness, but as metaphors for beauty. In this way, *ISC* is challenging racism and follows in the steps of the Black Power movement of the 1970s that declared 'Black is beautiful'. A danger however is that *ISC* reinforces thoughts of innate African male sexual savagery. This is why it was important when I was writing the play script that we reference 'good' South African men who would turn in their graves at the horrors inflicted on their sisters. At the memorial service, Charlie lays out the unopened boxes of wedding presents in a ritual-like action. The boxes on the floor look like a graveyard and each symbolically represents the women who have been killed. She reminds the audience of brave and beautiful black South African male heroes: 'Lionel Davis, Walter Sisulu and Mandela himself'.

Another danger in the discourse of beauty is in reinforcing the idea of symmetry and sameness as the norm. The abnormal as ugly is a pervasive nineteenth-century idea that fed eugenicist and racist ideologies. However, Joe Winston cites the disabled dancer Bill Shannon as an example of an artist who challenges perceptions of normalcy. Winston says: 'The first time we feel an appreciation of a painting, a poem a play or a disabled person *for their beauty*, we extend this acquaintance to others in that category with an innate appreciation of their potential and worth.'[49] Winston is saying that appreciating beauty is a value judgement. If a disabled person's art is considered beautiful, disabled people are then more valued in society. Beauty then is normalizing and increases visibility of those who have been shunned. It is important that the theatre made by people from marginalized groups is of high cultural value. Aesthetics can be empowering. When Nicola Miles-Wildin played Miranda from Shakespeare's *The Tempest* alongside the openly gay actor Sir Ian McKellen as Prospero, directed by Jenny Sealey of Graeae, at the opening ceremony of the Paralympics in 2012, it made a very clear statement to the world, the work of both of those performers is of equal value, both of these performers are ordinary human beings and extraordinary not for their disabilities or sexualities but for their artistry.

This is a potentially powerful idea that might equally be applied to *ISC* (and all work with oppressed groups of people). By merely increasing the visibility of beautiful black lesbian artists (and let us not forget that it is still very rare to see black and openly lesbian women performing on stage), we are raising their/our social status. We are making people think about our worth in the world. This is why the artistic quality of the work is so important. It is key to the success of the production that I am an accomplished actor and published playwright who has worked with the Royal Shakespeare Company. It is crucial that Mamela is a classically trained dancer who can still perform an arabesque at the age of 38 – and subvert it! It is important that the standard we set is, and is perceived as, high. This is not for vanity's sake. We are claiming our place as different and brilliant. By performing a beautiful work, we are asking people, do we deserve to be dumped in a rubbish bin like Zodwa was in the play and lesbians have been in

South Africa? The audience are compelled to think about the answer and engage with the arguments.

Beautiful moves

Winston draws attention to the idea that 'to experience beauty, we must, to some extent, lose ourselves.' That no matter how stressed we are, when we see, hear, feel, a beautiful thing, we forget ourselves, put our lives to one side and are immersed in that beautiful thing, for a time. Though many people who watch *ISC* may not be lesbian, because it is beautiful they are able to move away their own identity and prejudices for the time of the performance at least. Winston goes on: 'Beauty *as experience* inspires love and admiration as opposed to a sense of rejection.' If audiences find *ISC* beautiful, they will not reject it; they might accept or at least, respect, our argument. Herein exists the potentially transformative function of beauty. Winston asserts, 'in an encounter with beauty, rather than being protective of my identity, I acknowledge that it will in some significant way be changed. Not only do I acknowledge it, I desire it'.[50] It is possible that the beauty of *ISC* alters people's sense of self; enables people to move from their own fixed position and invariably, when something is beautiful and something has affected you, you want to share it.

So far I have gone some way to illustrating how beauty might make you think. What might it stir you to do?

Many people wept during *ISC* and many more said they wanted to. One man in South Africa told me he had not cried since his mother had died 10 years ago. He said he had lost many friends since that time, but he had not been able to cry. Yet watching me cry for Zodwa, he started to sob. I found his story very moving. He was grieving the loved ones in his life through identifying with Charlie's loss. He too was mourning for Zodwa. Mourning is an important part of the process of healing. When we mourn we move, we cry, we rock, we shake, our breathing changes; grief moves us and *moves* us. This in itself is powerful enough. Yet can the movement of mourning lead to marching? Can beauty aid justice?

Elaine Scarry asserts that 'beauty assists us in our attention to justice.' Justice, she points out, 'stands opposed to injury: "injustice" and "injury" are the same word.' She questions whether 'the symmetry in beauty and that in justice are analogous'.[51] Beauty is associated with that which is fair, symmetrical, balanced, equal, complete and, like justice, it must be seen to be done. Beauty is not merely imagined. It is associated with real things we can touch and hear and see. Yet as Scarry points out, 'The equality of beauty enters the world before justice and stays longer because it does not depend on human beings to bring it about.'[52] Like the Jewish musicians playing in the death camps, so beautifully illustrated by Joshua Sobol's play *Ghetto*, Mozart remains long after the Nazis have met their end.[53] Scarry's thesis is that beauty renews in us a desire for truth and justice. We experience something beautiful and we want for our world to be made right.

Moreover, beauty not only stirs a desire for justice but it also requires us to make a judgement. Daniel Herwitz discusses the eighteenth-century innovation that 'to think of the experience of the beautiful as itself a kind of *judgement*, to conceive of the pleasure taken in a beautiful thing as the ground for judgement, indeed the judgement itself'.[54] To experience beauty then is a decision-making process and crucially for the subject of so-called applied theatre, beauty requires participation.

Scarry says that 'Beauty is a call' that for me in the case of *ISC*, demands a response.[55] The people in the audience are witnesses at a wedding and witnesses to social justice. The implication is where we witness injustice, we must notice and speak up. Thompson states that, 'The call of beauty makes the case that, rather than being a distraction from radical politics, beauty can be positioned as central.' He draws our attention to the 'affect of beauty' rather than the 'aesthetics of injury', which he states, 'has come to dominate applied theatre and many forms of radical performance'.[56] For me *ISC* is doing both. We present the aesthetics of injury, of injustice through the opening scene with the bin. This physical metaphor for rape and murder, which lasts over 10 minutes, is situated at the very opening of the show, before the wedding commences. We then stimulate the affect of beauty through the senses, the sacred structure and the performer's signifiers. Yet whatever we see in the play, is in the context of that horrible opening scene where Zodwa is in the bin. Many people have said to me they did not understand what the opening scene was about, but they could not forget it and spent the rest of the play trying to figure out the significance of that ghastly imagery. By the end of the play, they realize that Zodwa has been dumped in a rubbish bin and set alight. The injury is startling when placed inside something beautiful. Our impulse then is to have that injustice put right. And if that feeling stays with us, perhaps the next time we receive an email asking us to sign a petition against corrective rape, or we hear a homophobic comment or we are invited to have our say on equal marriage, we may just remember that call to beauty, the call to justice and respond.

Looking forward

When we created *I Stand Corrected* we did not consciously plan to make a beautiful play but it seems we did. Nor did we realize that beauty itself could be a powerful political tool for personal and social change, but I have speculated on ways in which it could be. Though this chapter is not really about us, it is about you. I want to encourage all of us who study, teach and practice theatre, especially in community and educational contexts with groups of people who have been oppressed, to consider ourselves and those who we work with, theatre artists first and foremost, where if we are applying anything it is beauty and to ourselves as much as anyone else. To return to Boal, 'Our quest is for Beauty, like any other artist'.[57]

I have shown that our quest for beauty can stimulate the senses and appeal to the sense, it can humanize the other, it can be therapeutic and help us to cope with trauma, it has the potential to ritually engage people to participate in making change; beauty can help us identify what is ugly in the world, it can get us thinking rationally and critically about those who have been considered ugly by society in terms of race, gender, disability and sexuality, it can add value to the image of those who have been devalued; beauty can move us and *move* us, it can enable us to lose ourselves and identify with another experience, it can stir our desire for justice and limit our toleration of injustice; beauty requires us to make judgements, to call and to respond. If beauty really can enable us to do any of these things, then it is something we need to be concerned with as theatre artists who want to be part of making change and bringing equality.

My recent and most humbling participation at a high-level discussion at the German Bundestag (parliament) highlighted for me just how revolutionary harnessing the political power of art is. Godwyns Onwuchekwa of Justice for Gay Africans and I were invited by the German political think-tank, The Friedrich-Ebert Stifftung, to speak about homophobia in Africa.[58] Even these politicians recognized the powerful potential of the arts to make change. I spoke about *ISC* and also used the platform to provoke members of the German Christian Democratic party and all Christian politicians to take responsibility for the imposition of homophobia through evangelical missionary colonization. I said if they did not want LGBTQI people to be raped, killed and imprisoned in Jesus' name, then they should to take it upon themselves to dialogue with their African Christian brethren. I could not quite believe that I was given that platform because I was an artist and the politicians at the Bundestag were listening to me, a black lesbian theatre maker from South-East London who is (ironically), a former born-again Christian street rapping evangelist! It seems in this chapter I have not lost my proselytising streak but I have turned my rhymes to something more revolutionary. As I sat in the Bundestag, I was reminded of the quote by the Algerian author, Albert Camus: 'Beauty, no doubt, does not make revolutions. But a day will come when revolutions will have need of beauty'.[59] At a time when my fellow Nigerians are facing 14 years in prison for being lesbian or gay and anyone who knows us (including our families) faces 10 years in jail if they do not report us to the authorities, when homophobic hatred is the witch hunt of the twenty-first century from Russia to Uganda, Brunei to Jamaica, the time for beauty in the global revolt against homophobia, is now.

We shall not be corrected, nor shall we be applied to, we shall dialogue, play and engage, create, participate, educate, celebrate, call and respond . . . *Amandla / Awethu!* – the future / is ours! Such was the call and response of those who bravely struggled and won the battle against the state hate crime that was apartheid. The future is ours. The theatre is ours, and yours. May it be beautiful.

Competing International Players and their Aesthetic Imperatives: The Future of Internationalized Applied Theatre Practice?

Kirsten Sadeghi-Yekta

Introduction

'Cycle for sale. Wait here.' I pass by this hand-written sign on a side road opposite Battambang's busiest tourist hotel. Curious and in need of transport, I decide to wait. I am not in a rush. After half an hour, friendly Kazal shows up. For 15 dollars I am the new owner of a small bike, or for 10 dollars I can rent the bike for as long as I need. Moved by his negotiation skills, I choose the latter. Non-governmental organization and multidisciplinary arts school *Phare Ponleu Selpak* (PPS) is located on a dusty road in the city of Battambang in Northern Cambodia. The end of this road marks the beginning of endless rice fields, hundreds of miles only inhabited by farming communities. The road is crowded from early in the morning until the breath-taking sunset arrives: people are eating noodle soup in the shadow of the palm trees, and cows and bulls rest in the middle of the road. Joined by many children on bikes too big for them, I cycle here every morning at 7 a.m. to observe the theatre awareness group's rehearsals. *Phare Ponleu Selpak* – translated as 'the brightness of art', or interpreted in Khmer more literally as 'the light of the arts' – has its origins in 1986 in Site II refugee camp on the Thai border. Site II incorporated many older camps that had been invaded by the Vietnamese. This is where the civilian populations were transported after a period of violent Khmer Rouge rule. The workshops held for children in the camps' French orphanages developed the idea of a creative organization supporting young refugees in the process of overcoming war trauma. This idea remained with the refugees after they returned to Cambodia, and PPS was created in 1994 in Battambang, Northern Cambodia. After a few weeks of rehearsals, the actors of the group invite one of the European directors[1] and myself for a trip through the rice fields, ending up in a beautiful tiny bar in the middle of the fields. I slowly sip strong palm wine, while I amiably apologize for not eating two grilled rats. The ambiance is joyful, even though we are barely able to communicate with the actors. Then, two Cambodians crash their motorcycle. The accident happens right next to our dead rats. The driver looks severely injured; nevertheless, his friend does not seem to care about him. He picks up the side mirror of the broken bike and checks his *coiffure*. An elegant Cambodian custom of looking away, sparing the other person public humiliation. The director asks the actors if we should help the driver, but the actors advise us not to look. Our friends get nervous and we leave the rice fields. The sunset has arrived.

How can we discuss the aesthetics of applied theatre in a context where politeness equals looking away; even more so, in a country with a history of colonization, civil wars and post-conflict situations, invaded by foreign armies, fragmented by civil conflict and subject to arrivals of foreign peacekeeping and international aid personnel? In a country where at least 1.5 million Cambodians, including 80 per cent to 90 per cent of artists, perished in brutal killings or executions, forced hardships and starvation during the horrors of the Khmer Rouge years (1975–79)? What does aesthetics of applied theatre mean in a country undergoing a process of rediscovering, reshaping and at times reinventing its cultural identity? Finally, how can we define the terms 'aesthetics' and 'applied theatre' in this country, when both terms come from a foreign context with a different significance for Cambodia? How do this context and this history affect the sort of art that is being made, and the artists' artworks?

This chapter presents the aesthetics of a theatre initiative from a development setting: multi-disciplinary arts centre PPS in Cambodia. By focussing on how different judgements of social and aesthetic worth meet, conflict or interact within the programmes, processes and outcomes of this theatre organization, the chapter articulates the different kinds of 'values' attached to the (at times) competing aesthetic criteria for practitioners, government bodies and national and international non-governmental organizations that have stakes in this work. The majority of the data in this chapter is qualitative, generated by interviews, stories about theatre practitioners' experiences and my own observations of performances, workshops and rehearsals.

This chapter points out the ways in which international economics and global governance – manifest in funding decisions of international interveners and cultural policies of national governments – participate and intrude into both the aesthetic and social constructions of applied theatre's artistic value, therefore, framing its aesthetic sphere. The global pressure coming from the international humanitarian community seeking to shape applied theatre companies and make them respond to certain dynamics serves neither art nor community. This also makes it very difficult to locate an aesthetic of applied theatre in a way that is 'traditional' in discussions of aesthetics (through definition of the art 'product' alone and via reference to ideas of beauty, affect and the senses, and not linked to instrumentalism). This study therefore found a way of understanding the impact of international players on discourses of aesthetics in applied theatre in Arjun Appadurai's concept of the ethnoscape,[2] which offers an analytical framework for investigating the meaning of aesthetics of applied theatre in development settings.

I arrived in Cambodia in January 2010 and in total I carried out 27 semi-structured interviews with practitioners, NGO staff and academics in Cambodia. I conducted observations over a period of 6 weeks, five mornings each week, at the arts school during rehearsals for the theatre performance of *The Maids* by Jean Genet (1947). The rehearsals and workshops were all in Khmer, with translation available. Afterwards I would observe circus trainings, music trainings or drawing classes at the arts centre.

Aesthetics

During my fieldwork in Cambodia, the term 'aesthetics' or 'aesthetic' was used by my research participants as a synonym for production values, artistic quality, a system of artistic endeavour and realms of creativity, greater attention given to performance style, joy, pleasure and happiness, but also referred to the performance traditions of Cambodia and of intercultural theatre. All these definitions are equally valid and raise different questions – leading to different insights and implications; however, for the purpose of this study, I am inspired by a categorization of aesthetics by Jerrald Levinson in *The Oxford Handbook of Aesthetics*, as it covers all the synonyms for aesthetics mentioned by my research participants.[3] This chapter refers to aesthetics in relation to *aesthetic sphere, aesthetic practice, aesthetic criteria* and *aesthetic evaluation*. The *aesthetic sphere* is general and relates to the arena of art. The second focus involves *aesthetic practice* or *aesthetic object* – the practice of art, or the activity of making and appreciating art, the artistry. A third focus, *aesthetic criteria*, or *aesthetic terminology* enhances a kind of *property, feature* or *aspect* of things, which refers to the criteria of how we describe an art form, whether formal (composition, line and colour, innovation), extrinsic (content) or subjective (beauty, grace connotation, pleasure). The last focus, *aesthetic evaluation*, is the way we evaluate an artwork, asking questions about how the criteria interact with each other as well as the sensation-based aspect of the practice – or the role of audience members.[4]

Additionally, two terms that correspond with Levinson's foci are *aesthetic discourse* (the ways aesthetics are discussed and written about), and *aesthetic language* (the language used in performance, including sounds, senses, looks, colours, shapes and styles). The four foci and the two additional terms have allowed me to analyse the data from the interviews, rehearsals and observations via the practitioners' contexts, backgrounds and economic positions.

Ethnoscape – a way of looking

The practice of applied theatre takes place within a complex set of communicative exchanges and 'within a network which is historically and spatially located in a given system of action and behaviour'.[5] Ethnoscape is a useful tool for analysing the complicated flow of diverse actors, movements and systems that frame the aesthetics and aesthetic discourse of PPS. The concept of aesthetics within applied theatre is embedded in and part of histories, systems and economic and global flows. This raises questions such as: to what degree is the practice *determined* by its culture or context? Are the participants able to influence the determination of the meanings that are typical within this culture? Or is such a determination inseparable; that is, the participants are not able to influence this determination? This chapter looks at these questions from Appadurai's cultural anthropological standpoint, encapsulating this sense of 'moving' cultural identity by introducing the term *ethnoscape* (1991). By 'ethnoscape', Appadurai explains:

> I mean the landscape of persons who make up the shifting world in which we live: tourists, immigrants, refugees, exiles, guest-workers, and other moving groups and persons constitute an essential feature of the world and appear to affect the politics of and between nations in a hitherto unprecedented degree.[6]

The term ethnoscape approaches the question of how to address the complexities of identity and culture in an interpenetrated and cosmopolitan world, rather than one restricted by geography. 'Ethnoscape' is a neologism from two Greek root words, referring to people (ethno), rather than to ethnicity, and to landscape (scape); combining both terms offers an intercultural and transnational distribution of correlated people.

Significant for this chapter is the work of sociologist Anthony Smith who, following Appadurai, gives a pivotal précis of the term ethnoscape: he defines the concept as 'the belief shared by ethnic groups in a common spatial frame of origin, the territorialisation of shared ethnic memories'.[7] Shared memories attached to specific territories as a process can be found in many periods and countries. Cambodia's colonial and post-colonial status has produced a condensed net of knowledge and status attributions, within which individuals are tangled in every sphere of their lives. As Smith states:

> The symbolic content of this nation, building upon historical events, folklore, invented tradition, reinvented and reconstructed art-forms and cultural expressions, creates a picture of the national character both unique in content and standard in form.[8]

Following this, the aesthetics and aesthetic discourse of applied theatre in this context can be linked to how the mix of people, communicative exchanges, symbolization, relationships and networks can change.

Smith proposes two important sites of territorialized memory, which are relevant for the proposition of this chapter: 'miraculous or sacred sites'[9] and 'various fields of battle which marked critical turning points in the fortunes of the community'.[10] In this Cambodian case study, these can be described as the *sacred sites* of the Hindu temple complex Angkor Wat and the genocide commemoration Choeung Ek Killing Fields, but also the *fields of battle* of colonization, civil wars and most importantly genocide, which have affected the ways PPS's students struggle with their cultural identity. As Smith argues, for the members of a nation, it is not necessary to dominate or settle within their ethnoscape; it is sufficient for members to have a collective narrative related to a specific space.[11] Smith's view of the ethnoscape offers an understanding of the different ways collective memory is passed on in Cambodia, such as commemorations or international tribunals convicting Khmer Rouge leaders.

In the Cambodian context, I use the term *cultural ethnoscape* as my own critical framework, construed through all the different actors involved within PPS's culture, including: (i) refugees, the arts school's founders returning to their homeland after living in refugee camps on the Thai border for years; (ii) European international artists travelling to the arts school; (iii) tourists; and (iv) an international cast of donors providing their services as goods. These are all 'travelling' individuals or groups that shape a fundamental characteristic of the aesthetic discourse and politics of PPS. This chapter addresses all four categories within the cultural ethnoscape of PPS. The length of the four respective sections differs due to the diverse significance of the actors. Moreover, these participants are, I argue, intrinsically – at times unwelcoming, at times disruptively – interfering in the artistic process of PPS.

Refugees

Very early in the morning I have planned an interview
with a progressive Cambodian theatre director
We meet at his small theatre
on stage
He sits opposite me without a shirt
big heart shaped eyes
The smell of last night's performance is still present
props everywhere
I try to guess his age
but I fail to do so
The interview starts with some formal questions about
my research
the questions that are raised during my fieldwork
theatre in Cambodia

With no apparent reason he suddenly starts to talk about his
    childhood

during the Khmer Rouge years
I do not ask anything
His eyes fill with tears, however he does not drop his gaze
His voice shows no difference
He explains that he is the only survivor of four childhood friends
Two died of starvation and one was taken into the woods with him
Khmer Rouge soldiers killed his best friend with a bamboo stick
    in front of him
He was forced to watch
Thirty-five years ago
His friend was then eleven years old
my interviewee twelve years old
The tears coursing slowly down his face
even when he shows me the drums
he recently started to fabricate them himself
Drums in all forms and sizes
very impressed at the quality and care that had gone into shaping
    each piece
I buy one, a small one
I do not know why, I do not play drums
But the drums sound so differently beautiful when he plays

This poetic vignette from an interview with a Cambodian theatre director taking place in the winter of 2010 illustrates clearly the dichotomy of aesthetics in a place of horror. In Cambodia, the memories of traumatic events have lived on to 'scratch' those who were not there to experience these events. The children of PPS – children of survivors – have inherited disastrous histories not through remembrance but through post-memory – as Marianne Hirsch describes:

> inter- and trans-generational return of traumatic knowledge and embodied experience. It is a *consequence* of traumatic recall but . . . at a generational remove.[12]

Hirsh's definition of post-memory will be used here to understand the continuous impact and heritage of the Cambodian genocide by the Khmer Rouge between 1975 and 1979. This heritage affects and changes what kinds of art are produced in the country, and also how artists and spectators perceive these art-forms. Cambodia is still in the midst of a process of rediscovering, reshaping and at times even reinventing the country's cultural identity. This section describes the first actors of the cultural ethnoscape – refugees – originating in the aftermath of this brutal period. These are the founders of the arts centre, as PPS originated in 1986 in Site II refugee camp.

The traumatic history of civil wars, genocide and foreign peace-keeping, preserving the country as aid dependent, has influenced Cambodia's global position. Despite the many attempts of the international community, liberal peace-building in Cambodia so far has proven unsuccessful in many of its central goals, including the opportunity for collective remembrance.[13] In 2003, the Royal Government of Cambodia and the United Nations created a special court: 'Extraordinary Chambers in the Courts of Cambodia for the Prosecution of Crimes Committed during the Period of Democratic Kampuchea' (ECCC). Since 2007, the ECCC has struggled to adjudicate the remaining Khmer Rouge leaders and officials suspected of mass atrocities. Smith's view of ethnoscape offers an understanding of the different ways the collective narrative in Cambodia passes on, for example through the United Nations international tribunal convicting Khmer Rouge leaders. However, Cambodian collective remembrance is compromised by limiting the trial to only two remaining defendants – Nuon Chea and Khieu Samphan – both elderly and in failing health. For many – including the founders of PPS – who lost their relatives during the Khmer Rouge years, this is a permanent defect of the collaborative system between warlords, politicians and the United Nations. These developments all shaped the development of PPS. Cambodian culture was obliterated resulting in no secure Cambodian aesthetic or social domain – everything is 'developmental', provisional, transitional and ad hoc.

The refugees' first arts interaction came from a humanitarian project, that is, the on-site orphanages led by French NGOs used visual arts as a tool for children to express themselves and recover from their war trauma. NGO culture and French influence remains intact in PPS today: the French created the basic aesthetic of the arts centre, and PPS was born out of this intervention. The longstanding (13 years) but ultimately temporary displacement of the PPS artists did not help their attempts to reconstitute their social and cultural lives in the aftermath of the war. In 1992 the artists of PPS returned to Cambodia. Afraid that the young artists would have to leave their country again, they settled in Cambodia's second city, Battambang, the closest city to the Thai border.

The young adults from the orphanage in the Site II camp arrived in their home country with many traumatic stories. In order to understand these experiences, including the post-genocide period on the border, eight young artists (including two who remained directors of the arts school in 2010) decided to make a change for the next generation. They (re-)started creative workshops in Battambang with support from the French former workshop leaders. During interviews, the Cambodian circus director expressed that his positive experience with visual arts in the camp led him to believe strongly that arts could be used as a tool to overcome any sort of trauma, and he therefore chose to share this belief with other young people. The director and his colleagues first built a visual arts school for children. They then constructed a library to engage children in reading and writing. The social aims of the company were clearly more important than the artistic outcomes; however, the arts were used to achieve these goals. The social and aesthetic worth were connected.

The impetus behind the aesthetic discourse of theatrical practice within the arts centre is therefore mainly educational and social, supported by the international community. That is, firstly, the founders of the arts centre recognized that the Khmer Rouge had destroyed knowledge and awareness of Khmer cultural identity. Young children in particular had not been in contact with Khmer storytelling since they were born. The deliberate targeting of educated people and artists during the Khmer Rouge era resulted in a limited base of nationals with practical experience surviving. To a great degree, Khmer culture had vanished. International Non Governmental Organizations (INGOs) in

Cambodia interested in this *genocide narrative* were therefore willing to invest in the arts centre.[14]

Cambodians believe that traditional Khmer culture is not something you are simply born with; it is a kind of order, and is human-made. They believe that culture is something that is achieved, and that children should be raised and educated to become properly Khmer.[15] Experience and morality transmitted by Khmer folktales are vital aspects of traditional Khmer education.[16] During the Khmer Rouge years, parents and children were forced into labour and to attend indoctrination lessons where they were told that education was an imperialist tool. The children of PPS carry their parents' personal and cultural trauma through the actions and stories they remember from those they grew up with.[17] Due to the absence of many artists and traditional Khmer folktales, Khmer culture was invisible for the majority of children in Battambang, and did not exist prior to initiatives such as PPS.

Secondly, the majority of teenagers in Battambang are the first or second generation after the Khmer Rouge years. The elderly were separated from their families for the duration of the brutal regime, and the young adults were not educated to raise their children or to understand their own traumatic experiences. Most of them had been part of military groups, forced to fight for or against the regime. In 1998, the Cambodian director explained that they were starting families and their children easily got involved in gangs.[18] For these children to grow up with post-memory – an 'inter- and trans-generational return of traumatic knowledge and embodied experience'[19] – it was troubling to focus on visual arts, at that time the only existing art-form at PPS. The children's disconnection to visual arts forced the directors to develop a different art form that required a more physical concentration. The directors motivated the children to practise martial arts to protect themselves and gymnastics to keep in shape. Both sports were the basis for the development of the 'social' circus school.

The Cambodian and French directors clarified that they first focussed on the freedom for children to play, but the directors' desire was to professionalize the social circus school. After 3 months of successful circus trainings (from instructors of the The Royal University of Fine Arts [RUFA]) and performances, the directors realized that the natural behaviour of Cambodian children involved running, jumping and repetition of exercises. Circus was seen to be a suitable vehicle for teenagers with difficulties or homeless youngsters; a team-building activity in contrast to the lonely life on the streets. Their capabilities and strengths were tested and limits were taught. The concept of post-memory initially framed the social constructions of the theatrical practice. The picture below show a clear circus aesthetic based on endurance, strength, agility and flexibility. This aesthetic, however, is neither labelled nor discussed at the arts centre. The following categorization of ethnoscape players will demonstrate that due to the absence of aesthetic terminology, aesthetic discourse has been lost inside the centre.

In 1998 many children in Battambang suffered from drug-related issues due to the prevailing gang culture. The children experienced major concentration problems, and the founders of PPS argued that

Figure 5 The Circus School in 2010. (Photograph: Hanneke Smits).

theatre was easier and needed less concentration than circus. Therefore, the arts school organized a theatre show that toured around the country. Finally, the awareness theatre group of PPS was invented as a tool to reintegrate less competent young adults into the society.

There are specific dynamics at work in the connection between the social and the aesthetic. The struggles with post-memory, concentration, engagement and drug-use underpin the history of this connection. While the directors of the arts school attempt to engage the next generation, the ongoing trauma on different levels – the idea of post-memory – continues to generate a context of uncertainty and transition. The social and aesthetic are not just connected, but also un-pinnable, decentred, and related to crisis management rather than progressive 'development'.

In 2010, PPS staff members emphasized that the company's aims were to reconstruct children's identities and to rebuild their cultural habits and knowledge. Several questions were raised, such as: What is your (cultural) identity in Cambodia? Although the past is inextricably part of culture, what is the past today and what is the past tomorrow? What is the value of *Angkor Wat* today? Is it still part of Cambodia's cultural identity? These questions and many others were raised during hours of interviews with the Cambodian and French directors. The staff members explained that the children are taught to speak about their cultural identity and their traumas. However, PPS's directors recognized that the genocide would definitely take more than two generations to overcome.

One of the reasons why this process would take time is the imposition of the *genocide narrative*. Cambodia has a very young population, of which 32 per cent are between one and 14 years old.[20] Many are too young to remember the years of horror, and others do not believe the stories of violence and terror. The younger generation sometimes views the Khmer Rouge history as a myth: this generation questions and doubts these factual scenarios. Indeed, recent history is not mandatory in Cambodian schools. In 2009 the first textbook discussing the Khmer Rouge was distributed to schools. The children of PPS have inherited their ancestors' confusion: in general, it is not well defined who is a former Khmer Rouge soldier and who a victim; in particular, why certain families were killed and others were not. But the foremost question is how the Khmer could impose such violence and suffering on their fellow Khmer.[21] This confusion is a clear example of post-memory observed, and was mentioned in several interviews, including the one at the start of this section.

Furthermore, the constant change of ideology throughout their lives has left families confused: many Khmer Rouge survivors have witnessed five regimes, including colonization. After returning to their homeland in Battambang, close to the Thai border, where many former Khmer Rouge cadres reside, the artists and the perpetrators of violence live together. Growing up, their children could not always identify if their friends were offspring of victims or perpetrators. The confusing post-memory narrative is part of all the families living close to PPS and their children who visit PPS. Their frustration that only two remaining Khmer Rouge leaders will be prosecuted through the United Nations international tribunal for the genocide feeds the impression of the injustice of the tribunal. Although tribunals are answering the questions of the genocide, the staff of the arts centre argued that artistic practices have been helpful in communicating about the massacres. As Hawkes argues, within the genocide narrative, 'the gaps in healing that cannot be addressed through tribunals could possibly be addressed through art.'[22] The French director's viewpoint about healing from genocide is, however, derived from the international academic arena. 'Appropriate' ways of healing trauma vary by culture, and are not all necessarily applicable to Cambodia. At PPS, the children are therefore in the middle of clashes between the social discourses of the arts centre and the international community.

The influence of international discourses around genocide on Cambodian cultural practice was also visible during the specific moments when the interviewees talked about their traumas – described at the beginning of this section – only taking place *outside* PPS. The topic came up only when the interviewee started the conversation and when the interviewee had lived through the horrors of the Khmer Rouge. These meetings were always very emotional: the older artists cried about their past and described how they use the energy of their past in the creation of their performances. They use the medium – the body in theatre, shadow puppets in shadow puppetry and paint in visual arts – to create good energy, to forget their past and the deaths of their loved ones, the so-called 'way' to Buddhist *nirvana*.[23] This stage – the extinction of all suffering and longings – leads them through their artistic processes. The artistic final product generally does not consist of genocide narratives or Khmer Rouge-related props or sets. The artists only use the negativity of their past to their advantage by transforming this energy into an artistic product. The shows are very popular in Phnom Penh. This illustrates the aesthetic practice in a post-genocide setting: there is direct remembering of the horror that happened, but not elsewhere. This signals the impact of international discourses around genocide on Cambodian cultural practice. Relating to the opening story about looking away from the tragic during the road accident, Cambodian culture prefers to deal with history and tragedy in a different matter to international discourses. The latter aesthetic practice is contrary to the artistic products I observe at PPS.

As an outsider who does not speak Khmer I was aware that many conversations and meetings happened outside my awareness at PPS. Although the French director mentioned the importance of contemporary cultural identity for the new Cambodian generation, during my observations I did not witness any workshops where children were asked about their cultural identity, nor discuss the traumas of their families' past.

In contrast, I observed constant *silence* about the children's and their families' horrific past. During interviews, different translators emphasized avoiding questions about the interviewees' past, specifically the deaths of family members during the genocide.

This silence becomes 'deafening' during the weekly circus performances. A specific scene for a public show, directed by a French artist, exemplifies this silence and shows the impact of the genocide's visualization on PPS's artists and spectators. The scene starts with the circus artists entering the tent, each wearing a blue and white patterned scarf called a *krama*. As Stanton explains, these scarves were imposed by the Khmer Rouge Central Committee's cadres in Phnom Penh; the blue and white scarf was 'a symbol of classification, signifying that the person need not to be seen as an individual person but as a member of a class, determined by race, religion or education'[24] and was predominantly used to mark people for extermination. Stanton states that the scarf is one of the clearest pieces of evidence prosecutors have gathered of the Khmer Rouge's intent to commit genocide.[25] The specific circus scene shows how Cambodians wearing the *krama* are taken away and separated from their loved ones. With intense emotional and physical expression, the circus artists demonstrate the despair of fatal separation.

Observing this scene a few times during the weekly circus shows, I notice the elderly and older adults always turned their faces away during this emotional and intense moment. Many historians, scholars and survivors, as well as some interviewees, describe how Khmer Rouge survivors were forced to look at atrocities without dropping their gaze.[26] Loved ones were tortured and killed in front of survivors, and if they showed emotional or physical reactions they would be next. Elegantly looking away is a typical Cambodian custom: in uncomfortable situations it is a form of politeness, a gesture to make the other person feel at ease. When a Cambodian suffers, others will look away so as not to emphasize the sorrow or grief of the other. Several times in different settings in Cambodia I observed this gesture (including during the road accident described above) to avoid shame. During the circus performance it seems that the apparent representation of the past made the elderly turn around and avoid the images on stage, to look away. The spectators are confronted with situations they do not want to be reminded of: neither with the suffering nor with visual images of the past's atrocities. The Khmer Rouge horrors may have increased the necessity of the polite habit of looking away.

At an average circus show, the audience consists of tourists, children and a considerable number of elderly from nearby neighbourhoods and villages. The consequence of this mixed audience is that the circus artists can clearly perceive the moment when several spectators turn their heads and look away. In certain forms of therapeutic tradition arising from Euro-American practice, the sufferer's grief and sorrow is acknowledged. Nevertheless, Cambodians are used to looking away and are taught to do so. Here, the French artist forces the Cambodian audience to look at a horrific situation, therefore dominating the decision for them at the sensate level. The artist strongly dominates the aesthetic – the sensation-based aspects of the practice. Consequently, this does not only affect the artistic engagement and aesthetic value for the spectator, it also affects the spectator personally. In addition, it negatively affects the artist and the representation of their artwork on stage. Looking away is clearly a sign that what is shown is inappropriate; the people are visibly uncomfortable. The artistic quality vanishes as audience members turn their heads – the product has failed without the 'presence' of the audience. Khmer and 'Western' aesthetics clearly clash in this example. There is clearly not any room in Khmer aesthetics for this kind of uncomfortable material.

The different players and their aesthetic imperatives here make it impossible to locate the aesthetics of applied theatre in this context in a way that is 'traditional' in discussions of aesthetics as introduced in the first chapter by Levinson's four foci of aesthetics: *aesthetic sphere, aesthetic practice, aesthetic criteria* and *aesthetic evaluation*. The players all bring a different form of aesthetics. Appadurai's ethnoscape reveals that any cultural expression has 'external' influences: ideas of imposition or natural growth are both simplifications of intricate processes. It is an oversimplification to argue that the aesthetic of PPS is merely imposed, because this argument completely denies the agency of many Cambodian artists. Similarly, it is unreasonable to state that PPS is totally home-grown, as this ignores the flow of international money, ideologies and practices.

It does, however, exemplify James Thompson's argument that applying theatre to development settings needs to be translated to make it both understandable and meaningful in that place.[27] It must develop its own theoretical markers, its own local reference points, if it is to be believed, employed and settled in.[28] The danger is that practitioners struggle to avoid compromises and hold onto the 'artistic integrity' of their own 'Western' aesthetic. The external power could then impoverish local theatre practices and diminish cultural particularity.

As Thompson accurately notes:

> The belief that there is a global threat to local cultural practice will be more justifiable if knowledge and practice brought to the country is not properly understood as culturally particular with little immediate currency beyond the place of their inception.[29]

The presence of the French artist – the director of the show – is, however, vital for the survival of the circus group to link to powerful donors (which will be illustrated in the next section). Funding for post-memory initiatives has grown rapidly since the genocide. Here is an example of a shocking clash between the social discourse and the aesthetic of the centre, the donors, the performances – and the context of the work. The aesthetic discourse becomes an imposition if there is an assumption that the practice brought from Western settings *automatically* translates into the Cambodian context.

This relates to Smith's statement that shared memories attached to particular territories as a process can be found in Cambodia on different levels. The significance of the boundaries of nations for their inhabitants clearly derives from the joys and sufferings associated with a particular ethnoscape, even though 'they are determined by military, economic and political factors.'[30] Opposing agendas of international artists and international donors giving money for circus shows portraying the genocide compromises Cambodian collective remembrance in the circus scene described. The next section serves an understanding of these agendas and how international and national governmental organizations intensify the framing of the social circus's aesthetic discourses.

International interveners

During one of the warmest days of the year the French executive director of PPS invites me to lunch. The purpose of this meeting is to understand the history and aesthetic dimensions of the centre and how the school is embedded structurally and financially within the field of INGOs. The French director and I have lunch at his house. While we indulge ourselves with typical Cambodian delights such as fried mice and unidentifiable vegetables, he invites me to visit two prisons where new social circus projects will take place in future. PPS has received 175,000 Euros from the European Union to introduce social circus to Khmer prisons as a form of artistic leisure for the detainees. The idea is to train the school's third generation of circus artists to lead this project. The director explains that the project will focus on detained children aged 7 to 12 years old, with drug addictions.

Upon arrival at one of the prisons, I immediately notice that there are no children held in the prison – only men around 40 years old. The guard points out that the prisoners have been convicted for major drug crimes. The detainees are terribly thin and pale and have no energy to stand. The prison has neither beds nor mattresses on the stone floor. Ten guards accompany me inside the small low-rise building. The prisoners are forced to try to stand up, and start repeating Buddhist rhymes ten times as a way of welcoming me. Lacking any windows or ventilation, the temperature is above 45 degrees. After meeting the detainees, I am invited for a formal meeting with the main warden, the person in charge. He explains that the prisoners' favourite sentences of the Buddhist rhymes are: 'Don't drink, don't smoke, don't use drugs and don't do drug trafficking. Angry children always give misfortune to their parents, whilst gentle children give happiness to their parents.' He clarifies that the detainees receive 25 dollar cents a day for food, which means a bit of rice and porridge once a day. When we ask the warden why he has accepted this arts project while he is aware of an urgent need for proper food portions and better living conditions rather than circus tricks, my translator refuses to translate my question.

This scene in February 2010 during my trip to one of the designated detention centres for PPS's new social circus project gives a glimpse into the intricate nature of international donor funding, and describes the second player of the cultural ethnoscape: international interveners. Following Hughes, the term I use here for international donors, the United Nations and INGOs is 'international interveners' working together with local political players.[31]

This situation is an example of how humanitarian projects fail in these circumstances for numerous reasons. The initial funding application for this project, including the information I received about it beforehand, written by the French management of the company, entailed a completely different vision of the artistic project. The terms 'aesthetics' and 'social circus' that were used in the funding application clash in this context, because both terms clearly come from an alien cultural context and do not carry the same resonance in Cambodia. The French management explains that the initial project focuses on social circus activities for *young* detainees, combined with training skills for PPS's circus artists. However, the project clearly does not follow the aims of PPS.

First, the initial project target was interaction with *children* in Cambodian detention centres; however, PPS artists are now forced to work with *adults*. Secondly, the project does not concentrate on the significance of rehabilitating the artists' cultural identity and history as part of the organization's mission. On the contrary, the project's emphasis is mainly around the well-being of the detainees and *their* psycho-social needs. The workshop leaders in this project are fairly young adults, mainly circus artists, recently recovered from drug addiction. These artists will be spending a considerable amount of time each week with detainees, of which the majority are being forced to try to overcome their addictions. During project meetings the potential consequences for the artists regarding the sensitive 'addictive' situation in which they will work are stressed and noted. The risks and dangers the young artists may encounter are also discussed, albeit briefly, and considered. Nonetheless, the arts centre originally devised the basis of this artistic project and has now accepted the economic capital of the donor. By agreeing to take the monetary support, the project will have to be executed by PPS.

This project of PPS exemplifies the complications of the continuous narrative of the Khmer Rouge tribunal and the country's horrifying past – as well as the indication that at least one of five Cambodians are living in extreme poverty – attracts different international interveners, some with their own agendas and others their own causes. Of the total number of 4,000 NGOs, an estimated 1,300 NGOs are currently active[32] while there is only one NGO actively providing psychological services to trauma victims. Even the Killing Fields of Choeung Ek are internationalized and privatized: a Japanese company now controls the commemoration site. The international aid sector in Cambodia has seen substantial changes since its inception in 1992; the sector still gives the impression that everyone wants something for Cambodia, but not everyone wants what is best for the country and its citizens. A staff member of Documentation Centre Cambodia accurately states: 'Foreign aid needs other considerations of more important concepts, which are currently not included. Developmental aid ignores consequences of ethnic, language and cultural complexes.'[33]

The consequences of international intervention are highly ambivalent in Cambodia, in particular within PPS. The international sphere can offer several opportunities to local players – in terms of employment and infrastructure, but it can also function as a political tool, limiting the potential emergence of a sanctioned independent nation, as well as PPS's potential to become a strong community with moral authority. Ultimately, as this chapter argues, the award of foreign resources occurs in return for a decline of control, authority and sovereignty, which serves neither the aesthetic notions of the company, nor the community and audience members. This is not to suggest that all interveners' influence results in destructive and harmful situations. Nor does this one example stand for the general trend. The scenario of the detention centres offers just one example of the ways in which the ideals of sovereignty and community suffered a decline in the process of rearrangement into the notion of a strong community.

The person who frames is simply – 'he who pays the piper, calls the tune' – however, this analysis shows that the piper is the visiting or local artist, whose work is shaped by the financial structure. The INGOs have the finance and set the agenda. The tune of the piper seems to be important, but not indispensable. It is a show. The term 'show' is both theatrical and evaluative, and the verb 'showing' is linked to notions of accountability. That gives a clue as to where social circus fits into this analysis, because it is about proof. When receiving large amounts of money, PPS has to show a visual image in return. Moreover, the arts school has to show that the money is used appropriately. The study illustrates that the complexity is about the relationship between suffering, saving people from suffering, and showing people that you are saving people from suffering: hence, the *marketability* of saving people through art.

The organization and board of PPS during my fieldwork period in 2010 was mixed Cambodian/French, while the majority of staff were French. The French staff members emphasize the importance of fundraising and networking, both crucial for international acknowledgement. Appearing on international agendas with international qualifications is a great aspiration for the arts centre, the French staff stated. The French staff also argued that the artists should not only overcome the war but also overcome their borders. The survival and international future of the school depends on monetary and artistic resources from outside. Even though the circus division has been financially independent since 2006, and the circus group raises money through weekly tourist shows and hotel performances, monetary resources are still necessary for the survival of the school, and the opportunity for international acknowledgement. International interveners are willing to donate because of the historical origins of the company and their social aims, particularly their interest in the genocide narrative. The fairly lucrative practice of fundraising for utilitarian arts projects used within PPS raises questions of accountability and representation. These questions are – as mentioned before – important for debates about intervention. Although the poor, the community, the less privileged and the detainees are targets of assistance, the extent to which they have any kind of say over the assistance they receive and how much adequate assistance they receive is questionable here.

It should be noted, however, that the Cambodian staff believes in the ability of their international colleagues to deliver structure and organization. For example, the French Executive Director of PPS (in 2010) brought some crucial changes to the arts school and created a social project for educators with aid agency *Médecins Sans Frontières* to use circus as a tool. Although the Cambodian staff members shared their beliefs in the interveners' ability to increase fundraising contacts, international contributions were no longer regarded as necessarily excellent. During interviews I observed the Cambodians' appreciation for their international colleagues who had been residing in Cambodia for many years, and who were accustomed to their culture and language or were willing to return frequently.

Nonetheless, I also noted their weary annoyance at short-term and temporary international interveners, offering as their centrepiece hopes for development, aesthetic solutions featuring the reform of aesthetic notions, and overcoming Cambodia's past. Following independence from colonial rule and five ideological regime changes, Cambodian people – as I observed during meetings – have a more cautious perspective and a need for 'normality', in the sense that they would like to move on from the genocide narrative, after decades of conflict and violence.[34] The Cambodian staff members of PPS admitted that the genocide narrative had been repeated for many years, and that their development, particularly their artistic development, was at times conceptualized and depended exclusively on the country's past.

An aesthetic remains – focussed on endurance, repetition and strength – but the aesthetic is affected through the international funders. The mandatory thematic content focussing on Cambodian history is an example illustrating how foreign aid aims clashed with the arts school's goals. Its effect is profound on the weakest group – the children, including victims of human trafficking – for whom the projects are actually intended. These children are the target audience. It does not serve those who have any kind of say over the assistance they receive (the artists and the community in Battambang), nor does it serve the artistic quality of the educational projects. Arguably, the international interventions I observed attended to neither affect nor effect, but only required de-contextualized 'evidence' of efficacy, if that. Thompson's ideas resonate through my argument about international intervention: 'By failing to recognise affect – bodily responses, sensations and aesthetic pleasure – much of the power of performance can be missed'.[35] Thompson therefore claims that applied theatre is 'limited if it concentrates solely on effects – identifiable social outcomes, messages or impacts – and forgets the radical potential of the freedom to enjoy beautiful radiant things'.[36] It was in these shocking clashes that my search for an aesthetic for applied theatre in Cambodia came to an end. I abandoned the search here because for me, any meaningful notion of aesthetics in applied theatre needs to serve art and community.

Appadurai developed the term 'ethnoscape' to understand the fluid shapes caused by human groups and their cultural expressions linked to flows of international capital. Aid dependence seems to develop more and more as a condition arising from global structures and markets, rather than only from local shortfalls. While aid itself is most of the time well-meant, aid dependence encourages social and moral looseness in recipient communities such as PPS, and is executed by international interveners as a means to exercise power. Moreover, international capital directly interferes with the aesthetic dimensions and vision of PPS. The Khmer staff devotes large amounts of time to capture aid resources while deeply resenting the hierarchies of (human) power and obligation within which they are required to participate. I argue therefore that to a certain extent the aesthetic notions of applied theatre remain a dependent 'by-product' of funding with restricted artistic and social rules for those who require international support.

European artists

The director of DC-Cam commenting on the difficulties of regenerating cultural life in Cambodia, expresses his concern that:

> Nobody is in charge of or leads the Cambodian art forms, that is why the arts are so scattered. We (as in Khmer) prefer to follow, rather than leading. We fear to lead, fear to initiate, we are afraid to make mistakes.[37]

During that delightful lunch with the French executive director of the arts centre, I am intrigued to hear about the collaboration between PPS and Ariane Mnouchkine. The French theatre director is quoted as saying 'I am in the present and only the present matters to me' – while PPS's main focus is on Khmer cultural identity and how that relates to their past and possible future. Moreover, the 'fourth wall' is not Mnouchkine's ultimate restriction in the theatre: Mnouchkine's shows frequently consist of the actors getting ready in front of the spectators. The shows of PPS, however, are very traditional and always use the comfortable fourth wall. The moment I ask the director what the effect is of Mnouchkine's work and how 'theatre for theatre' influences the aesthetic dimensions of the company, a very young girl walks into the room. She holds a dead cat in one hand; obviously it died a few seconds ago. With my poor knowledge of the Khmer language, I understand that she killed the cat in the rice fields. She explains that she was very hungry.

This section illustrates the impact and power of the third player within the cultural ethnoscape: European artists travelling to PPS. The artists travel (mainly from Europe) on their own initiative to Battambang, in order to temporarily work with the young artists at the arts centre. The artists stay at the centre between 8 weeks and 6 months. Several artists return regularly to the centre. Observations during my fieldwork show that these artists all have their own agenda and reasons to visit the arts school: some desire to join groups with like-minded people for good causes; some have long-lasting relationships with the country because of their previous travel experiences or country of origin; some arrive in this remote arts centre wanting to offer *the Other* the hope for change, cultural modernity and artistic solutions that feature the reform of aesthetic notions. In more extreme cases, these artists at times try to counter this by using strategies to manufacture dependence beyond the control of the arts centre or international interveners. This section interrogates two examples of European artists travelling to PPS caught between the mechanisms of global governance and cultural misperceptions. The examples are interesting cases in that they form a bridge between the many difficulties players in the cultural ethnoscape face in terms of aesthetic notions in the context of a globalizing 'moving' world.

The first example illustrates how European discourses of social and aesthetic worth clash and therefore fail in their purposes. Since 2008 the arts school has been working in partnership with Ariane Mnouchkine's Parisian company *Le Théâtre du Soleil*. The rationale of Mnouchkine's new peace-building project is the play *L'Histoire terrible mais inachevée de Norodom Sihanouk, roi du Cambodge* ('The terrible but unfinished story of Norodom Sihanouk, King of Cambodia'), staged in Cambodia and France with 29 musicians and actors from PPS. In 1984 Mnouchkine and Hélène Cixous[38] were confronted with the refugee camps on the Thai – Cambodian border while travelling, and both realized that generally 'neither feelings of suffering nor dreams of hope are ever completely satisfied'.[39] Inspired by this trip, Mnouchkine began staging contemporary texts written specifically for *Le Théâtre du Soleil* by Cixous. This specific play centres on the double meaning of the French word *histoire*: between art and reality, between non-fiction and fiction. The story has an epic Shakespearian ancestry that explores a contemporary tragedy: the descent into Cambodian genocidal hell until the Vietnamese civil war and oppression.[40]

Ashley Thompson (2005), who has researched Cixous' theatrical texts of *Le Théâtre du Soleil*, argued that it would be refreshing for new Khmer generations to actively reclaim and reflect on their horrific history by staging this play. Thompson acknowledges that translating the epic theatrical text into Khmer involved high artistic and political risks; in particular, organizing the Cambodian *mise en scène* 'in a socially and politically morbid context'.[41] However, Thompson expected that the spectacle's themes of memory, forgiveness, presence, absence, life and death may assist the new Khmer generation giving meaning to these complicated themes.

PPS's students have noted the immense challenge of studying the complicated theatrical text and becoming accustomed to a rather foreign but very familiar piece of writing. The Cambodian directors explained during interviews:

> The project with Mnouchkine is important, because it is a unique chance for the artists to work with people in terms of understanding what theatre is, in particular, because it is the first time that the arts centre is working with 'theatre for theatre'. The students enjoy this form of theatre, however, they had to overcome two major thresholds. Firstly, we had to assure the young artists that the police would not harm them when the artists would talk about theatre. Secondly, we had to introduce them to theatrical texts, and again convince them that they would not be punished for reading theatre literature.[42]

The students were to a certain extent forced to overcome their fears (in the sense of discussing and reading theatrical texts) for Mnouchkine's causes. I doubt that these emotional processes should be part of applied theatre practice, in particular with regard to the vulnerable mental state of the artists. The Western 'aesthetic' was prioritized over the social state of the Khmer artists. This relates to the problem of Kant's theory of successful evaluation of artworks that requires a specific vocabulary to be learnt. However Joe Winston, agreeing with Geertz, notes that this is an entirely Western notion, because 'in all other cultures beauty is commonly understood by attending to the broader cultural concerns that it serves.'[43]

Thompson is convinced that this project is a transcultural contribution that does not impose; rather, Mnouchkine's methodology creates artistic freedom for the participating actors.[44] Mnouchkine's process also involves remembrance questions to make the young artists think about their pasts, including the French colonial period. The French executive director of PPS laughed infectiously when he explained: 'Perhaps we think this is very important, because I am French myself?'[45] This could indicate a forced social impact on the Khmer artists. As mentioned above, the ways to remember and to heal differ greatly between cultures; therefore, the French approach could clash with Khmer ways of remembrance.

The second example in this section of European artists travelling to Cambodia is the European theatre director of classical theatre performance *The Maids* by Jean Genet. The account offered here is drawn from 6 weeks of intensive study, five mornings a week, at the arts school during the performance's rehearsals. The European director had previously worked in South-East Asia and had visited Cambodia numerous times. Moreover, he had also performed this specific text on several occasions in different countries and was convinced that this was a suitable text for Cambodia's current situation.

Controversial French playwright Genet – orphan, prostitute and thief – transformed his life through literature and writing plays, desiring to be the spokesman of the oppressed. *The Maids* tells the story of two sisters, Claire and Solange, the maids of the so-called Madame. They admire their Madame, her independence, wealth and wardrobe, but they also despise her. The maids decide to poison the Madame's tea, but their attempt fails. In the final scene, Solange, 'playing' the maid, forces her sister Claire, 'playing' the Madame, to drink the poisoned tea.

Claire then shows courage and drinks the tea in the role of the Madame. Clearly, there is a playing-out of scenarios here – a deadly experiment with 'showing' and play-acting – in the play.

After rehearsals, the director expressed that he hoped intensely to open up space in the hearts and minds of the spectators by showing situations that would resonate with their own daily lives. The director anticipated that the audience would easily follow the story and would identify themselves with the maids. The Madame would symbolize upper-class people pretending to take care of their servants but never offering the maids the life they hope for. The director imagined that the audience would laugh at the attempts of the two maids to free themselves from the Madame, because of the naïve and humorous way the actresses would play the maids as two little children. As a result, the audience could have sympathy with the revolt of the maids, longing for some wealth and respect. The audience would agree with the outbursts of hatred towards the world that seemed to have abandoned the maids from the day they entered the Madame's house, but would also realize that hatred could fade.

Continuous and structured rehearsals took place only when the European theatre director was present. The rehearsals started on time and worked through 5 hours of intense practice with two breaks. The director worked with different Khmer translators, meaning that the stage directions of the director never travelled directly to the actresses. The second Khmer interpreter quickly took over the role of director in the sense that he gave stage directions himself and instantly hushed the actresses when in his opinion they made too much noise. It was obvious that the director was struggling to position the translator, and sometimes attempts to clarify his role as solely an interpreter failed. One significant moment demonstrates the mechanisms of cultural slippages, and the ways in which this player in the ethnoscape faced several difficulties in terms of aesthetic notions and discourses. The moment occurred as the European director was rehearsing one of the first scenes of the play: the Madame is out and the sisters build their own fantasy world. They open Madame's wardrobe: one sister plays the Madame completely dressed up, and the other sister acts as the maid. While the sisters were performing a game of 'snobby Madame and servile maid' to express their anger and to escape from the ties of dependence (again, there is a playing-out of scenarios here), the director asked one of the actresses to spit on the floor to provoke an exaggerated example of the role of the maid.

During this moment, when the stage direction was an exaggeration of the maid's role, the actress refused to spit on the floor. When she continued to resist making this gesture, tensions between the director and translator ran high. 'Could you please try to spit? I would like to see how it looks', the director amiably tried. 'Spit!' the translator shouted. 'Could you please ask her [the actress] to try it, so I can at least see how it looks?' – the director asked the interpreter in a friendly manner. 'SPIT!' the translator yelled. For a while, the intense conversation between the men continued, ending with a strong statement in which the director once more elucidated the interpreter's sole role as a translator. The actress then explained that spitting on the floor is an unacceptable and very disrespectful gesture on stage. Although the director attempted to persuade her that this gesture would be perfect for her role as a maid – particularly now he knew why she had refused, the actress was not convinced.

On the opening night, 3 weeks later, the actress spat. A little bit. With hesitation. I realized that the theatrical situation was implausible. The stylized and imposed aesthetic of the director led to a forced scene, in which the actress reluctantly followed the director's instructions, lacking both artistic understanding and appreciation. In an interview, the actress admitted that this creative process was hard, and through this process she had noticed the absence of a theatrical aesthetic vocabulary within the arts centre. At times she also doubted that the translation from English to Khmer was correct and nuanced, both in the text and via the interpreter. Moreover, she struggled with ideas and feelings about her character, as her ideas were not similar to the director's ideas, and did not suit the story. Due to the absence of an aesthetic terminology and reliable Khmer translation, the aesthetic discourse was lost during the rehearsals.

Observations throughout the rehearsals and the performances illustrated yet again Khmer people's difficulties in watching, and the motif of looking away. Sensitive or passionate moments brought about *despite* the European director produced instants of silence, of the artists slowly walking away, of spectators and artists in the audience turning around, looking away. As mentioned previously, looking away is an aspect of a conditioned response to avoid shame and to make sure that the other person does not feel ashamed. In numerous informal meetings, the European director discussed his struggle with this concept of cultural politeness and described the ways his Western theatre colleagues responded:

> Theatre is firstly observing or looking, and subsequently feeling the emotions. Experiencing theatre is never looking away, theatre is wanting to crawl into it. Creating theatre wants others to look and to observe. Being explicit. Inelegantly being explicit. Wanting to be seen. Is it possible to create theatre in Khmer culture? Is 'not looking and showing' then already the first social theme – independently of the theatrical text or the story?[46]

This demonstrates the European director's awareness and sensitivity about the work's 'territory', but also illustrates the unfeasible artistic situation for both parties: the Khmer artists and the European director. More importantly, this is about theatre aesthetics in Khmer culture: looking (*thea-*) is at the root of European theatre, and seemingly not at the root of Khmer performing arts. This clash is a vital part of my analysis, because it shows that this European aesthetic intervention clearly interfered with and differed from the Khmer aesthetic. The Cambodian artists and audience were expected to understand and work with a completely new aesthetic. This aesthetic is 'imposed', while the existing circus aesthetic of the arts centre is overlooked and unclear due to the lack of aesthetic terminology.

It could be argued that in both examples, Mnouchkine and the European theatre director, another struggle derives from their work: that is, their expectations of the audience and the young artists. As mentioned, both well-known directors had explicit expectations about coming to Cambodia: the ways they would work with the artists, how their work would contribute to the young artists' traumas and pasts, how the audience would respond and contribute, and how the show would possibly 'heal' the people. I argue here, however, in James Thompson's rhetoric, that the admiration focuses more on 'the skill of the lion tamer, rather than the performance of the lion itself.'[47] Intentionally or unintentionally, the international artists travelling to Cambodia decide on the issues and aesthetics in their performances on behalf of the people. As Ahmed argues regarding theatre for development, the issues do not come from the people themselves.[48] Unfortunately – though not in every case, one is then still left with a troubled perception, because, as Ahmed points out, it is not an accident that 'all these issues can be grouped under sectors which attract foreign donation'. This has consequences for the cultural ethnoscape of PPS. The aesthetic dimensions of the arts centre are imposed even if these notions conflict with the interests of the Khmer artists. Another example in which this is visible involves the next player in the ethnoscape: the tourists.

Tourists

This story is about a Khmer girl whom I will call Botum.

Botum keeps silent. She does not give an answer when I ask her opinion of the general Cambodian beauty image. Botum, the European theatre director and I are sitting in the restaurant, which seems to be the only somewhat cooler and mosquito-free space inside PPS. Unfortunately the two cooks do not notice our presence. Tonight the circus school will perform another tourist show and the cooks must prepare countless three-course meals, all included in the package deal. Forty-five minutes of complicated circus tricks plus a rich traditional meal is what you could call a bargain. While I am trying to understand Botum's judgements of her country, the school and herself, she immediately begins to talk about her appearance. 'I am not pretty, I am very ugly, but I try to compensate for my ugliness through my inner beauty.'[49] She explains that she will never get married. She will reside here – within the walls of PPS, for the rest of her life. Her girlfriends talk about boyfriends, getting married and other ideals. 'You [pointing at me] constantly tell me that I am beautiful, but Cambodians will never agree.'

Botum is physically disabled, like many other children at PPS, due to malnutrition, caused by poor living conditions or drug use, to the heavily mined areas around the arts school, or perhaps to psychological trauma. Botum has difficulties moving and using the left side of her body. The three main PPS directors know exactly what has happened to Botum and treat her problems confidentially. Botum is also illiterate. However, this does not hold her back from claiming the role of the Madame in The Maids. She learns the large amount of text by listening to her father's voice and imitating his lips movements. Botum's story is not unusual in this regard.

Today, around 2 million visitors travel through Cambodia annually. However, tourists avoided the country for decades until the mid-1990s. As tourists have returned after the civil war and the Khmer Rouge atrocities, the country has transformed 14 locations – including the place where Pol Pot was cremated, into tourist sites specifically relating to the genocide.[50] PPS is also a tourist attraction, explicitly advertised in the Lonely Planet and ranked ninth of all of Battambang's 31 tourist activities by Lonely Planet travellers.[51] The arts school puts on social circus shows for 8 dollars admission two or three times a week, depending on the season.

The final section only briefly describes the fifth player in the ethnoscape, tourists, because the actual actors are the disabled artists of PPS. The group of disabled individuals within the arts centre is

Figure 6 The Madame in Jean Genet's *The Maids* (March 2010). Photo: Kathy Barnhill.

treated as a minority as a direct result of the presence of tourists and the consequences of the globalized world.

The story that illustrates this result embedded in the pain and suffering of disabled Khmer people is Botum's story. The last actor in the ethnoscape explicitly demonstrates why this case study serves neither the community nor the art-form of theatre. Although the European director and I were not acquainted with the specifics of Botum's disability, the young actress was treated as a 'special' person, and at times even as an outlaw by the other artists of PPS. Botum was the only disabled actress in *The Maids*, and she insisted on playing the Madame against the wishes of the centre's directors. The arts centre's management preferred three circus artists or at least actresses without physical disabilities. Botum always had to take care of the lunch during the rehearsal's breaks, as the other young artists were convinced that job was meant to be for Botum. The other actors did not notice when the director or myself decided to prepare lunch; however, Botum was clearly embarrassed and showed that she did not appreciate the gesture. On opening night, Botum received great applause when she entered the stage dressed in a yellow evening dress. There was complete silence when Botum slowly removed the veil covered with embroidery, revealing her face.

During my time at the arts school, I was not able to find out which young people belonged to the theatre group and which did not. The theatre group was invisible to outsiders, and without a translator it was not possible to tell who was an actress or an actor. It was not until I heard Botum's story that I realized that the majority of the theatre group consisted of disabled children. Their disabilities varied and were not necessarily visible. I also became very conscious of the lack of materials and rehearsal space for the theatre group as opposed to the luxury circus department. Throughout the interviews and observations I identified a pattern: the artists participating in Mnouchkine's project, the artists invited to travel abroad for training *and* the artists challenged to work at the detention centres all belonged to the circus troupe. The arts school almost completely reflected an able-bodied circus and disabled theatre troupe. The different directors of the arts school emphasized that circus 'sells' and theatre does not. The circus division works independently: they are able to survive from the money they earn from the tourist shows. Since all circus performances are physically challenging and at times even fairly risky, the directors cannot *afford* to let disabled children participate in their popular tourist shows. This signals a worrying distinction between the disabled artists and the circus artists. The arts centre's aims have always focussed on inclusion and equality; however, the agenda of support from tourists is now prioritized. The disabled children are only accepted within certain parameters. This illustrates how tourist and economic flows have influenced the politics of the arts agenda, all in favour of the international image rather than the well-being of the children.

The decentred connections within the social and aesthetic landscape at the arts centre due to the agendas of the international interveners, the influence of the French staff and the significance of the global image confirms the overall argument of the chapter: the many ways in which economic and international players participate in the aesthetic and social constructions of applied theatre's artistic value. The players are *intrusively* depicted in the funding decisions of international interveners.

Conclusion

This chapter has attempted to articulate how the complex Cambodian historical context affects the sort of art that is being made at the Northern Cambodian arts centre PPS, and how this influences the artists' work. The cultural ethnoscape has proven to be a suitable tool for these intricate questions. The individuals and groups that make up the 'moving' community at PPS – refugees, international interveners, European artists travelling to the arts centre and tourists – affect the aesthetic dimensions and discourse of the arts school. The complexities of aesthetic notions within PPS's globalized community, rather than one restricted by geography, mean that these dimensions are influenced by each of the cultural ethnoscape's players, all carrying their own history and background. At the same time, they all attempt to interact with the diverse histories around them.

Moreover, aid dependence in Cambodia seems to be developing more and more as a condition arising from global structures and markets, encouraging social and moral looseness in PPS. This dependence is used by one of PPS's ethnoscape's players as a means to exercise power: international capital directly interferes with the aesthetic dimensions and vision of the arts centre. The four categories that arose from 'moments' of performance have shown us that there is no secure Cambodian aesthetic or social domain, and that there are clashes between the aesthetic and social discourses of the centre. Opposing agendas of international artists, commercialized tourist shows and international interveners donating money for genocide shows all affect the aesthetic dimensions of the arts centre. INGOs and NGOs have intensified this intrusion.

In order to understand the aesthetic of applied theatre, we cannot detach it from the *ethno* – something attached to the 'human' shapes and flows of life through economic, social and cultural channels. There is never any 'pure' serving of art or community. Therefore, a different tool is necessary to describe, practice, analyse and explore the implications of the aesthetics of applied theatre: the cultural ethnoscape has illustrated that the aesthetic of an art-form does not belong to one group or one nation. It shows that there is no original owner and that it is therefore very difficult to truly locate the aesthetic of the practice.

Applied theatre practices globally are seemingly becoming more and more uniform: the global pressure coming from the international humanitarian community seeking to shape applied theatre companies and make them respond to certain dynamics serves neither art nor community. The future of internationalized applied theatre could become a restricted internationalized unified place, far from the initial proposition of this chapter: the journey away from locating a pure and universal aesthetic of applied theatre. My concern is that this could imply the end of local practices, and create a form of 'flat' applied theatre practice. Aesthetic judgements will then shift towards universal criteria, resulting in internationalized and unified aesthetics of applied theatre.

This development will eventually force practitioners and audiences across the world to taste, smell and produce the same art-form. The practitioners will be forced to leave out secret local ingredients unique to their country and its mix of human flows and systems. This could unify and even reduce the taste of the applied theatre, and could leave the artists with artistic frustrations in the kitchen. My main concern is that this direction will suppress the expression of the situated interests of practitioners in their places of origin and cultivate an artificial global appreciation of the local, produced and consumed by the rest of the world. The local artists will then only produce one predetermined meal for one global audience, in which their own flavours and ingredients will slowly vanish. We should not ignore the qualities of local applied theatre practices in these sites, and consequently the potential of the artistry and its learning possibilities inherent in its astonishing performances. This is a call for a more nuanced understanding of applied theatre's aesthetic, including the identification of the relevant features of art practices and their relationship to broader social structures and the characteristics of a culture or community, whether that is Cambodian's social circus or any other practice. The naming of the practice is not significant; I merely believe that all cultural forms that have intimate connections with particular contexts, histories, traditions and cultures should have the right to maintain their artistry.

The Khmer practitioners I observed and interviewed showed their silent obedience towards this international terrain, accommodating the international interveners in *their* practice. As the DC-Cam director describes: 'We fear to lead, fear to initiate, we are afraid to make mistakes.' It was in these shocking clashes that my search for an aesthetic for applied theatre came to an end. I abandoned the search because any meaningful notion of aesthetics in applied theatre needs to serve art and community.

Aesthetic Play:
Between Performance and Justice

Ananda Breed

Introduction

This chapter explores the aesthetic interplay between juridical performances connected to due processes of law, alongside varied narratives
of justice and reconciliation. I argue that in the case of post-genocide
Rwanda's *gacaca* courts, the aesthetic frame of justice was used to
perform international norms and to provide legibility to the local
level courts, but that the actual courts themselves were eventually
manipulated for purposes ranging from revenge to extortion.[1] I
explore how the *gacaca* courts were implemented on a cell-to-cell level
between 2005 and 2012, by first illustrating the notion of protection
through international legalisms creating juridical subjects, then how
these norms were performed through the 'fictional frame' of *gacaca*,
navigating between the performance of the *gacaca* courts themselves
and narratives that emerged outside the predetermined government
script. I use the term script loosely as a 'dramaturgical blueprint' for
modes of justice and reconciliation that were to be performed post-
genocide.[2] For this analysis, I present two case studies of *gacaca* court
sessions that I attended between the initial data collection courts from
2004 to the culmination of the courts in 2012: one from an initial *gacaca*
court in the Eastern Province of Rwanda in 2005, and the other from
an appeal level *gacaca* court in Kigali in 2010. I analyse how *gacaca*
was used to reimagine an indigenous mediation system, followed by
the use of *gacaca* as a 'fictional frame' as it was manipulated for other

purposes. In this way, there are several layers of protection being explored – from the state level execution of Rwandanicity and *gacaca* to protect the Rwandan Patriotic Front (RPF) and ostensibly to prevent the occurrence of another genocide – to how systems of protection can also be used offensively to oppress versus to liberate.

I make the argument that state constructed scripts and the formation of *gacaca* – as a performance that rewrites the history of Rwanda from the vantage point of the genocide, is emblematic of the historic use of performance to record the Tutsi version of history through practices such as performances by actors or '*abiru*' during the Tutsi aristocracy and the use of performance by Tutsi artists-in-exile while in refuge, between 1959 and 1994. Tutsi artists-in-exile, such as Jean-Marie Kayishema and Kalisa Rugano, sought to use performance as a mode of cultural survival, both to preserve Tutsi culture in the countries of refuge and to fuel a militaristic return to Rwanda. In this case, theatre is used to protect a culture from annihilation and as preparation for war at the same time. The same construction of theatre as protection has been used on a national scale alongside international legalisms or speech talk to protect the current RPF and Tutsi-dominated government.[3]

Bert Ingelaere examines *gacaca* through concepts including numerical legibility, magic syllogisms and speech performances. He uses these terms to describe the strategy of *gacaca* advocates and the RPF to 'mask the absence of the actual and profound reference reality of the representation in question' based on numerical descriptions of *gacaca* or 'primarily based on law or law talk'.[4] I build the case that the noted 'magic syllogisms and speech performances' are characteristic of the historic use of theatre by the ruling RPF to maintain a dynastic past and that the *gacaca* serves as a 'fictional frame', another kind of theatre to perform justice and reconciliation at one level, but additionally to embed the RPF version of history to serve as victor's justice for the time period between 1990 and 1994 (the civil war leading up to the genocide against Tutsi in 1994) and to promote Rwanda as the poster-child for transitional justice systems. These varied performances may serve to protect, but simultaneously, these national performances may put individuals and the nation at risk.

In Chapter 1 of this volume, Gareth White notes how he will map ways in which questions concerning aesthetics take shape and attempts to present alternative ways to form questions for the purpose of interpreting these situations. For the benefit of this chapter, I would use his phrase as a question: How do questions take shape in conventional aesthetics, and how are they reshaped by applied theatre situations? Within the context of conflict and genocide and the literal destruction and reconstruction of cultural identity, bodies carry with them cultural histories and forms that contain political narratives. These bodies can continue to propagate identities under threat or to subvert narratives in opposition, as is often the case concerning ethnic conflict. The gacaca courts could not be considered applied theatre, but the fact that the courts were implemented on a mass scale involving every Rwandan citizen by law to attend the local level courts from 2004 to their culmination, evidences a different kind of participatory practice linked to the use of participatory art practices through sensitization and mobilization campaigns as part of the reconstruction of post-genocide Rwanda.

Gacaca as a performative

The mass exodus of Tutsi to neighbouring countries during periods of genocidal attacks, particularly after the Hutu revolution of 1959 in which power switched from the Tutsi to the Hutu, exposed them to the plight of exilic conditions in their host countries including Burundi, Uganda, and the Democratic Republic of Congo (DRC). In order to combat psychological and material loss exiled Rwandans sought to rediscover cultural identity through an artistic journey from a narrative of loss to a narrative of recovery. However, there is an agonistic tension between the use of the arts for creation and protection. Herbert Marcuse states in this regard, 'that aesthetic sublimation both has an affirmative character' (making suffering acceptable) *and* is simultaneously 'a vehicle for the critical, negating function of art. Art stands as reconciling other *and* rebellious subjectivity, at the same time.'[5] Marcuse notes that 'art does not change reality, but is another reality, and as such is always inherently revolutionary.'[6] The aesthetic form contains the political potential in art. Thus, art allows for another kind of dramaturgical blueprint in which scripts are imagined, recorded and eventually enacted.

The staging between these agonistic tensions is present within the reinvention of Rwandan traditions following the victory of the RPF who stopped the 1994 genocide, in which 1 million Tutsi and Hutu moderates were killed within a period of 3 months. One mode of staging the RPF version of history and to instil justice was the reinvention of the *gacaca* courts used to try the perpetrators of the genocide. Although touted as a 'traditional' practice, national theatre tours and sensitization campaigns used theatre to educate the masses about a practice that the majority of Rwandans had never heard of nor witnessed. In the aftermath of the genocide, the Government of National Unity was faced with enormous moral, legal and administrative challenges. At the request of the Rwandan government, the UN created the International Criminal Tribunal for Rwanda (ICTR) on 8 November 1994 to try high-level planners of the genocide but because of the extensive amount of time and money allotted for each case and the distance of the ICTR (in Tanzania) from Rwanda, there has been controversy concerning its effectiveness. To speed up the trials in classic courts in Rwanda and to lessen the load on the overburdened prisons, and to engage the active participation of Rwandans towards 'truth seeking' and 'fighting against impunity', the government sought a local solution that resulted in the establishment of gacaca courts.[7] *Gacaca* served as:

> A performative event in that rwandanicity was inculcated on a cell to district level and reinforced through the repeated portrayal of state power and the enactment of a 'moral community' in performances of justice, forgiveness and reconciliation. . . . Rwandanicity was inculcated both through the fictional staged renditions of *gacaca* courts and the real *gacaca* court proceedings . . . [t]he courtroom itself stages certain roles and scripts and is presented in a theatrical manner.[8]

Frank Rusagara of the Rwandan newspaper *The New Times* described rwandanicity as:

> An idea and philosophy that guided the people's conduct and perceptions. As an ideology, therefore, it is what the people of Rwanda understood themselves to be, what they knew about themselves, and how they defined and related to each other and their country as a united people (*Ubumwe*).[9]

Borrowing from J. L. Austin, the legal utterances staged within the Gacaca courts created a new national subjectivity. In this way, the inoculation and weekly ritual of Gacaca staged nationally has been a part of a national memory machine to produce Rwandanicity. As Judith Butler notes, drawing on Michel Foucault:

> Power works in part through discourse and works in part to produce and destabilise subjects. But then, when one starts to think carefully about how discourse might be said to produce a subject, it's clear that one's already talking about a certain figure or trope of production. It is at this point that it's useful to turn to the notion of performativity, and performative speech acts in particular—understood as those speech acts that bring into being that which they name.[10]

The pre-colonial past is the image or 'imagining' used to envision the future. Although an understandable pursuit in the wake of genocide, the use of culture to promote a legendary past is problematic because of historic power imbalances among Hutu, Tutsi and Twa. The reimagining itself is a rewriting of history and a reworking of culture to promote current political and social aims.

Performing justice and reconciliation – Art's sublimation (2005)

The following case study is an example of a gacaca court at the outset of the national implementation of gacaca in 2005. It presents an illustration of how the arts were used to meet the stated aims of gacaca to address both justice and reconciliation. Underneath a giant umunyinya tree, in the middle of an open dirt expanse, the gacaca court in the Eastern Province of Rwanda began with a dance by the Abiyunze Association.[11] Gacaca (pronounced ga-cha-cha) is Kinyarwanda for 'grass' or 'lawn'. The gacaca court is based on a traditional indigenous, pre-colonial form of mediation in which opposed parties 'sit on the grass and resolve community conflicts' (Umucaca is a type of grass eaten by livestock). The blending of reconciliation and justice took place as the association – comprising 30 perpetrators, 40 survivors and 60 community members, approached the meeting space where testimonies of the genocide would be heard. The performance started with drumming and clapping, and two lead dancers stepping into the centre of the gathering, their arms weaving over and under one another's while footwork patterns (right foot, left foot, left foot, right foot) kicked up dust as they circled one another.[12] The male dancer was a perpetrator who had killed the woman's uncle during the 1994 Rwandan genocide, the female dancer was a survivor. The gacaca was about to begin.

A single bench and table were placed in front of the now seated local audience. Ceremoniously, nine judges walked in single file across the dirt expanse to the desk, wearing sashes of the Rwandan flag across their chests. The sashes had the label inyangamugayo (persons of integrity, elected by the local population) written across the blue, green and yellow national colours. The crowd stood for a moment of silence. The dance space became an area to commemorate space for the atrocities of the genocide. The president of the gacaca began to recite several articles including Organic Law Article 34 that states that the cases to be tried in the gacaca courts are solely related to genocide or the extermination of an ethnic group.[13]

Emmanuel, an accused génocidaire (perpetrator of genocide), turned to face the audience of over 600 persons. He testified to the crimes committed, including the murder of David Twamugabo.[14] The perpetrator introduced the story by recalling that the interahamwe[15] was reluctant to go to the house of David, a giant man who was feared. When they first arrived, David stepped out of his house into the open air. Several members of the group attacked him, but were fought off. The group continued to attack him, throwing a grenade. The grenade did not explode. David picked up the grenade and warned them to leave or he would throw the grenade back at them, and he reentered his home. The interahamwe continued their attack from a distance, shooting arrows. Eventually, David was struck. The perpetrator recited the names of accomplices who first hit David with a hammer over his head, then struck his legs with a machete and, finally, sliced his throat with the machete. At this point in the confession, the perpetrator openly wept. The resident trauma counsellor made her way through the audience to offer him tissues. The audience simultaneously dried their eyes with shirtsleeves or collars. Following the gacaca, the grief counsellor stated that because the community participates in the gacaca and local association activities, people become comfortable round one another.

In this instance, justice and reconciliation are mutually supported through the integration of the arts with the local level gacaca courts – a model for transitional justice to encourage testimony related to atrocity by fostering trust and community building through the arts. However, the interplay between the arts for justice and reconciliation presents complex performances and performatives that are often contradictory. The use of performance in relation to justice includes the performativity of juridical systems themselves; this is particularly important in post-genocide Rwanda where the overarching justice project of gacaca frames any subsequent performances and utterances – one being intricately linked to the other.

The example illustrates an extraordinary link between how the arts were used for sensitization and mobilization for gacaca, but was not customary to the actual gacaca court proceedings in Rwanda. The reinvention of gacaca was promoted as a legacy of a pre-colonial utopian past. But Peter Uvin questions the role of gacaca as a traditional process: 'Why not assume that the "gacaca" appellation is there just to lend a sense of history and legitimacy, an invention of tradition'.[16] Indeed, mass media – newspapers, radio – and theatre, in particular, had been widely used to sensitize, mobilize and educate the nation concerning gacaca procedures and goals. According to a report on gacaca issued by the Norwegian Helsinki Committee, '[t]he authorities use large public gatherings to inform and discuss various issues with the people, for example, the gacaca or the new constitution. In addition, information videos and even drama, theatre, art and comics have been used'.[17]

A gacaca play directed by Rwandan playwright Kalisa Rugano, funded by the Rwandan Ministry of Justice and Johns Hopkins University, was created for this purpose. The play evoked the past, performing the history of how gacaca was used in pre-colonial times, inscribed with legendary status. It was a communal mechanism that few remembered; it was therefore the retelling, similar to the use of legends, which sensitized the public to the role of the gacaca in pre-colonial Rwanda and in service of the vision of Rwandanicity in the present. In my interview with Rugano, on 11 July 2005 in Kigali, he mentioned that the play went on national tour in 1999–2001 to educate the population and help them rehearse for the upcoming implementation of the courts. The play illustrated the gacaca laws through a performance of what a gacaca would look like, including the roles of the inyangamugayo, the community as witnesses and the apology of the accused. According to an evaluation report of the play:

> Persons interviewed are strongly convinced that the theatre requests them to be ready to tell the truth when the proceedings begin (73%). Nearly the total persons questioned think that the theatre is not only for sensitisation, but also educative (88%). The presentation of the theatre will be necessary for transmitting a variety of messages susceptible to bring the population to massively and voluntarily support gacaca courts.[18]

The gacaca play toured 10 out of 12 provinces in Rwanda. The evaluative sample was conducted with 220 people: men (54 per cent), women (46 per cent). The audiences primarily responded to the play by agreeing that the gacaca was created to address the rights of the victims and accused perpetrators by establishing the truth about the events of 1994, cell by cell. However, the production did not alleviate fears that those with incriminating information might be murdered or harassed, witnesses might refuse to testify or some people might not tell the truth. These anticipated problems were actually reinforced by the production. While the gacaca play was used for mass publicity, local associations also adopted theatre as a tool for mobilization and sensitization.[19]

Gacaca as *ikinimicu* (2010)

The next case study analyses court proceedings and varied narratives that emerged within the court session of Francois Mbarute to explore how gacaca served as a 'fictional frame' particularly towards the end of the gacaca process in 2010. Due to the social dynamics at play, court cases were increasingly identified by gacaca monitoring agencies as being manipulated following the speeding up of courts in 2007. Thus, it is important to identify at what point cases were filed and how varied social, political, and economic imperatives may have affected the lodging of case files and subsequent judgements. Through several interviews that I conducted with attendees and gacaca administrators, the case illustrates the multi-layered politics in Rwanda and how gacaca can be used for revenge and incrimination. According to a gacaca coordinator, witnesses were advised to not provide supporting testimonies for the accused, as they would often find themselves incriminated themselves or to have a case filed against them.

In this case, the concept of the 'fictional frame' is illustrated through the examination of discharging witnesses who were incriminated during the process of the trial. Thus, highlighting the fact that the defendant was already framed as guilty and anyone who might identify with him was likewise placed under suspicion as an accomplice. Here,

I also point out that Inyangamugayo were trained for 4 days in total to officiate court proceedings. Witnesses were often asked detailed questions by the Inyangamugayo (in random sequence) about time of day, timeline of activities, physicality of observations, and description of events. One observer who had attended each of the court trials of Mbarute stated: 'Think back to events sixteen years ago. Can you remember what happened with the detail in which the defendant and witnesses are being questioned? Then, listen to the accusers. They have their stories pre-scripted in full detail, including exact time of day. They are the ones who are lying. For those that can't quite remember, or may get some details wrong, those are the ones telling the truth.'[20] He stated that Mbarute had documents to fight his case, such as land dispute papers against one of the accusers, but that the Inyangamugayo would not acknowledge the documentation. Another gacaca researcher stated: 'During the last couple of years, gacaca has been used as a political device versus for justice.'[21]

The wife of Yusuf (someone killed during the genocide) stated the proceeding was like ikinimicu (Kinyarwanda term for theatre). Here, I provide a verbatim record of interactions between the Inyangamugayo, defendant and witnesses to further illustrate the function of gacaca as a 'fictional frame'. I attended the trial of Mbarute from 14 April 2014 to 16 April 2014. During the proceedings, I noted the dialogue, staging and interactions as if I were recording a staged script. The excerpts below come from these scripts.

President: Did you know the individuals whom *Mbarute* was charged with killing?

Witness One: No.

President: You made previous statements that *Mbarute* was amongst the gang that killed *Yusuf*. Why are you changing your statement?

Witness One: I didn't make that statement previously.

President: Who was training? Who was being trained?

Witness One: *Mbarute* notified me that they were planning to kill my wife, so I went past where they were conducting the training.

Mbarute was standing near the militia, but I cannot confirm that he was training with the militia.

President: Treat the courtroom as the trainees. How was *Mbarute* holding his body?

Witness One: The defendant was far away and I could not see any detail.

President: If you were able to see the accused, then you must have been standing on the side of the trainees and thus, *Mbarute* must have been facing the militia as a trainer.

Witness One: I am telling you what I know. I cannot lie.

Mbarute: The training was conducted in the valley, while I was a bystander. The person leading the training was a lieutenant.

In this exchange, the President frames Mbarute as a trainer for the militia. The testimony is questioned, although previous documents may have been falsely recorded. An attendee notes that several community members had made the claim that Mbarute used grenades and guns, to which Mbarute replied: 'This woman lies. For anyone who lives in the sector, they know her lies are commonplace.' The next witness provides a statement against the accused, that he had observed Mbarute at the Red Cross where Hutu and Tutsi were separated.

Witness Two: I witnessed the accused at the Red Cross register names.

President: Were the persons mixed whom registered?

Witness Two: They were mixed between Hutu and Tutsi. *Mbarute* registered their identity cards. He arrived in a white car, parked in front, and entered the Red Cross with another individual. *Mbarute* asked for identity cards.

Mbarute: I didn't enter the Red Cross. Why have you made that statement? (The witness does not respond).

Witness Two: He separated Hutu from Tutsi. He took these individuals by foot and they have never returned.

In this exchange, the case is made against Mbarute that he is working alongside the militia. Up to this point, there are no charges that actually claim Mbarute has killed any individuals. Statements infer that Mbarute may have been linked to training militia or registering identity cards, but no statements related to actually validating that Mbarute killed. In fact, the original witness claimed that Mbarute warned him about the planned attack of his wife, thus using Mbarute's role to warn and potentially to protect. The next witness provided testimony on behalf of Mbarute. However, during the course of the proceeding, a case file is made against him.

President: *Mbarute* was amongst a group of militia that went to kill *Yusuf*. Did you know that?

Witness Three: No, I didn't know that.

President: How did you come to be in ownership of a gun, and how were the Tutsi who were in hiding with you killed and buried?

Witness: *Mbarute* had put me in charge of guarding the Tutsi, to protect them. We were discovered and the Tutsi were killed. I was not killed because I had an identity card that said I was Hutu and with the former political party. I was commanded to put down my gun and that is when the Tutsi were killed.

Speaker from the floor: How did you get the gun? Why did you let the others die if you were supposed to be protecting them?

President: Have you been put in prison for this?

At this point, Mbarute approaches the bench with a letter from the President of Gacaca from one of the previous courts who declares that the current witness is an Inyangamugayo, or person of integrity. The president puts the letter to one side and continues to interrogate the witness.

President: Why didn't you defend the Tutsi?

Speaker from the floor: The declaration of character from the previous court must be false, if the witness had a gun.

President: How did you get a gun?

Witness Three: I was a soldier.

Speaker from the floor: If he had a gun, then he is responsible for the killing.

President: Who asked you to surrender?

Witness Three: Those that came from the market. They had lots of guns.

Speaker from the floor: If the witness didn't protect the Tutsi who he was given by *Mbarute* to protect, then he must have killed them.

Mbarute: When I arrived, he was kneeling. I had come to protect, but they were dead.

Speaker from the floor: You must have killed together. Who did you kill with?

Witness Three: No one.

Speaker from the floor: Why didn't the previous court make a case against this man?

The proceedings continued to question how the gun was passed between Mbarute and the witness. During the progression of the trial, the witness was cross-examined and eventually declared as being a conspirator with the accused. Individual proclamations from the attendees questioned how the witness could have survived as 'one who is hunted' (Tutsi). The secretary read out the court transcript and then the witness was asked to sign. It was evident that no witness was safe from incrimination. Mbarute owned several properties that were to be auctioned off as reparation and distributed among those who filed against the accused. In this way, although the court might have looked like it was following court procedures, I would postulate that the final judgement of the case was predetermined. Thus, the courtroom itself was an example of ikinimicu. Article 95 of Organic Law No. 40/2000 originally protected bystanders who provided testimony of genocide crimes, '[t]estimony made on offences of the crime of genocide and crimes against humanity committed between 1 October 1990 and 31 December 1994 can never serve as a basis to take proceedings against its author charging him with the offence of failure to render assistance.'[22] However, Article 95 was deleted from the subsequent Organic Law No. 16/2004, exposing bystanders who testify to potentially be charged as accomplices for not rendering assistance. Thus, the scripting of the court proceedings, both through the trial procedures and the testimonies given by defendants and witnesses, can be easily manipulated to either protect or frame individuals, depending on how narratives are crafted.

Conclusion

At the end of Rwanda's experiment, over a million Rwandans were accused of genocide, in over 12,000 community courts. What are the ramifications of *gacaca*, following *gacaca*? At the closing ceremony of *gacaca* in 2012, President Paul Kagame stated:

> Equally, the value and effectiveness of *gacaca* will be measured against the record of other courts, principally the International Criminal Tribunal for Rwanda (the ICTR). The ICTR has tried about sixty cases, cost 1.7 billion dollars and left justice wanting. Yet, at significantly less cost, the *gacaca* process has had the highest impact in terms of cases handled, and has delivered justice and reconciliation at a much higher scale.[23]

He further stated: 'It has been a period when we sought to reunite our nation, inspire confidence in the administration of justice and hold each other accountable for our actions.'[24]

Speeches often aim to legitimize policy (as evidenced by Kagame's closing ceremony speech). The proposed objectives of reconciliation and justice through the local-level courts were staged as a transitional justice model that originated from an indigenous mediation system, but may not have been administered or performed at a local level to achieve these objectives.

One of the main areas of tension relates to the traditional system of *gacaca* as a cultural form for *mediation* and the reinvented version of *gacaca* as a contemporary system for *justice*. Charles Villa-Vicencio stresses the importance of pre-verbal and non-verbal healing, and relationship building elements of traditional African reconciliation practices:

> As a pretext for rational debate and conversation to take place as a way of dealing with the violence and trauma of the past through ceremony and ritual, perpetrators and victims are encouraged to make an attitudinal and behavioural shift from a prelinguistic state to the point where they can begin to articulate their experiences in words and ritual.[25]

Several grassroots associations that I observed used performance (particularly dance and music as noted in the first case study) in correlation with the *gacaca* courts. Those particular case studies demonstrated strong links between arts-based grassroots associations and participation in the *gacaca* courts. Perpetrators were initially released into community service, or through presidential decree. Survivors responded with fear at the prospect of meeting face to face the murderers of their families and neighbours. At the same time, perpetrators have often found their wives or husbands in new marriages and their homes occupied. Within this context of mutual distrust, associations created an alternative space for communities to interact and to establish relationships. Several associations have been created by survivors, perpetrators and community members as a vehicle to build trust and community connections between individuals who uniformly express fear, distrust and grief at the outset. In this way, expressing another kind of protection through a creative, relational, and psychological response to the social and communal damage caused by the genocide – through the arts.[26]

The role of juridical performances for protection has been examined through the *gacaca* courts to illustrate the nebulous balance between the use of the arts – to protect Tutsi cultural identity and to construct *gacaca* as a reimagined participatory mediation system to try crimes from the 1994 genocide against Tutsi. I have noted that the same artists who used the arts to militarize a return to Rwanda between 1959 and 1994 are actively involved in the reimagining of the new Rwandan identity or Rwandanicity. In this way, artistic projects that reimagine citizenship and juridical subjectivity can be used for protection or conversely for the assertion of power – this agonistic relationship is intricately linked in the case of the *gacaca* courts in post-genocide Rwanda. The reinvention of *gacaca* for crimes solely related to the genocide against Tutsi may have altered traditional characteristics of *gacaca* to serve as protection versus mediation.

The Political Imagination and Contemporary Theatre for Youth

Anna Hickey-Moody

Introduction

Entertainment for youth is a pedagogy of consumption, or *pedagogy for consumption*, that produces little consumers as Disney et al shore up their market share. In between the cracks in the glowing orb of global media produced for youth, we find poachers[1] who are questioning the ubiquity and acquiescence of the youth position. Theatre makers, musicians, alternative game manufacturers and unconventional film producers are artists: technicians with a political imagination. It is with the works of such practitioners this chapter is concerned and, in a gesture towards the politics of such work, I examine C&T theatre as one of many possible examples of political theatre for young people. I read political theatre for young people through Peter Brook's[2] now classic writing on the 'Rough Theatre'. Such theatre should be made of imagination, direct audience engagement and is not necessarily defined by traditional ways of rendering plays. Theatre for young people should be Rough Theatre.

Through an expansive methodology for studying theatre for young people as a technology of the imagination that animates possibilities for political resistance, I draw on Appadurai's theories of global cultural flows,[3] opening up the machining[4] of traditional theatre and formal pedagogic practices to consider the pedagogical nature of global cultural flows.[5] Along with theatre, popular culture is a cultural pedagogy that youth machine through performing arts in order to create their own cultural pedagogies of youth, for youth, by youth. Drawing on Anderson's 'imagined communities'[6] Appadurai argues that in globalizing times, the imagination plays a new, critical role as a social practice:

> The image, the imagined, the imaginary . . . are all terms that direct us to something critical and new in global cultural processes: the imagination as a social practice. . . . The imagination is now central to all forms of agency, is itself a social fact, and is the key component of the new global order.[7]

For Appadurai, the imaginations of an increasing number of globally connected individuals and groups are constituted by a series of intersecting and disjunctive global flows, which he articulates in terms of five scapes. These are: ethnoscapes, mediascapes, ideoscapes, technoscapes and financescapes. These scapes are fluid, irregular, multiply constituted and perspectivally registered.[8] Theatre for young people, youth arts practices and cultures operate pedagogically across such scapes – particularly mediascapes and ideoscapes (e.g. mass media discourses, dominant cultural ideologies) – to orient the imaginations and subjectivities of young people involved in performing arts.

Groupings of young people that come together around shared imaginations and practices of performing arts articulate 'communities of sentiment'.[9] That is, such groupings of young people offer examples of how, in globalizing times, media flows and forces come together with theatre productions to mobilize groups of people 'to imagine and feel things together'.[10] Communities of sentiment that emerge around youth performing arts are privileged by different young people in diverse ways. Following, critiquing and responding to Habermas,[11] academic culture has come to see that communities of sentiment create performance texts that speak to critical publics. Media texts and dominant cultural positions on, and public framings of, young people's performing arts, shape how young people imagine and produce themselves through either participating in, or staying away from, arts practices. Young people's acquiescence to, or refusals of, dominant cultural positions around the value of performing arts can bear an intrinsic relation to young people's agentive possibilities. From this reading of theatre as part of a social imagination, I examine the work of C&T.

Political aesthetics

Applied Theatre is political in form, even if it is not always political in intent. The act of making theatre for young people is a political decision, whether the theatre is supposed to arouse political critique, teach curriculum or 'entertain' through re-creating a dominant status quo. The defining element of the aesthetics of applied theatre is the intent of the theatre makers, the means by which they question or acquiesce – or encourage young people to question or acquiesce. The aesthetic form is pedagogical in the most direct sense. It effects affective responses and modulates audiences' responses. The aesthetic form must not be underestimated, as Brook explains, the aesthetic is directly political:

> It is only by searching for a new discrimination that we shall extend the horizons of the real. Only then could the theatre be useful, for we need a beauty which could convince us: we need desperately to experience magic in so direct a way that our very notion of what is substantial could be changed.[12]

A new discrimination is clearly a critical framing of practice: a sensibility which redefines 'beauty' in a convincing fashion. Such persuasion is seemingly magic. As such, to the extend that they are persuasive, C&T Theatre highlight aesthetics as a political tool. They are a professional theatre for young people company that was founded 25 years ago and are the vehicle through which I think through the impact and the politics of the aesthetic form.

The acronym C&T stands for a number of pairings that characterize the work of the company. These foundational relationships include computers and theatre, citizenship and technology, community and training, creativity and technology and culture and theory. These pairings illustrate the obvious social intent in the company's work and the ways the company works with(in) popular mediascapes and ideoscapes of youth culture through utilizing 'new technology' as a platform for distribution and performance. Even though it was funded in Britain as a UK-based theatre company, C&T work between theatre, new media and education as disciplines and this interdisciplinarity is core to their technological and theatrical practices. As theatre for young people, or more specifically, theatre in education, it is clear that C&T aim to effect interpersonal and social change, to make a difference in a quantifiable, if qualitative way.

C&T sell their work to schools and/or community settings as 'apps' (applications which enrich life experience) and this broad arching conceptual design flags their use of new media as theatre. Brook's writings on Rough Theatre highlight the power of imaginative connections between the social world and theatre over the re-creation of traditional modes of theatre. Packaging theatre as a form of new media is exactly such an act of reading contemporary theatre through the lived world of youth.

The political nature of aesthetics in C&T's work comes to the fore with their transnational political theatre project *LipSync*. This is an app sold to schools, but it was also a transnational theatre exchange between Rio de Janeiro, Brooklyn and the East End of London. The young people involved respectively came from very disadvantaged backgrounds, and the global differences in disadvantage were made plain through the students in each site lip-syncing the British pantomime song 'My Favourite Things'.[13] The colonial history embedded in the songs' lyrics and distribution added critical affect when sung by a black non-English speaking Columbian teenage boy on the edge of Rio de Janeiro's Jardim Gramacho dump. On a number of levels, this transnational iteration of *LipSync* was a practice animated by what I characterize as 'technologies of imagination'.

Lip syncing is probably one thing every young person does when no one else is watching. Singing along, or pretending to sing, to a favourite song is a popular, if not private pastime of numerous youth. C&T's '*LipSync* app' is a process of theatre-based engagement that recontextualizes the usually private *LipSync* experience with a view to giving young people a voice in an available and appealing way, while also teaching skills in literacy, video editing, graphic design and music technology. C&T sell *LipSync* as a way that teachers and students can come together to work on key themes, subjects and issues through transforming them into music videos. Young people working with C&T take a song that has significance to them, and overlay their own meaning. Through this, the young people create their own drama but the song reinforces the drama and the drama reframes the song. C&T explain through saying:

> In schools, we use the C&T lip syncing process in a multiplicity of ways. We lip sync about social issues in PSHE, we lipsync in French and German in MFL,[14] we lipsync in approaching Shakespeare in English, and we lipsync in the extended day. There really are no limits regarding subject matter. You can create and share your videos within your school, or you can join our online global community of lip syncers, exchanging your lip syncs with young people in New York, Kenya or China! You will also have access to the C&T network – which is the engine behind every Application. It will be made available to you to facilitate collaboration between you and your collaborating schools. It is a secure, virtual space social media platform for creative learning that uses digital technology to help you to interact and connect. Young people can post comments, add videos and send texts to provide feedback to each other.[15]

Here, theatre becomes a platform for and network of technologies facilitating the art of make believe around, or in relation to, very real issues. A forum for the social imagination, theatre is imbued with the vital purpose to reinvent ideals. It is through such 'invention' that the theatre enters the world of make believe, as the young people enter an imagined world of music stars by lip syncing famous songs that connect them to global communities, or as performers enter the stage they become 'larger than life'; people who are temporarily not bound by day-to-day requirements of human behaviour. The theatre audience is presented with a group of young people who are endeavouring to explore and reestablish whatever it is they are crying out for. The exploration of popular modes of thought can be conducted only through the shared language of imagination.

Brook suggests that this capacity for facilitating collective imagination is one of theatre's primary strengths. His work credits the unparalleled magic created by theatre when an audiences' 'belief is caught'.[16] In the instance of C&T's work, it is also imperative that young participant's imaginations are caught. C&T's *LipSync* hears young people's screams to see themselves as that which they dream of being, to experience magic inherent in a shared and actual journey through the lives and minds of others. Their chosen popular music connects young people to the mediascapes and ideoscapes that mean the most to them. Yet the nature of the project, famed as it is around a lived issue, draws the fantastic back to the real so as to see the real in a new way. C&T do not change the lyrics of a lip sync, rather lip syncing is about 'repurposing': taking what exists already and making it appropriate to a new context. For example, young people in New York City are repurposing Pink Floyd's 'Money' to make a piece about the Occupy Wall Street campaign. Young people are always at the centre of creative choices, both in terms of issues and musical selection. Both sides have to reflect their interests to have credibility. The realization of C&T's *LipSync* is a process grounded in the power of make believe and the possibilities of impossibility.

Rough Theatre today

Audiences who witness huge social atrocities from a distance nearly every day of their lives and are desensitized to violence, sex and horror still become completely engaged in theatre performances. People's theatre, or as Brook refers to it 'Rough Theatre' is a far throw from the gladiatorial performances that entertained the masses in Rome. 'Performance' is no longer an appropriate term for the amazing feats we see depicted on the box – nor indeed the virtual reality[17] you can experience for less than half the price of a theatre ticket. Such media began as a spectacle, something amazing to behold, such amazement cannot be found within what is now the mundane – for in spite of its apparent intensity or ferocity, technological entertainment has become a mundane pass-time for many. Indeed, it has spawned a new culture of people who communicate across thousands of miles, represented by iconic symbols. There is no substitute for concrete interaction that embraces the senses and makes us aware of our human condition.

Part of the strength of C&T's work bringing popular media culture and theatre together is this affirmation of human ability. Brook articulates this capacity succinctly, stating: 'The closer we move towards the true nakedness of theatre, the closer we approach a stage that has a lightness and a range far beyond film or television.'[18]

Here Brook speaks not of a proscenium arch, but of the organic energy that forms the dynamic nature of theatre as engagement. The alive, real and boundless world created by theatre holds its strength in a visceral truth that can only be imitated on film. *The Empty Space* details the vital importance of the actor/audience relationship. It is this connection that draws the audience into the performers' world and charges theatre with the potential to move through the bounds of reality. Brook describes people's theatre as running from a kinetic energy; such power is generated through the shared focus of a group of people being reiterated by their audience. This is a finite relationship and can only be realized when the audience's or young participant's imagination is caught, their disbelief suspended.

It is a theatre facilitator's role to take an audience, or participants, on a journey that pushes them to relate to new worlds, and often difficult social issues and for this to occur both sides must relate to one another. Brook says, 'Actors must be as involved in the outside world as in the theatre.'[19] He is correct in suggesting that it is crucial to understanding theatre that the performers speak and share a social language and cultural imaginary. The 'Rough Theatre' of which Brook speaks is essentially a theatre that engages an audience's or participant's imagination, gains their respect and allows them to imagine otherwise. *The Empty Space* details Rough Theatre as being theatre designed specifically for its audience, or in this instance, participants.

Responding to young people's lives

The nature of C&T's work dictates that a performance of *LipSync* must be grounded in a strong participant/practitioner relationship. *LipSync* begins with the performers choosing their stage, namely, their song, for it is through locating themselves in the global mediascapes they value that they can look anew upon the issues troubling their lives at school. C&T's work thus speaks to contemporary youth imaginaries, asking the audiences to suspend their disbelief and step into the carefully constructed world of the music industry and the commodification of identity it brings.

Upon beginning the process, young participants are required to undertake a first aspect of pretence in that they are asked to bring their obvious surroundings into the clip they choose to mimic. From this point on, the role played by the young participant's imaginary world is intensified through character/audience interaction and improvisation. This relates directly to Brooks' ideas about Rough Theatre taking audiences out of the theatre, allowing audiences to 'join in and answer back'.[20] Indeed, in *The Empty Space* Brook suggests that: 'The Rough Theatre has apparently no style, no conventions, no limitations – in practice it has all three.'[21] C&T's use of traditional comedy techniques, (particularly timing and juxtaposition) and contemporary technology, craft work that appears comfortably simple and impromptu in performance and yet is structured through principles of levels of participant engagement and youth agency and it draws heavily on established theatre practices and performance techniques.

Perhaps ironically, one of the most sophisticated forms of theatre practice could be described as a game of make believe: the art of improvisation. This is a style of theatre vital to the process and performance of *LipSync*. Not only does the popular song as a text contain a wealth of opportunities for improvisation, the nature of the young people singing together requires that improvisation is employed in order to sing together.

'Rough Theatre operates on a level of invitation. Its strength is that of human truth rather than cultivated beauty.'[22] Brook articulates the power of improvisation. There is nothing more captivating than being witness to the energy of creation and such dynamism provides motivation. The ensemble skills and imaginative engagement necessary for performers to improvise are partly brought about then, by youth agency and the desire to belong to the mediascape in which they have chosen to position themselves.

Make believe not only constitutes the core theatre technique used when work-shopping and performing an iteration of C&T's *LipSync*, it also forms the basis of C&T's methodology for working with youth and its purpose as a form of Rough Theatre. *LipSync* asks its audience to make believe as much as it does its actors. It is such an important relationship between the performers and their audience, such an intensely human dynamic, that constitutes the particular kind of Rough Theatre I look to capture in the contemporary moment.

Peter Brook suggests that Rough Theatre may vary in form and lack all seemingly formal theatre conventions yet will always be defined through its possessing a 'human element which compels us'.[23] Rough Theatre changes according to its context and it is the 'human element', the magic of make believe which contemporary audiences look for in the Rough Theatre of today. C&T's work is based around various levels of make believe which entail pretence from both the participants and the facilitators. *Lipsync* not only speaks through imagination to the child in all of us, but presents the world as seen by a group of children

Figure 7 *LipSync.* (Photograph: C&T).

and draws from it striking parallels to the world of adults. Politics or play? *Lipsync* asks us. We might do well to ask ourselves why it is that select people in Western society (politicians, rock stars, those born into privilege) can act out their dreams of power with the support of a nation and yet dreams of change offered in the theatre have the support of only a few.

Imagination, popular culture, Rough Theatre

In articulating his theory of global disjunctive scapes of imagination, Appadurai does not engage with the concept of applied theatre or cultural pedagogy. However, his theory lends itself to a consideration of the pedagogical nature of theatre and culture. The kinds of global flows (scapes) described by Appadurai can be read as forms of cultural pedagogy that are disjunctive and processual; that is, global flows of youth culture are composed of diverse and intersecting components, which have pedagogical forces and comprise the tools C&T mobilize for Lipsync. For example, youth arts culture operates through channels as different as corporately produced music videos, histories of popular musical music performance, a young person's favourite costume or street wear, personal identifications with forms of speech and modes of 'dance comportment', television shows and movies that depict dance or theatre or which fetishise Hollywood and star culture, everyday youthful forms of cultural legitimation, school curriculum, and so on. These individual elements, upon which cultural meaning is inscribed, might not be pedagogical in themselves, but do become pedagogical when embedded in cultural narratives and processes of meaning making. Moreover, these diverse components interact with each other across lives, countries and continents, teaching different things and meaning different things to different young people. It is in these processes of making meaning (and the crucial roles played by materiality in these processes) in which Rough Theatre is constituted. Also, it is because of these intersections between public, private, people and things that Rough Theatre can be read as a cultural pedagogy that offers an intimate and pervasive expression of informal, unbounded, culturally mediated and subjective learning.

Acquiescence: The Rock Eisteddfod Challenge

Not all contemporary theatre for youth that engages with popular culture makes Rough Theatre. In fact, some makes Deadly Theatre: deskilled theatre with no horizons. As Brook suggests:

> If we try to simplify the problem by making tradition the main barrier between ourselves and living theatre we will again miss the real issue. There is a deadly element everywhere; in the cultural set-up, in our inherited artistic values, in the economic framework.[24]

To ensure I am not valorizing all engagement with popular forms, it is to Deadly Theatre I now turn. Like the work of C&T, but with a completely different politic, the Rock Eisteddfod Challenge (REC) offers an example of the complexity of many sites of youth culture. It brings together adult investments in what 'youth' theatre should be with young people's tastes and decisions about what constitutes a valuable investment of their time. The REC is a useful example of the tensions between commodification, capitalism, local school communities and everyday spaces of youth, which necessarily comprise corporate flows and acts of youth resistance and acquiesce. These are the tensions which I want to call to our attention as part of what makes C&T's re-politicization of popular culture so successful.

The REC started in Australia and is now global, corporatized and trademarked[25]: expanded to locations in Japan, New Zealand, the United Arab Emirates and Britain. While the REC provides an assessment focal point for some secondary arts units in Australian schools, REC National champion teams go on to compete against each other in the 'Global Rock Challenge.' The REC thus speaks to local-global imaginations to the extent that it cites the genre of the high school musical, which articulates across the history of colonial schooling and is given life in numerous media texts. And, insofar as those who participate in the REC do so by choice, and that this choice is a performance of investment in the idea that art contributes to public good through enriching community life, the REC brings together a critical viewing public. The REC website describes the event, stating:

> Rock Eisteddfod Challenge® events are produced by the Rock Eisteddfod Challenge® Foundation, a not for profit organisation. The event is a unique and exciting opportunity for schools to take part in a dance, drama and design spectacular where *the students are the stars.* Each year, the events are professionally staged in some of Australia's top entertainment venues.[26]

There is a discipline-specific model of arts practice underlying this event, which consistently produces performances that adhere to the genre of the high school musical/dance show. More than this, in the REC, the idea that young people can 'be a star' is explicitly concerned with teaching ways to be 'healthy' and 'active' citizens, an idea that is core to the organization of the competition. This echoes Habermas's early characterization of public spheres as places that feature 'competition among equals [in which] the best excelled and gained their essence – the immortality of fame'.[27]

The REC website cited above uses the trope of stardom as a mode through which it teaches 'healthy living'. The site has sections for students and teachers (as well as sponsors, ticket information and an 'about REC' section). The student section features 'get involved' and 'healthy lifestyle' hyperlinks, which detail lifestyle strategies that help in becoming a 'star'. The teachers' section features 'production tips' which link to genre-specific resources in costume design, set design, and lighting and have clearly been developed to furnish teachers with the know-how to reproduce the look of the high school musical. Here, popular cultural representations are assumed as cultural pedagogies of arts. The website requires knowledge of high school musicals and dance productions as popular genres to make sense and to be activated as a teaching resource.

The teachers' section also features links to the online teaching resource website 'Teachers' TV', in which possible classes are presented in video format. The videos are organized by levels of schooling (early childhood, primary, secondary) and subject areas (Arts, English, Health and P. E., Languages, Maths). Dance classes are displayed in Health and P. E. but not Arts, which only features media arts lessons on digital technology and music. These design features suggest the fact that the REC is a form of governance, within which dance and musical theatre are seen as ways of improving what is considered to be the health and well-being of the young people involved, rather than arts practices that extend young people's aesthetic vocabularies. The REC clearly sees itself as adding to the social value of young people through enhancing their health and well-being. The site explains:

> As part of the Global Rock Challenge,™ nearly 300 Australian schools and 25,000 students compete in Rock Eisteddfod Challenge® and J Rock™ shows across Australia. Teams as small as 20 or as large as 142 students plan an eight-minute performance based on a theme

of their choice and set it to contemporary commercially available music. Students, teachers and entire communities work together over a period of months planning and rehearsing, before competing against other schools at events in a 100% drug and alcohol free environment.[28]

In facilitating conversations between adults, young people, and the wider community, the REC forcibly shapes young people's voices through conventions of genre as much as it facilitates young people's expression. Both of these outcomes: giving young people a voice, albeit a carefully crafted voice, and fostering dialogue between socio-economically diverse communities, align with Habermas's[29] notion that conversations held in the interest of developing an understanding of public good need to be separated from the power of the church and the government. These outcomes somewhat 'bracket' social status through the inclusion of socially and economically diverse communities. Young people on stage at the REC are not equal to their teachers in terms of power, or influence, nor to their audience members in terms of social status. However, performing – rather than speaking or writing – offers a social voice and a scale of dialogue not otherwise afforded to secondary students as a community. Young people's performances in the REC are cultural pedagogies but more than this, they are the product of disjunctive scapes of global flows as cultural pedagogies. Rap music, musical films, T.V. talent shows, film clips and pop stars provide the resources that young people and their teachers machine in the REC in order to acquiesce to popular genres of youth performance.

The experiences of citizenship that accompany the REC are constituted through pleasure, disciplinarity, and affective responses to broad social imperatives for young people to have socially readable identities. Berlant,[30] Warner,[31] and Riley, More, and Griffin[32] argue that experiences of pleasure need to be considered as forms of citizenship which can be as powerful in terms of shaping identity as a person's legal citizen status. Youth arts and school arts projects are, in part, exactly such a pleasure-based citizenship. There is often great satisfaction in being disciplined enough to rehearse and perform, or make and show, a work. For example, during a 2-year ethnography of a low socio-economic school in north Melbourne, Australia, I spent 6 months working with a group of boys preparing a dance piece for their school Eisteddfod.[33] Their performance piece clearly articulates the ways arts can work as governance in the respect that the boys were all of non-white ethnicity and they performed hip-hop dance in a highly masculinized fashion that re-created dominant stereotypes of the 'black savage' in some ways. These boys were Vocational Education and Training (VET) students who mobilized their non-white ethnicities as a core resource that informed their dance. These boys were called to 'work' their ethnicity to perform the popular articulation of hip hop masculinity that was the figurehead for a hegemonic pattern of cool in the school context. They did so very successfully.

They crafted their performances of masculinity around a 'gangsta' style that has been associated with some articulations of hip hop and is positioned prominently in commercial culture targeted at the youthful consumer. The notion of gangsta was read as black style and has a long history in popular culture of being read this way. Richardson summarizes this history as:

> [A] very limited and questionable representational formula for black masculine subjects [which is] . . . in some ways quite regressive – far more regressive than it would appear to be on the surface. For it forecloses a broader and more diverse spectrum of black masculine representations.[34]

This act of foreclosure was assisted in the school by the fact that the VET boys' breakdance performances were celebrated on the promotional postcard for the school's dance programme, which features four students of colour wearing bright, baggy hooded tops, jumping in the air, bringing their bent arms in front of their bodies. These boys embody the hyper-hegemonic masculinity required to perform gangsta. However, unlike the often immobile, 'hard' modes of corporeality that characterize gangsta men, the VET boys were also 'soft' and kinesthetically skilled enough to dance. Being able to perform gangsta and breakdance is quite unique. These boys offered a very marketable version of 'blackness', which the school valued in light of its profile of leading Koori (Aboriginal Australian) education.

In a public aestheticization of localized racism, the teachers lauded the VET boys' depictions of non-white masculinity crafted through hip hop and referred to their dance performances as evidence of the performing arts programme's capacity to engage marginalized boys of colour. Reading these boys within the racial and socio-economic distribution of Australian society, the employment of European Australian and Asian Australian boys as signifiers of marginalized Australian youth could be said to possess aspects of truth. However, in the context of the school, these boys were not the most marginalized boys of colour, who were the Koori boys. The Koori boys were not break-dancers. In an unconscious performance of racism and sexism, the VET boys were encouraged to signify on the school's deployment of breakdance as a symbol of black empowerment.

In and out of school, arts practices can be considered a form of cultural pedagogy – they are part of what Willis refers to as 'common culture',[35] and they utilize formats that are publicly accessible. In making and speaking to very particular local-global communities, they constitute little publics. In the case of arts practices for youth run by adults, these little publics are often groups invested in 'the power of the arts' to better society through including marginalized young people in 'mainstream' culture and 'adding value' to young people as social commodities.

To better understand the cultural logics at play in the little publics made by youth arts, or the ways that young people are called to express their voices through arts practice, it is useful to think through the processes through which youth performances are made. Part of the way youth arts in schools operate is by mobilizing young people's knowledge of popular culture and their everyday literacies. This utilization of popular literacies is democratic to the extent that young people from all classes possess popular literacies and their collective knowledge can be mobilized through the arts. Dominant cultural presumptions that the arts are good for young people, that they mobilize youth 'at risk' for their own betterment and the good of society as whole, echo in many youth arts practices, especially those that adhere to, rather than mix, particular genres. For example, the REC is based on the premise that involvement in the performing arts makes young people better citizens. By improving young people through involving them in art, the REC partly advances what it sees as a public good: it makes young people fitter and less likely to strain healthcare systems. It correspondingly contributes to the democratic functioning of society through giving young people a public stage for a voice that is shaped and articulated through performance.

Popular culture as cultural pedagogy

The democratic valuation of everyday knowledge has a history in British cultural studies that is not normally equated with discussions of pedagogy. However, as I have suggested, popular culture is a powerful force in processes of cultural pedagogy and early work from the Birmingham Centre for Cultural Studies is so firmly concerned with the use of popular cultural knowledge as a vehicle for democratic voice that it seems fitting to explore popular cultural literacies here, as an extension of Appadurai's global mediascapes. The everyday knowledge taught through mediascapes are a core means through which young people craft performing arts texts. Williams' work on cultural forms and processes as pedagogical,[36] Hoggart's call to value everyday literacies[37] and Paul Willis's discussion of how class is learnt through culture and labour,[38] each value everyday or popular knowledge (knowledge outside 'the canon') as a way of democratizing education and involving those who might be considered on the 'margins'. Such means of employing popular literacies and cultural forms as a political strategy for engaging marginalized bodies, advancing calls for education as a democratic project and means of advancing 'public good' later became core to the ideas of public and popular pedagogy.

A framework for reading mediascapes as cultural pedagogies can thus begin with Richard Hoggart's *The Uses of Literacy*, written in 1957, a text that is described by John Hartley as having 'set the agenda for a generation's educational and disciplinary reform'.[39] The Uses of Literacy offers an account of Northern working-class life in Britain, in which Hoggart reads 'culture' as the experiences and habits of being part of 'everyday' community life, as opposed to 'popular culture' and popular (mass produced and widely distributed) publications. As the fields of audience studies and new media studies demonstrate, with the rise of new computer technologies and producer-user[40] media forms, the distinction between mass-produced and electronically distributed cultural forms and 'ordinary' community life is no longer as useful as it may have been in 1957. The grounds on which such a distinction might be drawn have shifted. However, the need for educators to think through the importance of considering the classed nature of practices of literacy, and to value 'everyday' literacies, endures. At the time, Hoggart claimed his focus on 'ordinary' literacy was anti-Marxist (i.e. disinterested in collective action by the working class), but to my mind it has clear parallels with Marxist critical literacy theorists' calls to engage students with the language(s) of their community, state and world. While the contribution of Hoggart and Williams to conversations about cultural studies and education is worthy of a more extensive treatment than I am able to offer here, I want mainly to note that these thinkers mark one kind of origin for considering popular culture as a site of learning and as a way of engaging marginalized learners. Youth arts projects can constitute an ideal vehicle for such a project as they work with young people's everyday tastes. More than this, youth performing arts texts are youth cultural pedagogies – cultural statements made by youth.

The REC is an example of a process of schooling that mobilizes texts from popular culture, a process that is partially grounded in young people's pleasures and tastes. Performances are set to popular music and, as I have noted, the REC event itself is modelled on the trope of the high school musical popularized within mainstream film and television. It offers one instance of learning via popular culture and it makes little publics that are called to hear and respond to youth (and adult) voices expressing genre specific images of healthy young citizens.

When a young person is involved in composing a dance routine or a song, they are required to draw on their knowledge of, and tastes in, popular culture – although critical reflection on these tastes is not necessarily a constitutive feature of practices of composition. Working with, and incorporating, the popular cultural tastes of students from marginalized and excluded social groups thus becomes critical when designing large popular events such as the REC as it is a means of social inclusion that is not condescending. School dance curriculum and many extra-curricular youth dance projects offer examples of the amalgamation of popular cultural forms into processes of teaching and learning. This inclusion of popular cultural forms in youth dance practices is an example of an educational process that mobilizes student knowledge and student taste as youth voice. These aspects of young people's lives are core to processes of teaching and learning through the arts.

Youth arts practices and school arts curriculum are generally optional extra-curricular activities for young people, which are not likely to succeed without young people's choice to invest in them. Further, at more senior levels, school arts curriculum subjects are selective areas of study, the pursuit of which obviously reflects youth taste and agency. Thus, youth arts practices and curricula utilize popular culture, but must also be considered popular to the extent that they are chosen. The articulation of youth arts practices and youth arts curriculum as either forms of disciplinarity or modes of activism ('education' vs. 'schooling') are site specific and these processes occur simultaneously – both political slants on these forms must be recognized, as youth arts practices and curriculum create and promote particular forms of subjectivities and social relations. For example, The REC brings together young people's knowledge of popular commercial music and dance with teachers' perspectives on how they feel their students should present themselves and what they think youth arts should look like. Popular cultural knowledge – knowledge about dance moves, different bands, musical styles and their meanings – is core to the ways young people communicate about arts. It is knowledge that is central to how youth arts texts are composed. Yet teachers ultimately have a final say in the work that makes it to the stage and as such, the 'youth voices' created in REC performance pieces are partly performances of adult ideas about youth because the teachers are shaping, monitoring and censoring their student's work.

Extending the idea of social inclusion through democratic parti-cipation, I want to critique the idea of social inclusion introduced above to the extent that it re-creates a concept of a privileged group. Working with little publics as a concept opens out and activates the politics that the term social inclusion signifies, but does so in a way that shifts focus from including youth in a dominant paradigm to having the possibility of youth creating their own dialogic space which might speak back to a dominant paradigm, or might acquiesce. Multiple little public spheres can be conceived as living alongside each other and young people's inclusion in them is constitutive – it is required in order for them to exist. As te Riele has shown us,[41] the term 'inclusion' privileges an existing social structure from which some youth are excluded. Although strategic engagement with discourses of dominant cultural forms is required in order to have a position of use in educational theory, the assumption of the hierarchy embedded in the idea of social inclusion brings with it models for thinking about young subjectivity to which I am opposed. These models are exemplified by the 'at-risk' youth discourse, which constructs specific young subjects as deviant. As Kelly and Tait express so clearly,[42] the 'at-risk' youth discourse needs to be understood as a governmental strategy that reproduces select young people as deviant and thus in need of control. Youth art projects are often means of governance developed in response to such risk discourses. Similarly, as I explain above, REC performances become vehicles through which adult ideas of youth voice are shaped. Both discourses of youth at risk and the REC are largely ways that adults control young people, or ways youth choose to govern themselves. They are also ways of contributing to the 'public' as a sphere and valuing everyday literacies as a way of engaging the socially marginalized in processes of schooling.

A critical political imagination is, then, crucial to the production as part of Rough Theatre for young people. As this chapter has shown, working with mediascapes and ideoscapes can enrich and extend the capacity of theatre to engage young minds. C&T's Lipsync project shows how social issues can be highlighted and reframed through make believe, in a contemporary example of what Peter Brook has called Rough Theatre. Yet on the other end of the spectrum of political aesthetics, Deadly Theatre asks young people to 'sing along' to their favourite songs in ways that re-inscribe existing power dynamics and problems. The REC is Deadly Theatre, theatre that cannot embrace change. What I have tried to show, is that critical and well-managed engagements with young people's everyday knowledge and lifeworlds can have profound impacts. More than this, such critical attitudes to engagement are crucial as badly managed displays of engagement with popular culture can damage the youth voice both as it is understood by adults and young people themselves. Theatre for young people should be Rough Theatre: a technology of the imagination that animates possibilities for political resistance.

The Aesthetics of Becoming; Applied Theatre and the Quest for Cultural Certitude

Brian S. Heap

Introduction

Any broad consideration given to aesthetics in relation to applied theatre tends to revolve around issues related to the perceived value of the art object, the emotional impact of the performance, and the quality of production values.[1] For Boal, the distinction between the making or aesthetic process and the finished work of art is central to his notion of the Aesthetics of the Oppressed.[2] From personal experience of working within the geographical and cultural context of the Caribbean, the various genres of applied theatre must also grapple with a complex and ever-changing landscape of aesthetic theory. Responding to the complex history and social structure of the Caribbean, theorist Edouard Glissant speaks variously of an aesthetics of the earth, an aesthetics of disruption and intrusion, aesthetics of rupture and connection, aesthetics of a variable continuum, of an invariant discontinuum and an aesthetics of chaos.[3] Caribbean theorist, educator and artist Rex Nettleford once wrote:

> Children growing up in untidy, indisciplined and disorderly environs cannot hope to be clear thinking, disciplined and orderly . . . many of our people will have to be de-socialised out of their negative perceptions about order and gentleness or compassion or tenderness, 'being against the rules' while violence, aggression, and terror spell manliness and courage.[4]

So for Nettleford, in the Caribbean aesthetics becomes a necessary organizing principle, not simply in the artist's organization of paint, colour, sound, objects and bodies in space and time, but in the organization of post-colonial societies in their pursuit of nation-building, identity and cultural certitude. Nettleford further asserts that within the narrative of 'becoming':

> The responsibility is clearly for us to define self, to delineate parameters of operation, experimentation and exploration, to bring to dramatic arts the texture and vitality which the process of cross-fertilization, all within historical memory, has bequeathed us.[5]

Personally my own engagement with applied theatre has been largely within the sub-genre of process drama applied within a broad educational context, as well as with theatre in education and theatre for development and social intervention, guided by the ideas of Dorothy Heathcote, and Caribbean arts education practitioners such as Dennis Scott, who studied with Heathcote during the early 1970s. Jonothan Neelands, in the Prologue to a published collection of his writings[6] cites Dorothy Heathcote's declaration in *Signs and Portents*:

> Finally, having spent a long time wondering why I have for years been irritated by the cry of 'let's have more drama in our schools'. I now realise why I always wanted to say don't lobby for dramatics, lobby for better learning![7]

Neelands then indicates that despite his enormous admiration for her work, Dorothy Heathcote's declared position in this statement marked a parting of the ways for him in that:

> I have always had absolute respect for Heathcote's decision to turn away from drama as an art to focus on developing a globally and historically significant pedagogic system, which uses some elements of drama for other ends. However my own path has always been as a drama and theatre educator wanting to lobby for more drama in our schools as a means of lobbying for better learning.[8]

Having similarly lobbied long and hard myself for drama to be included as part of the school curriculum in Jamaica, and having seen success to the extent that it is now included in the current school system at every level from the early childhood level through the primary and secondary levels, I begin to find that my own sympathies now lie increasingly with the views expressed by Heathcote. This is a result of the fact that during the period in which drama has been included in the curriculum, there appears to have been little noticeable increase in the teaching of or improvement in the aesthetic quality of Drama in Jamaican schools.

In addition, it is important to consider the full text of Heathcote's declaration which Neelands unfortunately omits from his citation. In fact Heathcote goes on to state her main reason for wanting to lobby for better learning in schools over lobbying for more drama:

> It is, of course, because the heart of communication in social situations is the sign. *All* teachers need to study how to exploit it as the first basis of their work. The theatre is the art form which is totally based in sign and the drama additive to learning gives the urgency possible through using now/imminent time. This is why we lobby for better schools when we ask that teachers wake up to the possibilities of the power of resonances in classrooms instead of verbal statements.[9]

In some respects, Heathcote, while highlighting 'the power of resonances in classrooms' echoes Nettleford whose concern appears to be for a similar power of resonances in confidently defining self and identity within developing societies.

Bearing in mind what Heathcote is really advocating for in this statement, it is important to make clear that simply introducing applied theatre to educational and other social settings ensures nothing. It is certainly not being touted in this chapter as a panacea to all the ills of modern education and society. I myself may be passionate about the demonstrated efficacy of drama in education in the hands of the many brilliant teachers I have been privileged to observe over the years of my personal drama practice, but I am not so naïve as to deny that without careful attention to planning and execution drama can become, in the words of Mary E. Styslinger, 'just another mechanism of domination'.[10] The introduction of applied theatre, process drama or theatre arts-based drama to curriculum or as social intervention in the first place does *not* automatically guarantee that it will necessarily be adequately delivered. And even where drama is delivered there is no guarantee that the aesthetic process of the teacher/facilitator will carry with it a transformative power or that it will lead to any meaningful form of emancipatory education or experience. Styslinger supports this view in her article *Relations of Power in Drama in Education: The Teacher and Foucault*, and goes on to cite Paulo Freire's argument that:

> Education either functions as an instrument used to facilitate the integration of the younger generation into the logic of the present system and bring about conformity to it, or it becomes 'the practice of freedom,' the means by which men and women deal critically and creatively with reality and discover how to participate in the transformation of their world.[11]

Highlighting this observation only serves to underscore even further the need for drama teachers and applied theatre practitioners to carefully negotiate 'critically and creatively with reality', if they are to be truly effective as transformational educators.

Aesthetic decisions in applied theatre settings

There are indeed, highly motivated, accomplished teachers, facilitators and administrators who remain persuaded that simply doing drama in schools and with other learning communities will almost always yield positive outcomes. However, if insufficient consideration is paid to the actual aesthetic qualities of the drama, or even to the possibility that drama, like anything else can be delivered badly, the risk arises that applied theatre practitioners may well reinforce the very stereotypical behaviour and power structures they are actually seeking to contest. One piece of drama work on 'The Trans-Atlantic Slave Trade'[12] conducted with 8 year olds at a school in Kingston, Jamaica, resulted from observing a very courageous and well-intentioned but inexperienced teacher using drama in her history lesson. She somewhat naively divided the class into groups taking the roles of planters and others enslaved Africans, and with no other guidelines offered to them, the children's role-play quickly devolved into a complete free-for-all. Those playing the enslaved were in no mood to be trifled with, and responded to orders from the planters with some very hair-raising flying karate kicks. Once order had been restored and the teacher had dismissed the class, I realized that these children were leaving the classroom with a completely distorted view of history, even though their speculative approach to the recognition that Africans had fought back might have been extremely empowering.

Once those same 8-year olds were given some responsibility in a follow-up session in which they interacted with experienced actors depicting enslaved Africans, and were provided with space to think about the condition of enslavement in a drama involving a wealthy philanthropist building a museum, their own questions, actually posed by them and not by a teacher, told a very different story. Two of the boys who participated in the class were grappling with a question which they had formulated, and that was 'What makes a good slave?' At first I had no idea where they wanted to take this line of enquiry until they qualified their first question with two others. 'Is a good slave one who does his work well? Or is a good slave one who resists and tries to escape?' And revealed in these questions was their dawning realization that they had begun to expose for themselves something of the terrible and utterly dehumanizing nature of enslavement. An enslaved person can never be good because he or she is robbed of the possibility of moral dignity. In addition, in their questioning, the two boys were also processing the conflicting messages of the contemporary Jamaican society of which they were a part, and the seemingly contradictory societal values which they were also trying to comprehend: the Establishment, on the one hand praising the virtue of industry as in, 'By the sweat of thy brow shalt thou eat bread,' and the forces of resistance on the other hand, expressed in the Rastafarian sentiment of resisting the 'system' encapsulated in the expression 'Fight down Babylon.' Through an encounter with history these young boys had seized an opportunity to explain themselves to themselves by formulating a question which demanded an answer. They had not simply produced a stock answer to somebody else's question, as is most generally the case in traditional models of education.

Again, Styslinger points out that:

> A need exists for critical and liberatory dialogue with the self(ves). Critical reflection on the presence of discourse and the exercise of power is wanted. Only through dialogue can teachers and students gain the 'will to truth.' We might re-examine the self constantly. We might recognise and take responsibility for oppressive roles in the current enactment of drama in education. Perhaps then, a new relationship might emerge, that of teacher-student with student-teachers. Perhaps then all the benefits of drama – improved literacy, multiple interpretations, increased collaboration, and problem solving – might truly be enjoyed.[13]

What remains somewhat disconcerting in Styslinger's article, however, is her apparent unwillingness to engage in any meaningful discussion about the teachers and students as artists in her analysis of their doing drama. Drama seems here to be treated primarily as yet another interesting teaching methodology, and while one can admire Styslinger's clarity on her discussion of the shifting power relations implicit in classrooms, her argument eventually leaves the impression that her analysis is somewhat lacking in balance. This is largely as a result of her own apparent unwillingness to engage with the aesthetic dimensions of drama, which constitute yet another set of serious challenges to be negotiated by teacher and students alike.

Aesthetic decision making constantly intersects power relations in applied theatre practice. In a teaching situation in Zambia I firmly refused to allow participants from the Anti-AIDS Teachers Association of Zambia in a drama about the stigma attached to HIV/AIDS to move too quickly towards the happy ending they craved at a very early stage in the proceedings.[14] This could easily be 'mis/read' by others, including the participants themselves in terms of all kinds of abuse of power – white European teacher abusing his power over black African subjects and, seemingly ignoring their creative input, doing it his way regardless. As teacher/facilitator, of course I must always be aware of the possibility of negative reading of my practice by others, since I exist, after all, in that kind of situation as a walking 'Primary Sign.' In other words, there is absolutely nothing I can do or would wish to do to alter the primary signifiers of my designated gender or ethnicity. However, I must also fervently be aware that as a teacher/artist I have an even greater responsibility to participants and administrators than simply attempting to present myself in a good light. I have to be able to negotiate my way around the eventuality of any negative personal projections or perceptions which may arise in order to fulfil my main responsibility, which is to challenge the participants as artists and provide them with as aesthetically engaging and meaningful a drama experience as may be possible. In the same way that a negative response can shut down a dramatic improvisation, a 'happy outcome' at that stage of that particular drama would have wrapped up the work there and then, removing any chance the participants might have had of confronting any major, meaningful challenge or dilemma. It would most certainly have denied the participants the opportunity of having to deal and engage with the depths of emotion resulting from depictions of family breakdown, forced separation, difficult reunion, guilt, and stigma, as well as having to further battle with the impact of HIV/AIDS introduced into a domestic household setting as part of a powerful and transformative drama. In other words, the aesthetic and learning outcomes were worth the struggle.

Like Styslinger, the Australian scholar Helen Cahill is also critical of the claims for drama as a 'safe space' for learning and addresses what she sees as some of the limitations of drama as 'a tool to investigate experience and to assist people to rehearse for change'[15] Her thesis also challenges the assumptions made about the fiction – reality boundary, particularly within drama's naturalistic tradition, and highlights the possibility of generating dramatic portrayals which 'can reinforce rather than challenge limiting stereotypes.' However, Cahill's analysis seems to me to be far richer than that of Styslinger, who, although she acknowledges the need to improve the quality of drama in terms of learning outcomes, appears to be less clear about the artistic implications of her new awareness of the 'hidden' power relations in classrooms. She offers as a solution to the challenges of her own situation in something she refers to as 'drama on the loose':

> Unobstructed by teacher governance, unregulated by textual truth, unimpeded by constraining discourse, this dramatic form (or lack thereof) attempts to introduce emancipatory content and liberatory practice into education. In collaborative settings, students are encouraged to interpret situations and problem solve with one another. It is one teacher's attempt to challenge the social forces and do battle against the oppressor consciousness embodied in the social institutions of power. The choice is ours. We may continue to wield power or offer alternatives.[16]

It is this apparent readiness to relax not only the use of the term 'drama' but also the rigour of the art form, which was raised as a major concern by my colleague Pamela Bowell and myself in a paper presented at the sixth International Drama in Education Research Institute convened at the University of Sydney, Australia in 2009:

> Many of the quite often legitimate claims for what drama can provide, including deep levels of engagement with curriculum content, providing opportunities to challenge all kinds of unjust power relations and hegemonic practices, building consensus through democratic processes, and nurturing a heightened sensibility to the importance of moral education, are all rendered invalid if teachers are not secure in the workings of the art form of drama, which is the means by which these very things are facilitated into existence in the first place.[17]

So here again it is the recognition of the role that applied theatre can play in the aesthetic strengthening of individuals and communities which is being emphasized. Cahill, by also centring her argument on dramatic style, demonstrates both a healthy respect for the art form of drama and what it can achieve in the learning situation as the prime elements of her focus, while at the same time she advocates for a greater awareness of what she refers to as 'genre shifts' in drama practice:

> For real change to occur, the drama must produce the possibility of doing ourselves differently. If people can play themselves out with and for each other, then this enactment becomes a form of 'knowledge', if only the knowledge that there are other possible modes of being. Having been enacted, this knowledge then becomes a part of our reality. It then becomes an option, and hence can be chosen.[18]

Inspired by the practice of deconstruction offered by Jacques Derrida as well as the notion of fantasy offered by Judith Butler, Cahill articulates for us a way of re-imagining ourselves and others, a meaningful alternative to the duplication of reality and strictures imposed by 'the rules of societal discourses' which frequently result from improvised naturalistic drama. In this way Cahill throws down something of a challenge to Styslinger and indirectly through her to Foucault, while still grounding herself solidly in the art form of drama. If naturalism sometimes supports existing power relations, then the shifting of genre into parody, thought tracking, alternative time frames and other dramatic sub-genres may disturb or challenge those same power relations without diluting the artistic experience. Cahill's consideration of 'genre shifts' also supports in a very concrete way, the paradox of the 'truth' of the theatre and the 'myth' of so-called reality:

> A reworking of identity requires a dismantling of the categorizing that has occurred. But for the dismantling to occur – we must first see how we are mantled. It is here that drama has a particular potency, for we trade in mantles. However, for the drama to contribute in this way, it must facilitate recognition of the constructed nature of identity, and of the constructing nature of dominant storylines. It must make visible the storying, rather than simply the story.[19]

Here Cahill's analysis resonates strongly with the notions of the constructed nature of identity through socialization as well as alternative experiences of reality.

'Baby Bird' drama: An example of genre shifts

Cahill's emphasis on the need for drama teachers and applied theatre facilitators to be able to execute 'genre shifts' which challenge participants is illustrated by an experience I had with teachers on the Caribbean island of St Lucia. On this occasion, I had the rare privilege of working with an accomplished professional dancer and a group of teachers who, I was informed, all worked with children and adults with special needs. Taking my cue from Dorothy Heathcote, my initial objective was to focus on getting the teachers to 'slow down' when working in the general area of special needs, and to test their patience as far as would be possible. The dancer and I had only just met one another at the venue, but I was already familiar with her work in New York where she worked in the outreach programme of a professional dance company with young dancers who were blind or visually challenged. My instinct was that she would have both the artistic sensitivity and the patience to carry out what I had in mind.

We planned out ahead of time what we would do together and the plan was simply this. I did not want to work naturalistically with the special needs teachers because of my concern that the role-playing of disabled and special needs constituents might be introduced into that approach to drama. Instead, I wanted to create some distance between the teachers and those with whom they worked, even though, at the same time the drama had to address issues of immediate concern to them. Eventually, we decided that the dancer would work in full role as a 'baby bird', which had been abandoned in its nest. The teachers would be expected to take care of the bird and help it, but the dancer would try to remain as unresponsive as she could be for as long as possible.

I would work as facilitator and 'baby bird' and I agreed that she could take her cue from me. If I felt the teachers were becoming too discouraged, I would indicate that she could then give them some slight response, which would serve as a reward to them by showing that some progress was being made. But the main aim was to make any progress only very, very, slowly.

In readiness for the drama session we prepared the room, which was in a local hotel. We borrowed some bed sheets and shaped them into a circular 'nest'. We got some broken eggshells from the kitchen and scattered them around the nest of bed sheets. The dancer also just happened to have with her a pack of coloured feathers which she had brought for another purpose. These too were strewn around the nest area. Dressed in plain leotard and tights, 'baby bird' had already taken up her place in a curled, foetal position in the nest before the participants entered. She remained there while I explained to the teachers about the kind of drama we were going to do, before I went into role as someone who had found this baby bird and needed some help in taking care of it. With hindsight I now realize that the teacher/participants readily entered into the fiction because they regarded themselves as persons of a helping disposition and the helping relationship was something that seemed almost instinctive to them. For the next 2 hours, the teachers worked with a human dancer in role as a helpless bird first trying to get her to open her eyes by giving her a name, and calling it to her, or by singing to her and just at the point where nothing seemed to be working and they seemed about to give up, she opened her eyes on cue very slowly and with great effort on her part. This went on from one stage of the drama to the next, getting her to sit up with a volunteer climbing into the nest with her and propping her up until she could do it by herself, with other participants offering advice from the side. This was followed by a period during which we struggled to get the bird to stand up, with the dancer continuing to make it so difficult and challenging for the teachers but rewarding them just sufficiently to keep them committed to their assigned responsibility.

At one point in the drama, one of the participants had the idea of making the nest bigger so that two or three people could get into it with the bird and walk her around so that she could get used to moving. So with all these people helping her, the bird began to take a few tentative steps. Then we had to try to get her out of the nest, which was achieved by making a gap in the sheets and walking her around the room. As I wondered aloud whether we would ever be able to teach her to fly, the teachers responded by taking up the coloured feathers and placing them in her hair, sticking them to her leotards and tights. Then they began making flapping motions with their arms which the bird imitated. This also being the Caribbean, some of the teachers began to beat out a rhythm on an empty water jug and started to sing the song 'If I had the wings of a dove.' With the lyrics of the song 'I will fly, fly away, fly away and be at rest', the participants had unconsciously introduced an idea to the dancer which I had not thought about as a possibility. She began to flap her 'wings' with greater confidence now, and elevated herself by jumping on to a chair. The whole room took on a very Carnival-like atmosphere. As she continued to 'fly' the bird/dancer slowly hopped from one empty chair to the next and I began to notice that she was moving closer and closer to the main door of the room. The Carnival revellers seemed oblivious to this as they appeared to be prematurely congratulating themselves on a job well done. Then without any indication to me or anyone the bird/dancer hopped down from the last chair, opened the door and 'flew' away. The singing stopped abruptly. The participants stood transfixed waiting for 'their bird' to come back into the room. Somebody eventually opened the door and looked up and down the corridor to find her, but there was no sign of her.

The teachers soon after began to express their feelings of annoyance, of disappointment, of being cheated or robbed, of having invested so much time and energy into an exercise that left them with nothing. I was quite taken aback by their strong reactions to the situation. Some of the participants were visibly devastated by the disappearance of the bird. It was not a conclusion that any of them had expected. Many of the teachers seemed to have been suddenly confronted with something they had been in denial about. The conclusion of the drama wasn't anything I had planned either but I then spent the next 90 minutes in frank discussion with the teachers getting them to work through the possibility that they might have built a dependence on the clients with whom they worked, just as much, if not more than the clients needed them. Subconsciously they needed to have their clients continue to depend on them. We had to work through the possibility that the helping relationship could in reality turn into one of mutual dependence. What the bird/dancer had given the teachers is what they had indicated they wanted, by reason of their professional status (i.e. to enable and empower another individual). But when confronted with the possibility of the emancipated as opposed to dependent individual they were not ready to let go. Many of the participants also began to rethink and express unease about the kinds of relationships they had with their own family members as well.

On the surface this example of applied theatre was about as far from anything in the naturalistic tradition as you could get. Here was a grown woman taking the role of a 'baby bird' inside a nest of bed sheets, eggshells and feathers, and a group of teachers nurturing this 'bird woman' to the point where she was able to 'fly' away. How could something that could have come straight out of the theatre of the absurd or which seemingly appeared to be quite childish on the surface, produce such an emotive response from this group of adult participants? But the aesthetic qualities of this apparently 'distanced' genre seemed to reveal so much to the teacher/participants about themselves and their working relationships, that at first they were reluctant to confront the very thing they had discovered.

If, as this example seems to illustrate, we are so reluctant to scrutinize our own teaching and learning experiences and relationships in order to see them in a new light, then training teachers and facilitators to use applied theatre within different kinds of learning community begins to reveal something of its complex nature. As Deborah Britzman points out so astutely in relation to teachers during the period of their initial formation:

> Learning to teach, like teaching itself, is a time when desires are rehearsed, refashioned and refused. The construction of the real, the necessary, and the imaginary are constantly shifting as student teachers set about to accentuate the identities and discursive practices of others. Theirs is a vulnerable position; the borders of borrowing and owning are not easily discernible, and the advice, support and guidance of others expresses an odd combination of authoritative and internally persuasive discourses.[20]

Becoming a teacher is undoubtedly a complex procedure. Becoming a successful teacher of theatre and drama adds the further complication of also developing the teacher as artist. What I and others do as applied theatre practitioners in educational contexts is something quite ephemeral. The drama happens and then it is gone, but like all art of a sufficiently high standard, not only do we remember it, but the most meaningful artistic experience seems to imprint itself on the memory so profoundly that we are able to revisit and re-process it over and over again.

In a personal correspondence to me a few years ago, Dorothy Heathcote was still reflecting on, analysing and drawing examples from dramatic encounters in which we had participated together 25 years earlier.[21] And why should that be at all surprising? I can't remember many of the ordinary classes, the 'telling' classes that I have taught over the years yet can vividly recall almost all the significant theatre/drama moments. So why should it be that such aesthetically charged experiences remain with us for so long? And not just in our memories. Does a meaningful dramatic experience somehow etch itself into our brains as permanent change? Whether or not future advances in cognitive neuroscience are able to yield new findings that lend solid support to such theories, it still seems to me that we remain affected because whenever applied theatre is successfully deployed, the result simply cannot be considered to be anything like an ordinary encounter, but rather, as a fact that has a mystical quality which derives from the engagement with the art form.

It is my contention here that the overall impact of the drama slowly develops as a result of all these aesthetic experiences which eventually 'grow' within us. Within the drama we may experience a range of different types of representation, the role of an African girl may be variously represented in space and time by a traditional shawl draped over a chair, as a baby by the shawl shaped into a bundle, as a silent man wearing the traditional shawl, or as a female who speaks her thoughts on the girl's behalf. Yet we may experience each of them as part of a cumulative process, which develops to such an extent that eventually we carry all these different representations from different times and locations inside us simultaneously. It is the complexity of interactive drama processes, which arise from the need for the teacher/facilitator to put on the mantles of playwright, director and actor, which facilitates this phenomenon. It becomes possible for teacher/facilitators to 'hold' different theatrical forms simultaneously, so that the aesthetic space becomes populated by a number of different representations from which they can choose as they need them. And the more we look at different examples the more we begin to understand that in view of what drama is capable of doing, Cahill is right to suggest as she does that in drama naturalistic representation alone may not be enough, because it represents only one sub-genre of the art form.

Quadripartite thinking/quadripartite response

In collaborative work together, Pamela Bowell and I have written about the complexity of the interactive drama processes referred to above. An even more complicated situation arises as a result of the fact that the *participants* must take on these functions as well. The complexity is further compounded because these functions are generally engaged simultaneously yet are driven by potentially different needs.

In educational settings the teacher/facilitator's object interest (what is to be imparted as part of a syllabus, or client brief) is frequently at variance with the need interest (the immediate concerns) of the student/participant. But within applied theatre practice yet another aspect of variance arises. The teacher/facilitator will be concerned primarily with achieving the learning objective of the drama experience, while the participants are concerned primarily with the storyline or the narrative of the drama. So the teacher/facilitator is faced with the challenge of selecting a dramatic narrative, which will deliver enough opportunities for learning to take place, in order for the required learning objective to be met. Yet another level of complexity arises from the fact that some aspects of applied theatre may be essentially spontaneous and improvisatory in nature unfolding in 'now time'. The successful teacher/facilitator, therefore, has to be sufficiently confident and well enough equipped to make decisions which are both creative and educative, in the 'present moment' of the drama. Preparing a teacher-artist to successfully deliver then, would seem to be next to impossible. Not only will that individual be required to negotiate all the variables of theatre and all the variables of education but also the variables of the broader community and culture and those of individual participants, including a range of negotiated power relations in addition to the rules of societal discourses. And yet such teacher/facilitators do exist and function at this level of complexity in teaching and learning situations every day, because they develop a very distinct level of high-order thinking skills.

In order to carry out the various artistic functions described above, the teacher/facilitator of the drama, needs to adopt what Pamela Bowell and I have referred to as 'quadripartite thinking'.[22] The adjustment in thinking needed to manage this complex, creative, educative process, means that the teacher/facilitator requires:

- The head of the playwright needing to think about how to help participants craft the narrative so the story unfolds in a way which carries within it the learning;

- The head of the director needing to steer participants to the learning within the narrative through the best dramatic performance structure;
- The head of the actor needing to give a performance which engages and beguiles participants and supports and challenges them in the creation of their own roles;
- The head of the teacher needing to hold all of the other thinking simultaneously, together with knowledge and understanding of the real context of the participants, classroom, school, community, culture and curriculum.[23]

The teacher/facilitator must therefore, fulfil *four* different functions simultaneously while moving between the two worlds on either side of the fiction – reality boundary. The perspective of the playwright, director, actor and educator will be brought to bear as part of the drama planning process. But it is at the point where the teacher and participants enter fully into the 'now time' of the drama, that all four viewpoints are not only brought into play, but must be applied to supporting, challenging and guiding participants in initiating, developing and bringing the drama to a satisfactory completion. For the successful teacher-artist, an appreciation of the nature of quadripartite thinking assists in both understanding something of the aesthetic complexity of the task at hand, and in confronting the challenges experienced in practice.

Jonothan Neelands connects each of the teacher/facilitator's functions outlined above, to the fundamental nature of theatre:

> Actors train so that they can control gesture, time and space. . . . Directors learn to weave all of the temporal, spatial and physical actions on the stage into the illusion of another world. Playwrights fill the artistic dimensions of time, space and presence with living and immediate representations of human behaviour and experience.[24]

Successful practitioners of applied theatre, in addition to the skills of actor, director and playwright, are also required to develop a fourth skill, which is that of teacher/facilitator. All four of these heads are brought into play not only as part of the pre-action, preparatory phase during which the teacher/facilitator plans the drama experience, but also during the active phase of the drama as it unfolds in 'now time'. Added to this is the dimension of the self-spectator, which is essentially a critical awareness of self which the teacher/facilitator maintains while operating in each of the functions outlined above. So the teacher/facilitator is operating simultaneously during the drama as self-spectator/actor, self/spectator/director, self-spectator/playwright and self-spectator/teacher/facilitator.

Also critical to the formation of a creative partnership with the teacher/facilitator is the need for participants to make a quadripartite response to what is happening in the drama. The participants:

- Learn how to contribute to the extension and deepening of the play they are in and to feel sufficiently empowered to initiate further developments of the narrative;
- Learn by acquiring knowledge of the art form by doing it (as well as knowledge of content) to have the confidence to initiate and implement directorial decisions;
- Learn how to respond and adjust behaviour within fictional circumstances, adjusting and demonstrating behaviour within that 'other' reality;
- Make sense of the layering of experience as it moves towards the possibility of some kind of self-transformation in the real context.[25]

So, the result of the quadripartite thinking of the teacher/facilitator, when experienced during the 'now time' of the drama, elicits a reciprocal quadripartite response from the participants and initiates a spiral of creative exchange whereby *both* experience the transformative power of drama. In this multifaceted spiral of creative discourse, the participants' feedback to the facilitator, who in turn responds, and so on. This corresponds with Freire's statement quoted by Styslinger earlier 'Perhaps then, a new relationship might emerge, that of teacher-student with student-teachers.'[26] Evidence would appear to confirm that the exchange does in fact take place – participants become part of the teaching/facilitation, the facilitator learns and all the participants are affected within this continuing cycle of exchange.

Aesthetic variables within the art form of drama

The exchange relationship, generated as it is by the spiralled input/ feedback interchange of feelings, ideas and perceptions between participants and facilitator, provides the basis upon which shifts in the shape and direction of the drama can be initiated by both participants and/or teacher/facilitator. However, rich though this relationship is, there are further elements that impact upon it and add further to its complex nature. There are a host of other potential shifts in the theatre/learning continuum which may derive from really quite small adjustments to the aesthetic building blocks of the drama.

The detailing of all such shifts, even if one could be at all confident that they had all been identified, is beyond the scope of this short chapter, and will no doubt form a foundation on which future applied theatre research can be developed. However, perhaps the major recommendation which emerges here is that in training teacher/ facilitators to work with applied theatre in future, greater emphasis must be placed on nurturing a greater understanding of the many *aesthetic variables* which operate when working with the art form of drama. Some of these variables about which we can appraise both facilitators and participants, and which increasingly they must have at their disposal as their skill as applied theatre practitioners grows, include the following:

There are aesthetic choices to be made relating to the structural framework of the applied theatre work.

These refer to the potentially dynamic interplay between the dramatic context of the applied theatre work, the roles being taken and developed, and their points of view within the work. The dramatic context of the work must resonate within the cultural context of the participants, as must the identity of the roles and their various or changing perspectives on the unfolding action of the work. Attention must be given to the ways in which even the slightest shift in one, two or all three of these key aspects of the drama can radically alter the nature of its interrogation. The main premise at work here is that these shifts in dramatic context, roles and point of view, working together with a range of applied theatre strategies, offer the opportunity for broadening and strengthening the drama experience for the participants and so provide a richer and more rounded learning experience through a set of changing lenses.

There are aesthetic choices relating to individual improvised performances within the applied theatre work – as well as to facilitator and participant register, out of role.

The dynamic at work here includes not only the facilitator conducting negotiations within the improvised performance of teacher in role (TIR), but also responding to the in-role behaviour of participants. The teacher/facilitator will also frequently be reflecting before negotiating new phases of the drama out of role, and will be carefully self-monitoring the register/mode of questioning and so on with the participants similarly adjusting to different demands of each change of phase in the session. Negotiations conducted out of role are just as important as those conducted by the teacher/facilitator in role. And while some negotiations may be conducted out of role, the chosen role, which the teacher/facilitator in role eventually adopts, may also have to be altered during the course of the drama, or the participants 're-framed' and 'keyed' according to Goffman[27] into taking another perspective on the fictional circumstances of the drama. Roles may also have to be represented in some kind of holding form, for example, indicating present absence or omnipresence for use as they are needed.

**Aesthetic choices also relate to signifiers within the applied theatre
work – sign may be generated by the drama and form the basis for
further negotiations of meaning.**

The applied theatre work will typically present a dense and constantly
changing semiotic field that must be carefully organized throughout
in order to generate the kinds of meaning which support the learning.
Facilitator and participants will be constantly generating new signs
which have to be negotiated and renegotiated in order to keep the
learning on track. Again, Dorothy Heathcote's suggestion cited above
that '. . . because the heart of communication in social situations is
the sign . . . all teachers need to study how to exploit it as the first
basis of their work,' once again resonates strongly here. Teacher/
facilitators have to develop enormous sensitivity to the 'informational
polyphony' and 'density of signs' which Barthes[28] uses to characterize
the multiple semiotic dimensions of theatre, and which are mirrored
in the dramatic signifiers and general modes of communication used
in education.

**Aesthetic choices also relate to the use and perception of space
in applied theatre and the strategies and theatre conventions
of space.**

Drama is an art form which unfolds in space and time, so that an
understanding of how the facilitator can best make use of even limited
space and alter the participants' perception of it through the way in
which that space is used is a key dynamic area of applied theatre. The
space in drama is in a constant state of flux, so this dynamic requires
not only an understanding of strategies associated with space, like
defining the space in a physical way, or using sound effects to define it,
but also an understanding of those transformations of space which are
related to proxemics, the socially conditioned spatial factors in ordinary
human relations, or the physical body such as the gaze, relationships
between movement and stillness and so on. For example, within the

confines of a small room the feeling of a wide open space can be created by gazing beyond the ceiling of that room as though to the heavens above, reinforcing this by pointing to distant stars or galaxies. By simple modulation of the voice, a teacher can transform the students' perception of a classroom for example, by whispering or speaking in hushed tones to create a situation of confinement as participants huddle together indoors as a storm rages outside, or by calling to them as though across a wide distance to give an impression of being in an open outdoor area.

Other aesthetic choices relate to the use and perception of time in applied theatre as well as the strategies and theatre conventions of time.

As part of the recognition of the central importance of the Time-Space continuum in which drama unfolds, the dynamic of time can also be singled out for particular attention. Here the facilitator and participants must be cognizant of the myriad ways in which time manifests itself in drama. The dozens of available strategies relating to the depiction of time whether oriented to the past, present or future are always made manifest in the 'now time' of the dramatic action. In addition, there is the real time of life and of the applied theatre session, along with different perceptions of time passing as with the entry into the Mythic Time of ritual for example. So the teacher/facilitator must develop a further sensitivity to the fact that throughout the dramatic action there are likely to be multiple manifestations of time operating, and that these are frequently experienced by the participants all at the same time. A good example of this can be found in Polly Teale's play *After Mrs Rochester* in which the actor playing the Dominican writer Jean Rhys sits in a room in a house in Devon in 1957, remembering herself as a young girl around 1900 portrayed by a younger actress, reading Charlotte Bronte's *Jane Eyre*, whose main characters in the 1840s are also depicted onstage.[29] The three time periods are here experienced simultaneously.

Finally, there are those aesthetic choices relating to progression, assessment and evaluation undertaken as praxis by both facilitator and participants in applied theatre.

Within the dynamic of the unfolding drama, the teacher/facilitator is reflecting on and refining the theoretical aspects of the art form in practice. Much of this reflection in action is conducted in conjunction with the teacher/facilitator using the art form as diagnostic tool in evaluating participant achievement, while they too are reflecting on their own grasp of the content concepts contained within the drama, as well as their ability to use and appreciate the intricacies of the art form. An interesting illustration of this arose out of work conducted in a primary school in Jamaica by three teachers working as a team during their teaching practicum. They devised a process drama which involved students as customers in a restaurant selecting their lunch choices from a menu. They were given paper plates and invited with crayons and coloured pencils to choose a dish from the menu and draw their dinners on their plates. The exercise went well until one of the teachers noticed that one particular little boy had done something different from the other students. While all the other children had all made their selection and drawn their impressions of cooked food on their plates, the boy in question had selected 'curried goat and rice' and drawn a beautiful, and quite detailed picture of a goat, along with a bag marked 'rice'. For some reason the boy had not projected himself through the cooking process to draw cooked food as the other children had done. The teachers handled the exception very sensitively, but in their discussions together afterwards concluded that this was a reminder that as applied theatre practitioners we can take nothing for granted.

Conclusion

Cognizant of the expressed national goal of most post-colonial societies of empowering their citizens to achieve their optimum potential, it is imperative, that applied theatre be recognized as having the potential to make a fundamental contribution to the organization of national social life. Aesthetic strengthening is particularly critical for those populations and communities whose individual and collective identities have been compromised by the experience of colonialism, and whose indigenous cultures might well have experienced possible forms of aesthetic degradation. As Rex Nettleford observes:

> Tom Mboya, a former Kenyan leader, once told the world that Africa's poverty (expressed in recycled motor-tyre sandals and semi-nudity) should not be mistaken for its culture.[30]

The social and economic development of any society depends on individuals who can think and act creatively, approach challenges positively, and show initiative, as well as find imaginative solutions to problems.

Participants in applied theatre, have the potential to take greater responsibility for shaping the aesthetic qualities of their own personal encounters with performance while they are situated inside the drama. The social and personal skills developed in the process of 'becoming' as a result of education through applied theatre, coincide with those which appear to be highly valued in contemporary society. These include a greater ability to interrogate issues of national and cultural identity in a globalized world.

Not just the countries of the Caribbean and other former colonized nations, but those of Europe and North America, as well as Australia and New Zealand must continually adjust their identities to keep pace with the fluctuations of a rapidly changing global community. Many of these countries' own identities are now being increasingly challenged and destabilized by the emergence of increasingly diverse populations resulting from demographic shifts and migration. Aesthetic adjustment, strengthening and development through the creative arts including applied theatre promises to be one of the most effective ways of meeting these challenges in the future.

Epilogue

Gareth White

In the February 2014 edition of *Research in Drama Education*, Matt Omasta and Dani Snyder-Young published a meta-analysis of methods in applied theatre research. In their survey of journal articles in English over a decade (2002–12), they categorized 428 examples, finding the majority to be either taking qualitative approaches (37 per cent), conceptual or theoretical approaches (32 per cent) or to be documentations of practice (11 per cent); quantitative research accounts for only 4 per cent of examples. Of 203 that made a claim about the effectiveness of the practice they examined, 90 per cent reported successful practice rather than unsuccessful, neutral or mixed results. For Omasta and Snyder-Young these are reasons to question 'whether our own field [has] adopted a research paradigm that allows us – or even encourages us – to neglect certain questions and approaches'.[1] Though they conclude by calling for a broader range of methodologies and openness to genuine and challenging evaluation,[2] what stands out from their analysis is the lack of the kind of quantitative research that might be thought best for presenting an unambiguous evaluation of efficacy; and that the vast majority of reports on efficacy confirm it. These findings raise the question of whether research into applied theatre is structurally biased towards advocacy rather than independent evaluation, and whether the methodological preferences of the discipline play a part in this tendency.

The various 'aesthetics approaches' taken in this book range across conceptual, qualitative and documenting methodologies; obviously, they neither fill the gap of qualitative evaluation nor use research to only advocate for the work. Shaughnessy, Adebayo, Heap, and I all advocate for modes of practice, with an analysis of that practice, but Sadeghi-Yekta, Breed and Hickey-Moody all critique models and iterations of practice. Turning our attention to aesthetics is about remembering that applied art is art as much as social practice, and that artistic quality matters. As the chapters here evidence, it's about asking rigorous questions related to quality, and about what kind of quali*ties* matter; it examines the conceptual basis of quality, and adds rigour to evaluation. Aesthetics research can do more than advocate for the work we approve of, it can be used, as several contributors here have done, to discern the problems: to describe value and to critique where value is mistaken.

Omasta and Snyder-Young cite Eleonora Belfiore's article in *The International Journal of Cultural Policy*, which draws on moral philosopher Harry G. Frankfurt's *On Bullshit*. This 1985 text itemizes disingenuous discourse in public life, with categories including vagueness, obfuscation and especially a pervasive indifference to the truth. Belfiore finds all of these at work in the discourse of cultural policy, both political and academic, such that assessment of and communication about cultural activity makes use of material that fits preconceptions and best serves predetermined ends. If Belfiore is right about cultural policy, and if Omasta and Snyder-Young are right about applied theatre research, then we need to be vigilant about avoiding a tendency to fall into habits of advocacy and celebration at the expense of independent evaluation; we must resist the temptation of bullshit.

For Belfiore this necessitates an intellectual humility, recognizing that research will not be able to capture the diverse experiences and multiple impacts of the arts on people and communities:

> Any simple, straightforward solution to this riddle, or any impact evaluation toolkit that promises to evaluate the transformative power of any form of aesthetic experience in '10 easy replicable steps', thus bypassing or refusing to address such complexity, is likely to be – let us be honest – bullshit.[3]

Aesthetics takes this complexity as a starting point. It turns our attention to the difficulty of artistic value, so that speaking of beauty is not merely celebratory. There is a place for applied theatre research that is not dispassionate: that is practice-led, embodied, partisan or polemic. The language of aesthetics adds rigour to these approaches so that they properly complement independent evaluation; it is also part of the arsenal of evaluative research, it is an additional strategy of critique.

Notes

Introduction

1 Nicholson, Helen, *Applied Drama: The Gift of Theatre*. Basingstoke: Palgrave Macmillan, 2005, p. 2.

2 I don't share her rejection of the term, seeing it as a usefully broad church under which to gather diverse practices, where the impulse to seek an orthodoxy – of politics or practical approach – can be more easily avoided. But those of us who teach applied theatre need to remain aware that it is a discursive compromise rather than a coherent discipline, and share with our students a critical perspective of it.

3 van Erven, Eugene, *Community Theatre: Global Perspectives*. London, Routledge, 2001.

4 in Landy, Robert and David Montgomerie, *Theatre for Change: Education, Social Action and Therapy*. London: Palgrave Macmillan, 2012, p. 163.

5 van Erven, pp. 248–51.

6 O'Connor, Peter, in Jackson, Anthony and Chris Vine, *Learning Through Theatre: The Changing Face of Theatre in Education*. London: Routledge, 2013, pp. 305–20. See also the introduction to the website of *The Aesthetics of Applied Theatre*, a research project funded by the European Research Council. Their project aims for an approach which:

> promises precise insights into the aesthetic forms of applied theatre, which constitute the (hitherto barely researched) foundation of its political effects. It will furthermore bring to light the ethical issues of applied theatre: intense aesthetic experiences often linked with risks when it comes to performances do not readily fit in with the claim to restore children, youngsters, patients, and other target groups to health, integrity, and self-confidence through theatrical practice. The project aims to show how aesthetic, political, and ethical aspects interact in the practice of applied theatre.

Each instance here is in the adjectival form, but the aesthetic forms, aesthetic experiences and aesthetic aspects, each have different relationships to the question of whether quality lies in the eye of the beholder or in the object. *The Aesthetics of Applied Theatre* (found 18/10/13) http://www.applied-theatre.org/about-us. The project celebrates the 'many different types of applied theatre, which set in motion constructive social processes while upholding theatre's aesthetic claim'.

7   O'Connor, p. 307.

8   Ibid., p. 312.

9   Ibid., p. 315.

10 See also Cohen, Cynthia E., Roberto Gutiérrez Varea, and Polly O. Walker (eds), *Acting Together: Performance and the Creative Transformation of Violence: Volume I: Resistance and Reconciliation in Regions of Violence*. New York: New Village Press, 2011, p. 9: 'A wide variety of word views and aesthetic traditions, and drawing in varying degrees on ancient practices and modern innovations', p. 3; 'engaging people in embodied, collaborative and temporal aesthetic experiences, performances generate – for artists, witnesses and participants – unique opportunities for reflection learning and imagination', p. 5. '. . . The extent to which some of these approaches prioritise social and psychological outcomes over and above aesthetic concerns places them outside the focus of this work, which examines the contributions to peacebuilding of performances that are composed with significant attention to aesthetic values.'

11 Haseman, Brad and Joe Winston, 'Why be interested? Aesthetics, applied theatre and drama education', *Research in Drama Education* 15, 4 (2010): 465–75.

12 Haseman and Winston, p. 466.

13 Ibid., p. 469.

14 Cohen, Variea and Walker, p. 6.

15 Winston, Joe, *Beauty and Education*. London: Routledge, 2010.

16 Thompson, James, *Performance Affects*. London: Palgrave MacMillan, 2009.

17   Thompson, p. 111.

18   Scarry, Elaine, *The Body in Pain*. Oxford: Oxford Paperbacks, 1988.

19   Thompson, p. 140.

20   Dewey, John, *Art as Experience*. London: Pedigree, 1980 (1935).

21   Thompson, p. 11.

22   Shaughnessy, Nicola, *Applying Performance: Live Art, Socially Engaged Theatre and Affective Performance*. London: Routledge, 2012.

23   Machon, Josephine, *(Syn)Aesthetics: Redefining Visceral Performance*. London: Palgrave Macmillan, 2009.

24   Lehmann, Hans-Thies, *Post-Dramatic Theatre*, trans. Karen Jurs-Munby. Abingdon: Routledge 2006.

25   Shaughnessy, p. 75.

26   Ibid., pp. 135, 147, 181 respectively.

27   Shusterman, Richard, 'Somaesthetics and Education: Exploring the Terrain', in Liora Bressler (ed.), *Knowing Bodies, Moving Minds: Towards Embodied Teaching and Learning*. Dordrecht: Kluwer, 2004, p. 177.

28   Brook, Peter, *The Empty Space*. Victoria: Penguin Books Australia, 1968, p. 42.

29   Though C&T began in the 1980s as Collar and TIE, their website now states: 'Today, C&T stands for many more things: Citizenship & Technology, Computers & Theatre, Community & Training, Creativity & Technology, or, even Culture & Theory.' C&T website (found 23/07/2014), http://www.candt.org/about/what-does-c-t-stand-for/.

Chapter 1

1   Leonard Koren's *Which Aesthetics Do You Mean: Ten Definitions* suggests the dimensions of the problem; he gives the following titles for his definitions: Appearance, Style, Taste, Philosophy of art, Thesis or exegesis, Artistic, Beauty, Beautification, Cognitive mode, Language. Among his rough synonyms are adjectives and nouns, and nouns for

properties, actions, categories and faculties. I do not intend to follow his taxonomy, as I find that there are further overlapping ideas that are relevant to this discussion.

2 There is a '. . . non-reciprocal relationship between an audience and the actors in a drama. The audience may see and feel, but is powerless to act or communicate. The actors are enclosed in the action they are in. This is why attempts to include the audience in the space of a play are so peculiarly embarrassing and irritating.' A. S. Byatt, 'The Age of Becoming', *The Guardian*, Saturday 16/12/2006.

3 'Questions of ontology. (What is the nature of a work of art? What is the difference between the work and a copy? How do performances relate to the work?); Questions of phenomenology. (What is the nature of our reactions to a work of art? How do they affect us?); Questions about judgement. (What sort of judgement are judgements of value and critical interpretations of works of art? How do we support them by the reasons we offer?).' Sharpe, R. A., *Contemporary Aesthetics: A Philosophical Investigation*. Brighton: The Harvester Press, 1983, p. 12.

4 Jackson, Anthony, *Theatre, Education and the Making of Meanings: Art or Instrument*. Manchester: Manchester University Press, 2007.

5 Carey, John, *What Good Are the Arts*. London: Faber and Faber, 2005.

6 Carey, p. 7.

7 It is remarkable that there is no modern edition of *Aesthetica* in English, and it was only as recently as 2007 that it was translated in full from the original Latin into German (though Italian translations pre-date this). See Allen, Jennifer, *Frieze* 113, March 2008, https://www.frieze.com/issue/article/the_beautiful_science/ [accessed 29 September 2013].

8 See Davey, Nicholas, in David Cooper, *A Companion to Aesthetics*. Oxford: Blackwell, 1992, pp. 40–1.

9 Though according to John Kirwan, 'Kant's text inaugurates nothing', coming as the culmination of a century of enquiry into the nature of taste as a subjective response to objective phenomena, largely by

British philosophers such as Shaftesbury, Hume and Burke (1–5). Kant's intervention is to look for the non-subjective element in the response itself rather than in the object.

10 Kant, Immanuel, *Critique of Judgement*, trans. J. H. Bernard. New York: Dover Philosophical Classics, 2005 (1914).

11 Kant, p. 33.

12 Ibid., p. 34.

13 I owe this particular phrasing to Kirwan (Op. Cit., p. 12).

14 Givenness: that is, that they arrive unbidden and are not dependent on a conscious synthesis of sensible perception with the cognitive faculty, but provoke it unconsciously.

15 Hegel, G. W. F., *Introductory Lectures on Aesthetics*. London: Penguin, 1993.

16 In *Aesthetic Theory*. London: Athlone Press, 1997, and his essays in *Aesthetics and Politics*. London: Verso, 1980.

17 See Hanfling, Oswald, *Philosophical Aesthetics: An Introduction*. Milton Keynes: Open University Press, 1992, pp. 20–4.

18 Williams, Raymond, *Keywords*. London: Fontana, 1983, p. 32.

19 Bourdieu, Pierre, *Distinction: A Social Critique of the Judgement of Taste*. London: Routledge 1986.

20 'Everything takes place as if the "popular aesthetic" were based on the affirmation of form to function, or, one might say, on a refusal of the refusal which is the starting point of the high aesthetic', Bourdieu, ibid., p. 32.

21 Eagleton, Terry, *The Ideology of the Aesthetic*. Oxford: Blackwell Publishing, 1990.

22 Wolff, Janet, *The Aesthetics of Uncertainty*. Chichester: University of Colombia Press, 2008, pp. 12–17.

23 Wolff, p. 33.

24 Scarry, Elaine, *On Beauty and Being Just*. London: Gerald Duckworth and co., 2006, p. 61.

25 Armstrong, Isobel, *The Radical Aesthetic*. Oxford, Blackwell, 2000, pp. 2–3.

26   Heidegger, Martin, 'The Origin of The Work of Art', in David Farrel
     Krell (ed.), *Basic Writings*. London: Routledge, 2010; Apollon, Willy
     and Richard Feldstein (eds), *Lacan, Politics, Aesthetics*. New York: New
     York University Press, 1996; Derrida, Jacques, *Writing and Difference*.
     London: Routledge, 2001.

27   Rancière, Jacques, *The Politics of Aesthetics*. London: Continuum,
     2004, pp. 20–30.

28   Rancière, Jacques, *The Emancipated Spectator*. London: Verso, 2009.

29   Dewey, John, *Art as Experience*. London: Pedigree, 1980 (1935).

30   Dewey, pp. 1–19.

31   Ibid., pp. 36–59.

32   Ibid., p. 18.

33   Ibid., p. 108.

34   Armstrong, p. 162.

35   Alexander, Thomas, 'John Dewey', in David E. Cooper, *A Companion to
     Aesthetics*. Oxford, Blackwell, 1992, p. 119.

36   White, Gareth, *Audience Participation in Theatre: Aesthetics of the
     Invitation*. London: Palgrave MacMillan, 2013.

37   Boal, Augusto, *Aesthetics of the Oppressed* (2006), p. 18.

38   Landy, Robert and David Montgomerie, *Theatre for Change: Education,
     Social Action and Therapy*. London: Palgrave Macmillan, 2012, p. 67.

39   Landy and Montgomerie, pp. 48–51.

40   Ibid., p. 49.

41   Thompson, James, *Performance Affects*. London: Palgrave Macmillan,
     2009, p. 140.

42   Ibid., p. 131.

43   'In contemporary art, the shifting emphasis from artist to spectator (via
     participatory, collaborative and public modes of art) similarly challenges
     traditional notions of aesthetics as well as the notion of art as object
     and commodity. As in applied theatre, the distinctions between creator/
     performer/perceiver are blurred as performers and participants engage
     in creative dialogue through action/interaction.' Shaughnessy, Nicola,
     *Applying Performance: Live Art, Socially Engaged Theatre and Affective
     Performance*. London: Routledge, 2012, p. 11.

Interlude

1 The company has been in existence since 1976, firstly as 'Rainbow Drama Group', and since 2009 as 'Access All Areas', http://accessallareastheatre.org/ [accessed 13 January 2014]. Their community theatre group is known as 'Black Cab Theatre', while the seven performers in *Eye Queue Hear* are drawn from a core group of actors that make up their 'Performance Company'; other activity includes 'Spinning Yarn', a multi-sensory project for people with severe and profound disability.

2 White, G., interview with Nick Llewellyn Central School of Speech and Drama, London, 4 December 2013

3 Performing company: Paul Christian, Kazeem Esso, Dayo Koleosho, Imogen Roberts, Jolene Sampson, Lee Phillips, Jehrius Shepherd-Whyte; Video: http://www.youtube.com/watch?v=6wRop65bstE; Trailer: http://www.youtube.com/watch?v=6wRop65bstE [both accessed 13 January 2014].

Chapter 2

1 Saito, Yuriko, *Everyday Aesthetics*. Oxford: Oxford University Press, 2010, p. 211.

2 Shusterman, Richard, *Pragmatist Aesthetics*. Oxford: Rowman and Littlefield, 2000, pp. 34–61.

3 Armstrong, Isobel, *The Radical Aesthetic*. Oxford: Blackwell, 2000.

4 See Scarry, Elaine, *On Beauty and Being Just*. London: Gerald Duckworth and co., 2006; and Wolff, Janet, *The Aesthetics of Uncertainty*. Chichester: Colombia University Press, 2008.

5 Kant, Immanuel, *Critique of Judgement*, trans. J. H. Bernard. New York: Dover Philosophical Classics, 2005 (1914), p. 114.

6 Boal, Augusto, *The Aesthetics of the Oppressed*. London: Routledge, 2006, p. 18.

7   Kant, Immanuel, *Critique of Judgement*, p. 117.

8   Chignell, Andrew, 'The Problem of Particularity in Kant's Aesthetic Theory', in Paideia: Aesthetics and Philosophy of The Arts, online at http://www.bu.edu/wcp/Papers/Aest/AestChig.htm [accessed 25 April 2014].

9   Ibid., p. 144.

10 Ibid.

11 Ibid., p. 37.

12 Ibid., p. 30.

13 Kirwan, James, *The Aesthetic in Kant*. London: Continuum, 2004, p. 46.

14 Immanuel Kant, *Critique of Judgement*, p. 35.

15 Ibid., p. 36.

16 Saito, Yuriko, *Everyday Aesthetics*, p. 239.

17 Docherty, Thomas, *Aesthetic Democracy*. Stanford, CA: Stanford University Press, 2006, p. 66.

18 Berleant, Arnold, *The Aesthetic Field: A Phenomenology of Aesthetic Experience*. Christchurch, New Zealand: Cybereditions, 2000 (1970), p. 16.

19 Ibid., p. 29.

20 Ibid., pp. 50–1.

21 Ibid., p. 70.

22 Shusterman, op. cit., p. 40.

23 Ibid., p. 5.

24 Ibid., p. 6.

25 Shusterman's discussion of Moore and Derrida are in his chapter 'Organic Unity: Analysis and Deconstruction', ibid. pp. 62–83.

26 Ibid., p. 81.

27 See 'Postmodern Ethics and Art of Living', ibid., pp. 236–61.

28 Ibid., p. 263.

29 Johnson, Mark, *The Meaning of the Body: Aesthetics of Human Understanding*. Chicago: University of Chicago Press, 2007.

30 Metzinger, Thomas, *The Ego Tunnel*. New York: Basic Books 2009; Damasio, Antonio, *Descartes Error*. London: Vintage, 2006; Lakoff, George, *Women, Fire and Dangerous Things: What Categories Tell Us About the Mind*. Chicago: University of Chicago Press, 1987;

Gibson, James J., *An Ecological Approach to Visual Perception*.
New Jersey: Lawrence Ernbaum Associates, 1986; Merleau-Ponty,
Maurice, *Phenomenology of Perception*. Abingdon: Routledge, 2002.

31 Ibid., p. 273.

32 Ibid., p. 266.

33 Ibid., p. 268. In phenomenological terms, meaning is 'intentional': it
occurs when our attention is directed towards something.

34 Ibid., p. 273.

35 Ibid., p. 44.

36 Ibid., p. 47.

37 Ibid., p. 212.

38 'Dewey's seminal contribution to aesthetic theory – his Big Idea – which
is that *every fulfilled experience is individuated by a pervasive unifying
quality*.' Johnson in Bhatt, Ritu, *Rethinking Aesthetics: The Role of Body in
Design*. Abingdon: Routledge, 2013, p. 38.

39 'Even if we can experience such a quality, we certainly cannot describe it,
since any proffered description will involve discrimination of particular
qualities of the experience, and so will lose the unifying quality itself.'
Johnson in Bhatt, Ibid., p. 42.

40 Johnson 2007, op. cit. p. 71.

41 Metzinger, Thomas, *The Ego Tunnel: The Science of the Mind and the
Myth of the Self*. Philadelphia: Basic Books, p. 51.

Chapter 3

1 Isobel Armstrong, *The Radical Aesthetic*. Oxford: Blackwell, 2000, p. 19.

2 Janet Wolff, *The Aesthetics of Uncertainty*. New York: Columbia
University Press, 2008, pp. 24–8.

3 Michael Mangan, *Staging Ageing: Theatre, Performance and the Narrative
of Decline*. Bristol: Intellect, 2013, p. 43.

4 *Ballroominating* by Sian Stevenson, was performed in Canterbury in
July 2006 as a Practice Research project at the University of Kent.

5 Armstrong, p. 8.

6 Mike Featherstone and Mike Hepworth, 'Images of Aging: Cultural representations of later life', in Malcolm L. Johnson (ed.), *The Cambridge Handbook of Age and Ageing*. Cambridge: Cambridge University Press, 2005, pp. 354–92.

7 See Michael Murray, et al., 'Understanding and Transforming Ageing through the Arts', in Alan Walker (ed.), *The New Science of Ageing*. Bristol: Polity Press, 2014, in press.

8 Mangan, p. 43.

9 'On Ageing', Fevered Sleep, 27 September – 9 October 2010, programme note.

10 Mangan, p. 45.

11 Stevenson and Thompson are collaborating with researchers at the Sydney de Haan Research Centre for Arts and Health; Fevered Sleep worked with gerontologists and psychologists at the Centre for Research on Ageing, University of Southampton and drew upon the Mass Observation Project, based at the University of Sussex. See also accounts emerging from 'Ages and Stages' (Miriam Bernard, Jill Rezzano, Lucy Munro, David Amigoni, Michael Murray), an interdisciplinary project based at Keele University, exploring social representations of ageing, community identity and 'the impact of theatre on ideas about, and the experience of ageing'. The collaboration with the New Vic Theatre draws upon the extensive archives of the documentary theatre maker, Peter Cheeseman as well as ethnographic and practice-based research. See http://www.keele.ac.uk/agesandstages/.

12 Mangan, *Staging Ageing*, p. 5.

13 A palimpsest is a manuscript or parchment from which the writing or image has been partially erased (scraped or washed off but often still detectable) in order for the paper to be used again. I use the term palimpsestic to refer to the process of layering, where the traces of previous versions (the original stories) are part of the performance textures.

14 *The Diary of Anais Nin*, 1944–47, cited in 'On Ageing' programme note.

15 Armstrong, p. 2.

16 Joe Winston, *Beauty and Education*. London and New York: Routledge, 2011.

17 James Thompson, 'Performance of pain, performance of beauty'. *Research in Drama Education: The Journal of Applied Theatre and Performance* 11, 1 (2011): 47–57 (p. 57). See also Thompson's *Performance Affects: Applied Theatre and the End of Effect*. Basingstoke: Palgrave, 2011.

18 This terminology refers to James Thompson's critique of performance practice motivated by *effect*, as evident in the subtitle of his book (*Applied Theatre and the End of Effect*). He posits *affect* (and the importance of embracing pleasure and passion) as the basis for a new political-aesthetic performance practice.

19 I refer here to my experience working with autistic children on an AHRC -project, Imagining Autism, and publications arising from this work exploring what I have referred to as a 'neurodivergent aesthetic.' See, for example, 'Imagining Otherwise; Autism, Neuroaesthetics and Contemporary Performance', in Carina Bartleet and Kirsten Shepherd-Barr (eds), *Interdisciplinary Science Reviews*, Special Edition: 'Experiments in Theatre: New Directions in Science and Performance', December 2013, pp. 321–34. See also *Applying Performance: Live Art, Socially Engaged Theatre and Affective Practice*. Basingstoke: Palgrave, 2012, for discussion of affect and aesthetics in a range of case studies in community, educational and social contexts.

20 Interview with author, 23 December 2013.

21 Wolff, p. 13.

22 Ibid.

23 John Lutterbie, 'The State of the (Inter) Discipline: Time-Based Aesthetics and Cognitive Science', unpublished paper for the *American Society for Theatre Research Annual Conference*, Dallas, November 2013.

24 See John O'Mahoney's Review of the production at the Barbican Theatre, London, 19 April 2011, 'Christ, what's that smell?' www.theguardian. com/stage/2011/apr/19/romeo-castellucci-concept-face-son [accessed 21 November 2013].

25 See Vilayanur Ramachandran, *The Tell Tale Brain: A Neuroscientist's Quest for What Makes us Human*. New York and London: W. W. Norton, 2011.

26 Lutterbie, 'The State of the (Inter) Discipline'.

27 Ibid.

28 Ibid.

29 Fischer-Lichte, Erika, *The Transformative Power of Performance*. London and New York: Routledge, 2008, p. 150.

30 Ibid., p. 144.

31 Jane Willis, 'A Shift to Sharing Values', *Arts Professional*, http://www.webmaster@artsprofessional.co.uk [accessed 12 April 2014].

32 Fischer-Lichte, p. 150.

33 Wolff, p. 28.

34 Steven Connor, 'Isobel Armstrong's Material Imagination', Unpublished paper for 'Radical Aesthetics: the work of Isobel Armstrong', Institute for English Studies, 21 June 2002, http//www.stevenconnor.com/isobel [accessed 11 November 2013].

35 Ibid.

36 Ibid.

37 Wolff, p. 28.

38 Sian Stevenson, interview with author, 23 December 2013.

39 Evaluation of the work of StevensonThompson is being undertaken by Trish Vella-Burrows, registered nurse and arts and health researcher (specialist in music in dementia care), and Lian Wilson, expressive dance therapist and arts and health research assistant, from the Sidney De Haan Research Centre for Arts and Health, Canterbury Christ Church University. A range of methods are being developed to include the 'Prosper Involvement Scale' and the 'Prosper Well Being' scale.

40 *More Please* was performed at the Gulbenkian Theatre Canterbury and the Theatre Royal in Margate in November 2013 as part of a double bill with *Moving on Moving*, a reworking of a previous production. *Moving On Moving* was first premiered as part of the Canterbury Festival. See www.stevensonthompson.com.

41 Armstrong, p. 2.

42 Ibid.

43 Ibid., pp. 16–17. Armstrong refers to Gillian Rose, *The Broken Middle: Out of Our Ancient Society.* Oxford: Blackwell, 1992.

44 Ibid., p. 18.

45 Evelyn Tribble and John Sutton, 'Cognitive Ecology as a Framework for Shakespearean Studies', unpublished paper presented to American Society for Theatre Research, November, 2013, Dallas. See www.johnsutton.net/Tribble [accessed 1 November 2013].

46 This is discussed in my introductory chapter to *Affective Performance and Cognitive Science:* Body, Brain and Being. London: Methuen, 2013.

47 Willis, 'A Shift to Sharing Values'.

48 In her professional theatre career, extending over 20 years, Sian Stevenson has worked as a freelance artist, performing, directing and choreographing. Companies she has worked with include The Hairy Marys, Gloria Theatre Co, Shared Experience, Plain Clothes, English Touring Opera, The Guildhall and Grange Opera. For her own company, Scratch Arts, she produced numerous community and education based projects. She is a long-term collaborator with Bobby Baker and Daily Life Ltd and lectures in Drama at The University of Kent.

49 Jayne Thompson is a lecturer in Drama at the University Kent and the subject specialist for the Faculty of Humanities. She has a range of experience in theatre and performance, and her specific areas of interest are naturalist representation, verbatim theatre, site related performance, and applied drama. Jayne has worked as a performer and facilitator in a number of different community and educational contexts and participated in work created by Rosemary Lee and Wendy Huston. In her role as subject specialist she works closely with local schools developing arts-based projects.

50 Interview with author, 23 December 2013.

51 Names have been changed.

52 The Veleta waltz, originally written by Arthur Morris in 1900, is often cited as the originating 'sequence' dance, eventually referred to as 'Old time' and 'New Vogue' (a style originating in Australia)

later on. Consisting of a 16-bar waltz, couples begin by holding hands and dance in relation to each other in a series of exchanges apart and together.

53 The company collaborate with multi-media specialists 'Butch Auntie'. http://www.butchauntie.com.

54 Interview with Sian Stevenson and Jayne Thompson, 23 December 2013.

55 Armstrong, pp. 39–40.

56 Ibid.

57 See D. W. Winnicott, *Playing and Reality*. Harmondsworth: Penguin, 1971.

58 Doreen Massey, 'Landscape/Space/Politics: an essay', http://www. thefutureoflandscape.wordpress.com [accessed 30 October 2013].

59 Armstrong, p. 19.

60 See Shaughnessy, *Affective Performance and Cognitive Science*.

61 Tribble and Sutton, 'Cognitive Ecology'.

62 See Helen Nicholson, *Applied Drama: The Gift of Theatre*. Basingstoke: Palgrave, 2005.

63 Armstrong, p. 13.

64 See www.butchauntie.com.

65 *Engineers of the Imagination* is the title of the *Welfare State Handbook*, by Baz Kershaw and Tony Coult. London: Methuen, 1983.

66 Amelia Jones, 'Preface', in Deidre Reynolds and Matthew Reason (eds), *Kinesthetic Empathy in Creative and Cultural Practices*. Bristol: Intellect, 2011.

67 Ibid., p. 12.

68 *Psychology Dictionary*, http://www.psychologydictionary.org/ entrainment [accessed 12 November 2012]

69 Stevenson, Interview with author, 23 December 2013.

70 Nicholas Bourriaud, *Relational Aesthetics*. France: Les Presse Du Reel, 2002, p. 113.

71 The evaluative methods consisted of focus group discussions (recorded and transcribed in July 2013 and September 2013) in which participants reflect on process; interview questions and consultations with the team; observations of rehearsals, filmed footage and performances using

two coding measures which focus on well-being and engagement.
The researchers subsequently developed a new evaluative tool
(Prosper Involvement Scale), which uses a five-point scale to measure
commitment, energy, creativity and embodiment, and verbal and
non-verbal communication, with one being very low and five being
very high. The scale was developed over the course of the project and
piloted over the course of five of the creative workshops, rehearsals and a
performance undertaken by the Moving Memory Company.

72 Wolff, p. 50.

73 See James Thompson and Richard Schechner, 'Why Social Theatre?'.
TDR: The Drama Review 48, 3 (2004): 1–16.

74 Gregory Minissale, *The Psychology of Contemporary Art*. Cambridge:
Cambridge University Press, 2013, p. 346.

75 Ibid., p. 346.

76 Ibid., p. 335.

77 Ibid., p. 333.

78 Fevered Sleep, *On Ageing* Young Vic Theatre, 27 September–10
October 2010.

79 Rebecca Johnson, unpublished report: 'On Ageing Case Study:
Evaluation Report', Centre for the Research on Ageing, University of
Southampton, June 2011, p. 23.

80 Ibid., p. 27.

81 Ibid., p. 241.

82 Ibid., p. 46.

83 Ibid., p. 5.

84 Ibid., p. 246.

85 Programme note, *On Ageing*.

86 Adrian Kear, 'Cooking Time with Gertrude Stein'. *Performance Research*
4, 1 (1999): 44–55 (p. 44).

87 Johnson, *On Ageing*.

88 See Shannon Jackson, *Social Works: Performing Art, Supporting Publics*.
London and New York, Routledge, 2011.

89 Ibid., p. 242. In her discussion of children performing theatre for adults
Jackson refers to Josse De Pauw's *Ubung*, Rimini Protokoll's *Airport Kids*,

Tino Sehgal's museum-based pieces, *The Progress* and *This Success or This Failure*, described as 'situations' in which children interact with visitors.

90 *On Ageing* script (2010).

91 Jackson, p. 247.

92 See Reynolds and Reason, *Kinesthetic Empathy.*

93 Jackson, *Social Works,* p. 6 citing Vivian Sobchack, 'choreography for One, Two and Three Legs (A Phenomenononological Meditation in Movements)'. *Topoi* 24 (Spring 2005): 55–66.

94 Ibid.

95 Fevered Sleep, *Men and Girls Dance.* Pilot project, The Point, Eastleigh, August 2013.

96 Jimmy Savile was a British media celebrity, a DJ and television presenter, charity fundraiser and philanthropist who was highly respected until his death in 2011. During 2012, a series of allegations by victims of sexual abuse, exposed Savile as a serial sexual offender, with over 400 testimonies from children and women. Widespread media coverage of the Savile controversy and an ensuing investigation led to a series of reports, corroborating the evidence against Savile. See, for example *Giving Victims a Voice*, published by the UK's National Society for the Prevention of Cruelty to Children (NSPCC).

97 Harradine, 'Men and Girls Dance', http://www.Feveredsleep.co.uk [accessed 30 October 2013]

98 Ibid.

99 Harradine, interview with author, 20 November 2013. For further information on the project see www.feveredsleep.co.uk

100 Jackson, p. 245.

101 Harradine, *Men and Girls Dance.*

102 Interview with author, 20 November 2013.

103 Ibid.

104 Jackson, p. 12.

105 Tribble and Sutton, 'Cognitive Ecology'.

106 Harradine, http://www.feveredsleep.co.uk [accessed 21 November 2013]

107 Lutterbie, 'The state of the (inter) discipline'.

108 Jackson, p. 42.

Chapter 4

1   See the Centre for Artistic Activism webpage http://www. artisticactivism.org/2009/03/camus/ [accessed 1 February 2013].

2   Augusto Boal, *The Aesthetics of the Oppressed*. London and New York: Routledge, 2006, p. 38.

3   This is one of the many references to beauty on audience feedback slips in relation to the production *I Stand Corrected*, Artscape, Cape Town and Ovalhouse Theatres, 2012.

4   See the e-debate by Kramer, Chamberlain, McNamara, et al., 'Applied Theatre/Drama: an e-debate in 2004. *Research in Drama Education* 11, 1 (February 2004): 90–5.

5   In the Rastafarian African-Caribbean linguistic sensibility that I draw on many words in the English language are played with to reveal their true meaning. The use of the word politricks in place of politics highlights that politics is a means of playing power games, it is often deceptive, slippery and tricky to pin down. Other examples include saying overstanding rather than understanding and downpressor instead of op(up)ppressor.

6   The 'umbrella' is a phrase used in Tim Prentki and Sheila Preston (eds), *The Applied Theatre Reader*. London and New York: Routledge, 2009, p. 9.

7   See http://www.pan-arts.net/pages/myanmar-burma.html for more information on the ongoing work in Burma and elsewhere.

8   See Mojisola Adebayo, John Martin and Manisha Mehta, *The Theatre for Development Handbook*. London: Pan Intercultural Arts, 2011. The book is only available to order online through www.pan-arts.net. All proceeds go to VIDYA Educational and Charitable Trust, India.

9   Judith Ackroyd, 'Applied Theatre an Exclusionary Discourse?', 2007, p. 3. Accessed at http://www.griffith.edu.au/__data/assets/pdf_file/0005/52889/01-ackroyd-final.pdf [accessed 7 April 2014].

10 Jan Cohen-Cruz, *Engaging Performance: Theatre as Call and Response*. London and New York: Routledge, 2010, p. 6.

11 See http://www.headlinestheatre.com/theatre_for_living.htm on Power Plays.

12 Stella Barnes quoted in Frances Rifkin, *The Ethics of Participatory Theatre in Higher Education: A Framework for Learning and Teaching*. London: Palatine, 2010, p. 7.

13 Ackroyd, 2007, p. 7.

14 VIDYA is an NGO whose vision is: 'To be a significant force of change for India's less privileged'; see http://www.vidya-india.org/who-we-are. htm [accessed 29 July 2014].

15 See http://www.graeae.org/ for more on Graeae Theatre Company.

16 Victor Ukaegbu, 'The Problem with Definitions', in Judith Ackroyd and Jonathan Neelands (eds), *Drama Research*, vol. 3, 2004.

17 See http://www.thetriangleproject.org/ for more.

18 For the original version of the game see http://www.youtube.com/ watch?v=B0r9MmTgsuk.

19 There are clips of the show online as well as interviews with Mamela and I. Feel free to look to get a sense of the show. See http://www.vimeo. com/58992789 and http://www.vimeo.com/80282830.

20 Boal 2006, p. 29.

21 Thompson 2009, p. 140.

22 Roger Scruton, *Beauty*. Oxford: Oxford University Press, 2009, p. 22.

23 Scruton, p. 23.

24 I first learnt about Namatjira through the performance of the same name by Big Hart Theatre Company from Australia on Friday 29 November 2013 in the Purcell Room at the Southbank Centre London. *Namatjira* was led by Trevor Jamieson and featured members of Albert Namatjira's family.

25 Joe Winston, *Beauty and Education*. London and New York: Routledge, 2011, p. 77.

26 John Carey, *What Good Are the Arts?* Oxford: Oxford University Press, 2006, p. 77.

27 See my website http://www.mojisolaadebayo.co.uk/2012/09/19/moj-bloj-in-the-beginning/.

28 Umberto Eco, *On Beauty: A History of A Western Idea*. London: MacLehose Press, 2010, p. 45.

29 Naomi Wolf, *The Beauty Myth*. London: Vintage, 1991, p. 94.

30 Wolf, p. 18.

31 Ibid., p. 86.

32 In Sarah Nuttall (ed.), *Beautiful Ugly: African and Diaspora Aesthetics*. Durham and London: Duke University Press, 2006, p. 93.

33 The words in the brackets are illegible to my eye. *Enkosi* means 'thank you' in Xhosa.

34 James Thompson, *Performance Affects: Applied Theatre and the End of Effect*. Basingstoke: Palgrave Macmillan, 2009, p. 152.

35 Eco, p. 102.

36 Ibid., p. 133.

37 Ibid., p. 144.

38 Sianne Ngai, *Ugly Feelings*. Cambridge and London: Harvard University Press, 2005, p. 354.

39 Ngai, p. 354.

40 Ibid., p. 334.

41 Ibid., p. 335.

42 Eco, p. 238.

43 Ibid., p. 53.

44 Boal, 2006, p. 19.

45 Elaine Scarry, *On Beauty and Being Just*. London: Duckworth, 2006, pp. 28–9.

46 Scarry, p. 30.

47 Ibid., p. 3.

48 Nuttall, pp. 8, 9.

49 Winston, p. 84.

50 Ibid., pp. 51–2.

51 Scarry, pp. 86, 99, 107.

52 Ibid., p. 108.

53 Joshua Sobol, *Ghetto*. London: Nick Hern Books, 1989.

54 Daniel Herwitz, *Aesthetics: Key Concepts in Philosophy*. Continuum: London and New York, 2008, pp. 24–5.

55 Scarry, p. 109.

56 James Thompson, *Performance Affects: Applied Theatre and the End of Effect*. Basingstoke: Palgrave Macmillan, 2009, p. 146.

57   Boal 2006, p. 38.

58   Bundestag, Berlin, Germany, 1 February 2013.

59   See the Centre for Artistic Activism webpage http://www. artisticactivism.org/2009/03/camus/ [accessed 1 February 2013].

Chapter 5

1   The interviewees prefer to remain anonymous. They are therefore referred to as the Cambodian, European or French circus or theatre director.

2   Appadurai, Arjun, 'Global ethnoscapes: Notes and Queries for a Transnational Anthropology', in Richard Fox (ed.), *Recapturing Anthropology*. Santa Fe, New Mexico: School of American Research Press, 1991, p. 192.

3   Levinson, Jerrald, *The Oxford Handbook of Aesthetics*. Oxford: Oxford University Press, 2003, pp. 3–4.

4   Ibid.

5   Mills, C. Wright, *Power, Politics and People*. New York: Oxford University Press, 1963 in Melossi, Dario, 'The Cultural Embeddedness of Social Control'. *Theoretical Criminology* 5, 4 (2001): 404–24.

6   Appadurai, Arjun, p. 192.

7   Smith, Anthony, 'Culture, Community and Territory'. *International Affairs* 72, 3 (1996): 445–58.

8   Smith, Anthony, 1981, quoted in Hughes, Caroline, *Dependent Communities. Aid and Politics in Cambodia and East Timor*. Ithaca: Cornell Southeast Asia Program, 2009, p. 4.

9   Smith, p. 454.

10   Ibid.

11   Smith, Anthony, *Myths and Memories of the Nation*. New York: Oxford University Press, 1999, pp. 149–59.

12   Hirsch, Marianne, *The Generation of Postmemory: Visual Culture after the Holocaust*. New York: Colombia University Press, 2012, p. 6.

13 Richmond, Oliver P. and Franks, Jason, 'Liberal Hubris? Virtual Peace in Cambodia'. *Security Dialogue* 38, 1 (2007): 27.

14 French theatre director, interview with Kirsten Sadeghi-Yekta, Battambang, 22 February 2010.

15 Nee, Meas and McCallum, Wayne, *Roads to Development. Insights from Sre Ambel District, Southwest Cambodia.* American Friends Service Committee: Graphic Roots, 2009, pp. 21–3.

16 French, Lindsay, 'Displaced Lives: Stories of Life and Culture from the Khmer in Site II, Thailand', in IRC Oral History Project, Bangkok: Craftsman Press, 1990, p. 5.

17 Hirsch, Marianne, p. 6.

18 DC-Cam staff member, interview with Kirsten Sadeghi-Yekta, Phnom Penh, 12 March 2010.

19 Hirsch, p. 6.

20 Worldbank 2012.

21 DC-Cam 2012.

22 Hawkes, Martine, 'Transmitting Genocide: Genocide and Art' [Online] *M/C Journal* 9, 1 (2006). Available at: http://journal.media-culture.org. au/0603/09-hawkes.php [accessed 15 September 2013].

23 *Therevada* (Teaching of the Elders) Buddhism is the strongest religion in Cambodia. Its definite goal is *nirvana*, exterminating all suffering and longing to reach the ultimate stage of reincarnation.

24 Stanton, Gregory, *Blue Scarves and Yellow Stars: Classification and Symbolization in the Cambodian Genocide* [Online] lecture notes distributed in Faulds lecture at Warren Wilson College, Swannanoa, North Carolina, March 1987, p. 4. Available at: http://www. genocidewatch.org/images/AboutGen89BlueScarvesandYellowStars.pdf [accessed 15 September 2013].

25 Ibid.

26 See for example Burridge, Stephanie and Fred Frumberg, *Beyond the Apsara: Celebrating Dance in Cambodia.* Delhi: Routledge India, 2010.

27 Thompson, James, *Digging up Stories: Applied Theatre, Performance and War.* Manchester: Manchester University Press, 2005, pp. 5–6.

28 Ibid.

29 Thompson, James, in Anheier, Helmut and Raj Isar, Yudhishthir (eds), *Conflicts and Tensions. The Cultures and Globalization Series*. London: SAGE, 2007, p. 302.

30 Smith, p. 455.

31 Hughes, Caroline, *Dependent Communities. Aid and Politics in Cambodia and East Timor*. Ithaca: Cornell Southeast Asia Program, 2009, p. 1.

32 CCC, 2012.

33 PPS staff member, interview with Kirsten Sadeghi-Yekta, Phnom Penh, 12 March 2010.

34 Documentation Centre Cambodia, located in Phnom Penh, has a slightly different take on this: remembrance in the form of archives plays a significant role in nurturing elements essential for Cambodia's recovery, that is, accountability, truth and memory. See DC-Cam.org.

35 Thompson, James, *Performance affects. Applied Theatre and the End of Effect*. London: Palgrave Macmillan, 2009, p. 7.

36 Ibid., p. 6.

37 Director DC Cam, interview with Kirsten Sadeghi-Yekta, Phnom Penh, 12 March 2010.

38 Hélène Cixous is the University of Paris 8's emeritus professor and *Le Théâtre du Soleil*'s playwright.

39 Cixous, Helen, 'Le Théâtre se Tenant Responsible', in Phay–Vakalis, S. and Bayard, P. (eds), *Cambodge, Mémoire de l'Extrême*. Paris: Université Paris 8, 2011, p. 26.

40 Thompson, Ashley and Prenowitz, Éric, 'Un Théâtre Épique non Aligné', in Soko Phay–Vakalis and Pierre Bayard (eds), *Cambodge, Mémoire de l'Extrême*. Paris: Université Paris 8, 2011, p. 24.

41 Ibid.

42 Cambodian directors, interview with Kirsten Sadeghi-Yekta, Battambang, 22 February 2010.

43 Winston, Joe, *Beauty and Education*. London: Routledge, 2010, p. 26.

44 Thompson, Ashley and Prenowitz, Éric, pp. 24–5.

45 French director, interview with Kirsten Sadeghi-Yekta, Battambang, 22 February 2010.

46 European theatre director, interview with Kirsten Sadeghi-Yekta, Phnom Penh, 13 March 2010.

47 Thompson, James, 'From the Stocks to the Stage', in Michael Balfour (ed.), *Theatre in Prison: Theory and Practice*. Bristol: Intellect, 2004, pp. 57–76.

48 Ahmed, Jamil, 'Wishing for a World without "Theatre for Development": Demystifying the Case of Bangladesh'. *Research in Drama Education* 7, 2 (2002): 207–19.

49 Botum, interview with Kirsten Sadeghi-Yekta, Battambang, 4 March 2010.

50 Buncombe, Andrew, 'Cambodia puts the cremation site of Pol Pot on "historic" tourist trail', *The Independent,* 11 March 2010.

51 Ray, Nick and Robinson, Daniel, *Cambodia*. Victoria: Lonely Planet Publications Pty Ltd, 2008, p. 243.

Chapter 6

1 'Gacaca was first launched in June 2002. Following a two-and-a-half year pilot phase, it was rolled out nationwide in January 2005, and trials of lower-level perpetrators finally got under way throughout the country in July 2006. Most of those trials were completed by the end of 2007, partly as a result of an increase in gacaca benches hearing cases concurrently. In late 2008, gacaca courts began hearing cases involving higher-level suspects (including those accused of rape). In 2009, the government opened a new information-gathering phase. After trials had largely ended in August 2010, gacaca continued hearing some appeals. Gacaca officially closed in June 2012 having tried more than 1.9 million cases involving just over a million suspects. Most remarkably, the vast majority of those trials occurred in a four-year period–from mid-2006 to mid-2010' (Lars Waldorf, in email correspondence, August 2013).

2 Fujii, Lee Ann, *Killing Neighbors: Webs of Violence in Rwanda*. New York: Cornell University Press, 2009, p. 12.

3   The use of the phrase theatre for protection was first used for this
     essay at the conference 'Politics of the Applied, Theatre and Art as
     Intervention' between 31 January and 1 February 2014, Freie Universitat,
     Berlin.

4   Bert Ingelaere uses the terms numeric legibility, magic syllogisms
     and law talk in his article 'From Model To Practice. Researching and
     Representing Rwanda's "Modernised Gacaca Courts"'. *Critique of
     Anthropology* 32, 4 (2012): 388–414.

5   Miles, Malcolm, *Herbert Marcuse: An Aesthetics of Liberation*. London:
     Pluto Press, 2012.

6   Miles, p. 131.

7   An important distinction between the ICTR and the gacaca was the
     temporal jurisdiction: gacaca addressed genocide crimes between
     1 October 1990 and 31 December 1994, whereas the ICTR addressed
     crimes between 1 January and 31 December 1994. Although the
     Rwandan government was one of the initiators for the ICTR, the
     tribunal was voted against in the end because it did not include the
     period between 1990 and 1993 as inclusive of the genocide. Further, it
     did not allow the death penalty and was located outside Rwanda.

8   Ananda, Breed, *Performing the Nation: Genocide, Justice, Reconciliation*.
     Chicago: Seagull Press, 2014.

9   Rusagara, Frank K., '*Gacaca*: Rwanda's truth and reconciliation
     authority', *The New Times*, 16 May 2005, http://allafrica.com/
     stories/200505170174.html.

10 Butler, Judith, 'Extracts from *Gender as Performance: An Interview with
     Judith Butler*'. Interview by Peter Osborne and Lynne Segal, London,
     1993. Available at: http://www.theory.org.uk/but-int1.htm [accessed on
     23 April 2014].

11 *Abiyunze* is Kinyarwanda for 'united'.

12 The current government of Rwanda claims that there is only one culture,
     with the same dances and language. However, several government
     officials have differentiated between dances as being regional and loosely
     connected to divisions between Tutsi, Hutu and Twa. In this way, dances
     of reconciliation may actually have stronger political affiliations.

13 For the full text of Organic Law No. 16/2004 of 19/6/2004, Article 34, see Government of Rwanda (2004).

14 The *gacaca* trial of Emmanuel was held on 4 August 2005, which I attended. This description is adapted from Ananda Breed (2007, pp. 306–12).

15 *Interahamwe* (youth militia) is Kinyarwanda for 'we who stand/work/ fight/attack together'. Mahmood Mamdani (2001) states that the *interahamwe* was formed as a youth organization in 1990 and was eventually trained to execute the genocide as death squads largely responsible for the mass killings of 1994.

16 Uvin, Peter, 'The Introduction of a Modernised Gacaca for Judging Suspects of Participation in the Genocide and the Massacres of 1994 in Rwanda'. Unpublished discussion paper prepared for the Belgian Secretary of State for Development Cooperation, 2000. p. 7.

17 The Norwegian Helsinki Committee (NHC), *Prosecuting Genocide in Rwanda: The Gacaca System and the International Criminal Tribunal for Rwanda. Report II/2002*. Oslo: NHC, p. 22.

18 Ministry of Justice, *Evaluation Report for 'Gacaca Play'*. Kigali, Rwanda, 16 September 2004.

19 The information based on the Gacaca play and the use of theatre for the sensitisation and mobilisation of gacaca is adapted from empirical research by Ananda Breed (2014, pp. 99–100).

20 Interview with attendee of Gacaca Court of Appeal, Nyarugenge District, Kigali. 14 April 2010.

21 Ibid.

22 For more information about court proceedings and the analysis of gacaca in regard to 'scripting' see: Breed, Ananda, 'Discordant Narratives in Rwanda's Gacaca Courts', in Maddalena Campioni and Patrick Noack (eds), *Rwanda Fast Forward: Social, Economic, Military and Reconciliation Prospects*. Hampshire: Palgrave, 2012, pp. 36–7.

23 Paul Kagame H. E, Speech at the Official Closing of Gacaca Courts, available at http://www.presidency.gov.rw/speeches/654-speech-by-he-paul-kagame-president-of-the-republic-of-rwanda-at-the-official-closing-of-gacaca-courts, Rwanda, 18 June 2012.

24 Ibid.

25 Charles Villa-Vicencio. *Walk with Us and Listen: Political Reconciliation in Africa*. Washington, DC: Georgetown University Press, 2009, p. 138.

26 The information based on the use of grassroots associations see Ananda Breed (2014, p. 133).

Chapter 7

1   de Certeau, Michel, *The Practice of Everyday Life*. Berkeley: University of California Press, 1984.

2   Brook, Peter, *The Empty Space*. Victoria: Penguin Books Australia Ltd., 1968.

3   Appadurai, Arjun, *Modernity at Large: Cultural Dimensions of Globalization*. Minneapolis, MN: University of Minnesota Press, 1996.

4   Guattari describes machine and the machinic stating: 'Machines, in the widest sense, that is, not just technical machines but theoretical, social, esthetic, etc., machines, never function in isolation, but by aggregates or assemblages. A technical machine, for example, in a factory, interacts with a social machine, a training machine, a research machine, a commercial machine, etc.' (Guattari, Felix, *The Anti Oedipus Papers*. Los Angeles: Semiotext (E), 2006, p. 418)

5   Savage, Glenn and Hickey-Moody, Anna, 'Global Flows as Gendered Cultural Pedagogies: Learning Gangsta in the "Durty South"'. *Critical Studies in Education* 51, 3 (2010): 77.

6   Anderson, Benedict, *Imagined Communities: Reflections on the Origin and Spread of Nationalism*. New York: Verso, 1983.

7   Appadurai, p. 31.

8   Appadurai 2000, p. 95.

9   Anderson, Benedict, *Imagined Communities: Reflections on the Origin and Spread of Nationalism*. New York: Verso, 1983, p. 8.

10 Appadurai, p. 31.

11 Habermas, Jürgen, *The Structural Transformation of the Public Sphere: An Inquiry into a Category of Bourgeois Society*. Cambridge: Polity Press, 1962.

12 Brook, p. 108.

13 Rodgers, Richard and Oscar Hammerstein, 'My Favourite Things', *The Sound of Music*, Twentieth Century Fox, 1965.

14 Modern Foreign Languages.

15 C&T 2014: personal communication.

16 Brook, p. 78.

17 I refer to Second Life.

18 Brook, p. 98.

19 Ibid., p. 86.

20 Ibid., p. 73.

21 Ibid., p. 80.

22 Ibid., p. 74.

23 Ibid.

24 Brook, p. 20.

25 See http://www.globalrockchallenge.com/Article/140/About/ [accessed 2 April 2014].

26 Rock Eisteddfod Challenge, 2011: online NP, Emphasis added.

27 Habermas, p. 4.

28 Rock Eisteddfod Challenge, 2011: online NP, Emphasis added,.

29 Habermas, p. 99.

30 Berlant, Lauren, *The Queen of America Goes to Washington City: Essays on Sex and Citizenship*. Durham, NC: Duke University Press, 1997.

31 Warner, Michael, 'The Mass Public and the Mass Subject', in Craig Calhoun (ed.), *Habermas and the Public Sphere. Cambridge*, MA: MIT Press, 1992; Warner, Michael 'Publics and Counterpublics'. *Public Culture* 14, 1 (2002): 49–90.

32 Riley, Sarah, Morey, Yvonne, and Griffin, Christine, 'The 'Pleasure Citizen': Analysing Partying as a Form of Social and Political Participation'. *Young* 18, 1 (2010): 33–54.

33 See Hickey-Moody, Anna, *Youth, Arts and Education*. Routledge: London, 2012.

34 Richardson, Rene, *From Uncle Tom to Gangsta: Black Masculinity and the U.S. South*. Athens, GA: University of Georgia Press, 2007, p. 237.

35 Willis, Paul, *Common Culture*. Open University Press: Milton Keynes, 1990; *The Ethnographic Imagination*. Polity: Cambridge, 2000.

36 Williams, Raymond, 'Culture is Ordinary', in Norman Mackenzie (ed.), *Conviction*. London: McGibbon and Kee, 1958; reprinted in John Higgins (ed.), *The Raymond Williams Reader*. Oxford: Blackwell, 2001; *Culture and Society*. New York: Columbia University Press; first published 1958; London: Chatto and Windus, 1963; *The Long Revolution*. Harmondsworth: Penguin; first published 1961; London: Chatto and Windus, 1965; *Communications*. New York: Barnes and Noble, 1966.

37 Hoggart, Richard, *The Uses of Literacy: Aspects of Working-Class Life With Special Reference to Publications and Entertainments*. Harmondsworth: Penguin, 1957.

38 Willis, Paul, *Learning to Labour*. Aldershot: Gower, 1977.

39 Hartley, John, *The Uses of Digital Literacy*. St. Lucia: Queensland University, 2009, p. 1.

40 Bruns, Axel, *Blogs, Wikipedia, Second Life and Beyond: From Production to Produsage*. New York: Peter Lang, 2008.

41 te Riele, Kitty, 'Youth "At Risk": Further Marginalizing the Marginalised?' *Journal of Education Policy* 21, 2 (2006): 129–45.

42 Kelly, Peter, 'Governing Individualised Risk Biographies: New Class Intellectuals and the Problem of Youth at Risk'. *British Journal of the Sociology of Education* 28, 1 (2001): 39–53, and Tait, Gordon, 'Shaping the "At-Risk Youth": Risk, Governmentality and the Finn Report'. *Discourse* 16, 1 (1995): 123–34.

Chapter 8

1 Prendergast, Monica and Saxton, Juliana, *Applied Theatre*. Bristol, UK: Intellect, 2009, pp. 191–2.

2 Boal, Augusto, *The Aesthetics of the Oppressed*. New York: Routledge, 2006, p. 18.

3 Glissant, Edouard, *Poetics of Relation*. Ann Arbor: University of Michigan Press 1997, pp. 150–1.

4 Nettleford, Rex, *Jamaica in Independence: Essays on the Early Years*. Kingston, Jamaica: Heinemann Caribbean, 1989, p. 126.

5 Nettleford, Rex in Heap, Brian (ed.), *Caribbean Quarterly: The IDIERI Papers* 53. 1. 2007, p. 3.

6 Neelands, Jonothan, *Creating Democratic Citizenship through Drama Education: The Writings of Jonothan Neelands.* Ed. Peter O'Connor. Stoke on Trent: Trentham, 2010, p. xviii.

7 Heathcote, Dorothy, *Collected Writings on Drama and Education.* Eds. Liz Johnson and Cecily O'Neill. Evanston: Northwestern, 1991, p. 169.

8 Neelands, p. xix.

9 Heathcote, p. 169.

10 Styslinger, Mary E., 'Relations of Power and Drama in Education: The Teacher and Foucault'. *Journal of Educational Thought* 34, 2 (2000): 195.

11 Freire, Paulo. *Pedagogy of the Oppressed.* UK: Penguin Books, 1972.

12 Heap, Brian, 'New Reals: Drama in Education as a Process of Realization'. Unpublished Diss. U of Newcastle upon Tyne, 1984.

13 Cahill, Helen, 'Re-thinking the fiction-reality boundary: investigating the use of drama in HIV prevention projects in Vietnam'. *Research in Drama Education: The Journal of Applied Theatre and Performance* 15, 2 (2010): 155–74.

14 A detailed account of this work in Zambia is given in 'Process Drama: An Investigation into the Paradox of Negotiating Fictional Contexts for Meaningful Learning.' Unpublished Doctoral Thesis: University of the West Indies, Mona, Jamaica, 2011.

15 Cahill, p. 155.

16 Styslinger, Mary E., 'Relations of Power and Drama in Education: The Teacher and Foucault'. *Journal of Educational Thought* 34, 2 (2000): 196.

17 Bowell, Pamela and Brian Heap, 'Drama is not a Dirty Word: Past Achievements, Present Concerns, Alternative Futures'. *Research in Drama Education* 15, 4 (2010): 587.

18 Cahill, p. 172.

19 Ibid.

20 Britzman, Deborah P., *Practice Makes Practice: A Critical Study of Learning to Teach.* New York: State University of New York Press, 2003, p. 221.

21 Dorothy Heathcote, Personal written communication with the author. 28 June 2008.

22 Bowell, Pamela and Brian Heap, 'Drama on the Run: A prelude to mapping the practice of process drama'. *Journal of Aesthetic Education* 39, 4 (2005): 58–69.

23 Adapted from Bowell and Heap, ibid.

24 Neelands, Jonothan, 'Three Theatres Waiting: Architectural Space and Performance Traditions', in *The Research of Practice, The Practice of Research*. Victoria: IDEA Publications, 1998, p. 149.

25 Bowell, p. 66.

26 Freire.

27 Goffman, Erving, *Frame Analysis: An Essay on the Organization of Experience*. Cambridge, MA: Harvard University Press, 1974.

28 Barthes, Roland, *Critical Essays*. Evanston: Northwestern University Press, 1972.

29 Teale, Polly, *After Mrs. Rochester*. London: Nick Hern, 2003.

30 Nettleford, p. 126.

Epilogue

1 Omasta, Matt and Dani Snyder-Young, 'Gaps, silences and comfort zones: dominant paradigms in educational drama and applied theatre discourse'. *Research in Drama Education* 19, 1 (2014): 7.

2 They call for a range of methodologies, and a 'need to clearly distinguish between research for its own sake and research in service of advocacy', Omasta and Snyder-Young, p. 19.

3 Belfiore, Eleonora, 'On bullshit in cultural policy practice and research: notes from the British case'. *International Journal of Cultural Policy* 15, 1 (2009): 355.

References

Introduction

Brook, Peter, *The Empty Space*. Victoria: Penguin Books Australia, 1968.

Cohen, Cynthia E., Roberto Gutiérrez Varea, and Polly O. Walker (eds), *Acting Together: Performance and the Creative Transformation of Violence: Volume I: Resistance and Reconciliation in Regions of Violence*. New York: New Village Press, 2011.

Dewey, John, *Art as Experience*. London: Pedigree, 1980 (1935).

Haseman, Brad and Winston, Joe, 'Why be interested? Aesthetics, applied theatre and drama education', *Research in Drama Education* 15, 4 (2010): 465–75.

Jackson, Anthony and Chris Vine, *Learning Through Theatre: The Changing Face of Theatre in Education*. London: Routledge, 2013.

Landy, Robert and David Montgomerie, *Theatre for Change: Education, Social Action and Therapy*. London: Palgrave Macmillan, 2012.

Lehmann, Hans-Thies, *Post-Dramatic Theatre*, trans. Karen Jurs-Munby. Abingdon: Routledge, 2006.

Machon, Josephine, *(Syn)Aesthetics: Redefining Visceral Performance*. London: Palgrave Macmillan, 2009.

Nicholson, Helen, *Applied Drama: The Gift of Theatre*. Basingstoke: Palgrave Macmillan, 2005.

Scarry, Elaine, *The Body in Pain*. Oxford: Oxford Paperbacks, 1988.

Shaughnessy, Nicola, *Applying Performance: Live Art, Socially Engaged Theatre and Affective Performance*. London: Routledge, 2012.

Shusterman, Richard, 'Somaesthetics and Education: Exploring the Terrain', in Liora Bressler (ed.), *Knowing Bodies, Moving Minds: Towards Embodied Teaching and Learning*. Dordrecht: Kluwer, 2004.

Thompson, James, *Performance Affects*. London: Palgrave MacMillan, 2009.

van Erven, Eugene, *Community Theatre: Global Perspectives*. London: Routledge, 2001.

Winston, Joe, *Beauty and Education*. London: Routledge, 2010.

Chapter 1

Adorno, Theodor, *Aesthetic Theory*. London: Athlone Press, 1997.

Adorno, Theodor, Walter Benjamin, Ernst Bloch, Bertolt Brecht and Georg Lukacs, *Aesthetics and Politics*. London: Verso, 1980.

Allen, Jennifer, *Frieze* 113, March 2008, https://www.frieze.com/issue/article/the_beautiful_science/ [accessed 29 December 2013].

Apollon, Willy and Richard Feldstein (eds), *Lacan, Politics, Aesthetics*. New York: New York University Press, 1996.

Armstrong, Isobel, *The Radical Aesthetic*. Oxford: Blackwell, 2000, pp. 2–3.

Boal, Augusto, *The Aesthetics of the Oppressed*. London: Routledge, 2006.

Bourdieu, Pierre, *Distinction: A Social Critique of the Judgement of Taste*. London: Routledge, 1986.

Byatt, A. S., 'The Age of Becoming', *The Guardian*, Saturday 16/12/2006.

Carey, John, *What Good are the Arts*. London: Faber and Faber, 2006.

Cooper, David, *A Companion to Aesthetics*. Oxford: Blackwell, 1992.

Derrida, Jacques, *Writing and Difference*. London: Routledge, 2001.

Dewey, John, *Art as Experience*. London: Pedigree, 1980 (1935).

Eagleton, Terry, *The Ideology of the Aesthetic*. Oxford: Blackwell Publishing, 1990.

Hanfling, Oswald, *Philosophical Aesthetics: An Introduction*. Milton Keynes: Open University Press, 1992.

Hegel, G. W. F., *Introductory Lectures on Aesthetics*. London: Penguin, 1993.

Heidegger, Martin, 'The Origin of The Work of Art', in David Farrell Krell (ed.), *Basic Writings*. London: Routledge, 2010.

Jackson, Antony, *Learning Through Theatre*. London: Routledge, 2013.

—*Theatre, Education and the Making of Meanings: Art or Instrument*. Manchester: Manchester University Press, 2007.

Kant, Immanuel, *Critique of Judgement*. New York: Dover, 2005.

Kirwan, James, *The Aesthetic in Kant*. London: Continuum, 2004.

Koren, Leonard, *Which Aesthetics Do You Mean*. Point Reyes, CA: Imperfect Publishing, 2010.

Landy, Robert and David Montgomerie, *Theatre for Change: Education, Social Action and Therapy*. London: Palgrave Macmillan, 2012.

Machon, Josephine, *(Syn)aesthetics*. London: Palgrave MacMillan, 2011.

O'Connor, Peter, *Learning Through Theatre: The Changing Face of Theatre in Education*. London: Routledge, 2013.

Rancière, Jacques, *The Politics of Aesthetics*, trans. Gabriel Rockhill. London: Continuum, 2004.

—*The Emancipated Spectator*. London: Verso, 2009.

Scarry, Elaine, *On Beauty and Being Just*. London: Gerald Duckworth and co., 2006.

—*The Body in Pain*. Oxford: Oxford Paperbacks, 1988.

Sharpe, R. A., *Contemporary Aesthetics: A Philosophical Investigation*. Brighton: The Harvester Press, 1983.

Shaughnessy, Nicola, *Applying Performance: Live Art, Socially Engaged Theatre and Affective Performance*. London: Routledge, 2012.

Thompson, James *Performance Affects*. London: Palgrave MacMillan, 2009.

White, Gareth, *Audience Participation in Theatre: Aesthetics of the Invitation*. London: Palgrave MacMillan, 2013.

Williams, Raymond, *Keywords*. London: Fontana, 1983.

Wolff, Janet, *The Aesthetics of Uncertainty*. Chichester: Colombia University Press, 2008.

Chapter 2

Armstrong, Isobel, *The Radical Aesthetic*. Oxford: Blackwell, 2000.

Berleant, Arnold, *The Aesthetic Field: A Phenomenology of Aesthetic Experience*. Christchurch New Zealand: Cybereditions, 2000 (1970).

—*Sensibility and Sense: The Aesthetic Transformation of the Human World*. Exeter: Imprint Academic, 2009.

Bhatt, Ritu, *Rethinking Aesthetics: The Role of Body in Design*. Abingdon: Routledge, 2013.

Boal, Augusto, *The Aesthetics of the Oppressed*. London: Routledge, 2006.

Chignell, Andrew, 'The Problem of Particularity in Kant's Aesthetic Theory', in Paideia: Aesthetics and Philosophy of The Arts, online at http://www.bu.edu/wcp/Papers/Aest/AestChig.htm[accessed 25 April 2014]

Damasio, Antonio, *Descartes Error*. London: Vintage, 2006.

—*Experience and Nature*. New York: Dover, 1998 (1927).

Docherty, Thomas, *Aesthetic Democracy*. Stanford: Stanford University Press, 2006.

Gibson, James J., *An Ecological Approach to Visual Perception*. New Jersey: Lawrence Ernbaum Associates, 1986.

Johnson, Mark, *The Meaning of the Body: Aesthetics of Human Understanding*. Chicago: University of Chicago Press, 2007.

Kant, Immanuel, *Critique of Judgement*. New York, Dover, 2005.

Kirwan, James, *The Aesthetic in Kant*. London: Continuum, 2004.

Lakoff, George, *Women, Fire and Dangerous Things: What Categories Tell Us About the Mind*. Chicago: University of Chicago Press, 1987.

Merleau-Ponty, Maurice, *Phenomenology of Perception*. Abingdon: Routledge, 2002

Metzinger, Thomas, *The Ego Tunnel*. New York: Basic Books 2009.

Saito, Yuriko, *Everyday Aesthetics*. Oxford: Oxford University Press, 2010.

Shusterman, Richard, *Pragmatist Aesthetics*. Oxford: Rowman and Littlefield, 2000.

Wolff, Janet, *The Aesthetics of Uncertainty*. Chichester: Colombia University Press, 2008.

Chapter 3

Armstrong, Isobel, *The Radical Aesthetic*. Oxford: Blackwell, 2000.

Bourriaud, Nicholas, *Relational Aesthetics*. Paris: Les Presse Du Reel, 2002.

Connor, Steven, 'Isobel Armstrong's Material Imagination', unpublished paper for *Radical Aesthetics: the work of Isobel Armstrong*, Institute for English Studies, 21 June 2002, http//www.stevenconnor.com/isobel/ [accessed 11 November 2013].

Featherstone, Mike, and Mike Hepworth, 'Images of Aging: Cultural representations of later life', in Malcolm L. Johnson (ed.), *The Cambridge Handbook of Age and Ageing*. Cambridge: Cambridge University Press, 2005, pp. 354–92.

Fischer Lichte, Erika, *The Transformative Power of Performance*. London and New York: Routledge, 2008.

Jackson, Shannon, *Social Works: Performing Art, Supporting Publics*. London and New York: Routledge, 2011.

Johnson, Rebecca, unpublished report, *On Ageing Case Study: Evaluation Report*. Centre for the Research on Ageing, University of Southampton, June 2011.

Kear, Adrian, 'Cooking Time with Gertrude Stein'. *Performance Research* 4, 1 (1999): 44–55

Kershaw, Baz and Coult, Tony, *Engineers of the Imagination: Welfare State Handbook*. London: Methuen, 1983.

Lutterbie, John, 'The State of the (Inter) Discipline: Time-Based Aesthetics and Cognitive Science', unpublished paper for the American Society for Theatre Research Annual Conference, Dallas, November 2013.

Mangan, Michael, *Staging Ageing: Theatre, Performance and the Narrative of Decline*. Bristol: Intellect, 2013.

Massey, Doreen, 'Landscape/Space/Politics: an essay', http://www. thefutureoflandscape.wordpress.com [accessed 30 October 2013].

Minissale, Gregory, *The Psychology of Contemporary Art*. Cambridge: Cambridge University Press, 2013.

Murray, Michael, et al., 'Understanding and Transforming Ageing through the Arts', in Alan Walker (ed.), *The New Science of Ageing*. Bristol: Polity Press, 2014.

Nicholson, Helen, *Applied Drama: The Gift of Theatre*. Basingstoke: Palgrave, 2005.

Ramachandran, Vilayanur, *The Tell Tale Brain: A Neuroscientist's Quest for What Makes us Human*. New York and London: W. W. Norton, 2011.

Reynolds, Deirdre and Matthew Reason (eds), *Kinesthetic Empathy in Creative and Cultural Practices*. Bristol: Intellect, 2011.

Rose, Gillian, *The Broken Middle: Out of Our Ancient Society*. Oxford: Blackwell, 1992.

Shaughnessy, Nicola, *Applying Performance: Live Art, Socially Engaged Theatre and Affective Practice*. Basingstoke: Palgrave, 2012.

—'Imagining Otherwise; Autism, Neuroaesthetics and Contemporary Performance', in Carina Bartleet and Kirsten Shepherd-Barr (eds), *Interdisciplinary Science Reviews, Special Edition: Experiments in Theatre: New Directions in Science and Performance*. December 2013, pp. 321–34.

—(ed.), *Affective Performance and Cognitive Science: Body, Brain and Being*. London: Methuen, 2013.

Thompson, James, 'Performance of Pain, Performance of Beauty'. *Research in Drama Education: The Journal of Applied Theatre and Performance* 11, 1 (2011): 47–57.

—*Performance Affects: Applied Theatre and the End of Effect*. Basingstoke: Palgrave, 2011.

Thompson, James and Richard Schechner, 'Why Social Theatre?'. *TDR: The Drama Review*, 48, 3 (2004): 11–16.

Tribble, Evelyn and John Sutton, 'Cognitive Ecology as a Framework for Shakespearean Studies', unpublished paper presented to American Society for Theatre Research, November, 2013, Dallas. See www.johnsutton.net/Tribble [accessed 1 November 2013].

Willis, Jane, 'A Shift to Sharing Values', *Arts Professional*, http://www.webmaster@artsprofessional.co.uk [accessed 12 April 2014].

Winnicott, D. W., *Playing and Reality*. Harmondsworth: Penguin, 1971.

Winston, Joe, *Beauty and Education*. London and New York: Routledge, 2011.

Wolff, Janet, *The Aesthetics of Uncertainty*. New York: Columbia University Press, 2008.

Chapter 4

Ackroyd, Judith, 'Article 1 Applied Theatre Problems and Possibilities', in *Applied Theatre Researcher*, published by Griffiths University and IDEA, ISSN 1443-1726 Number 1, 2000, online at http://www.griffith.edu.au/__data/assets/pdf_file/0004/81796/Ackroyd.pdf/ [accessed 31 March 2013].

—'Applied Theatre: An exclusionary discourse?', 2007. Available at http://
www.griffith.edu.au/__data/assets/pdf_file/0005/52889/01-ackroyd-final.
pdf [accessed 7 April 14].

Adebayo, Mojisola, John Martin and Manisha Mehta. *The Theatre for
Development Handbook*. London: Pan Intercultural Arts, 2011.

Boal, Augusto, *Theatre of the Oppressed*. London: Pluto Press, 1978.

—*The Aesthetics of the Oppressed*. London and New York: Routledge, 2006.

Carey, John, *What Good Are the Arts?* Oxford: Oxford University Press, 2006.

Cohen-Cruz, Jan, *Engaging Performance: Theatre as Call and Response*.
London and New York: Routledge, 2010.

Eco, Umberto, *On Beauty: A History of a Western Idea*. London: MacLehose
Press, 2010.

Freire, Paulo, *Pedagogy of the Oppressed*. London: Penguin Education, 1996.

Herwitz, Daniel, *Aesthetics: Key Concepts in Philosophy*. London and New
York: Continuum, 2008.

Kramer, Chamberlain, McNamara, et al. 2004. 'Applied Theatre/Drama: an
e-debate in 2004'. *Research in Drama Education* 11, 1 (February 2006):
90–5.

Ngai, Sianne, *Ugly Feelings*. Cambridge and London: Harvard University
Press, 2005.

Nicholson, Helen, *Applied Drama: The Gift of Theatre*. Basingstoke: Palgrave
Macmillan, 2005.

Nuttall, Sarah (ed.), *Beautiful Ugly: African and Diaspora Aesthetics*. Durham
and London: Duke University Press, 2006.

Prentki, Tim and Sheila Preston. *The Applied Theatre Reader*. London and
New York: Routledge, 2009.

Rifkin, Frances, *The Ethics of Participatory Theatre in Higher Education: A
Framework for Learning and Teaching*. London: Palatine, 2009. Available
online at http://78.158.56.101/archive/palatine/files/ethics.pdf

Scarry, Elaine, *On Beauty and Being Just*. London: Duckworth, 2006.

Scruton, Roger, *Beauty*. Oxford: Oxford University Press, 2009.

Shaughnessy, Nicola, *Applying Performance: Live Art, Socially Engaged Theatre
and Affective Practice*. Basingstoke: Palgrave Macmillan, 2012.

Sobol, Joshua, *Ghetto*. London: Nick Hern Books, 1989.

Taylor, Phillip, *Applied Theatre: Creating Transformative Encounters in the Community*. Portsmouth, NH: Heinemann, 2003.

Thompson, James, *Applied Drama: Bewilderment and Beyond*. Oxford: Peter Lang, 2003.

—*Performance Affects: Applied Theatre and the End of Effect*. Basingstoke: Palgrave Macmillan, 2009.

Victor Ukaegbu, 'The Problem with Definitions', in Judith Ackroyd and Jonathan Neelands (eds), *Drama Research*, Vol. 3, National Drama, 2004.

Winston, Joe, *Beauty and Education*. London and New York: Routledge, 2011.

Wolf, Naomi, *The Beauty Myth*. London: Vintage, 1991.

Chapter 5

Ahmed, Jamil, 'Wishing for a World without 'Theatre for Development': demystifying the case of Bangladesh'. *Research in Drama Education* 7, 2 (2002): 207–19.

Appadurai, Arjun, 'Global Ethnoscapes: Notes and Queries for a Transnational Anthropology', in Richard Fox (ed.), *Recapturing Anthropology*. Santa Fe, New Mexico: School of American Research Press, 1991, pp. 164–92.

Buncombe, Andrew, 'Cambodia puts the cremation site of Pol Pot on 'historic' tourist trail', *The Independent*, 11 March 2010.

Burridge, Stephanie and Fred Frumberg, *Beyond the Apsara: Celebrating Dance in Cambodia*. Delhi: Routledge India, 2010.

Cixous, Helen, 'Le Théâtre se Tenant Responsible', in Soko Phay–Vakalis and Pierre Bayard (eds), *Cambodge, Mémoire de l'Extrême*. Paris: Université Paris 8, 2011.

French, Lindsay, 'Displaced Lives: Stories of Life and Culture from the Khmer in Site II, Thailand', in *International Rescue Committee Oral History Project*. Bangkok: Craftsman Press, 1990, p. 5.

Hawkes, Martine, Transmitting Genocide: Genocide and Art' [Online] *M/C Journal* 9, 1 (2006). Available at: http://journal.mediaculture.org. au/0603/09-hawkes.php [accessed 15 September 2013].

Hirsch, Marianne, *The Generation of Postmemory: Visual Culture after the Holocaust*. New York: Colombia University Press, 2012.

Hughes, Caroline, *Dependent Communities. Aid and Politics in Cambodia and East Timor*. Ithaca: Cornell Southeast Asia Program, 2009.

Levinson, Jerrald, *The Oxford Handbook of Aesthetics*. Oxford: Oxford University Press, 2003.

Mills, C. Wright., *Power, Politics and People*. New York: Oxford University Press, 1963 quoted in: Melossi, Dario, 'The Cultural Embeddedness of Social Control'. *Theoretical Criminology* 5, 4 (2001): 403–24.

Nee, Meas and McCallum, Wayne, *Roads to Development. Insights from Sre Ambel District, Southwest Cambodia*. American Friends Service Committee: Graphic Roots, 2009, pp. 21–3.

Renan, Ernest, 1882, quoted in Smith, Anthony, 'Culture, Community and Territory'. *International Affairs* 72, 3 (1996): 445–58.

Richmond, Oliver P. and Franks, Jason, 'Liberal Hubris? Virtual Peace in Cambodia'. *Security Dialogue* 38, 1 (2007): 27–48.

Smith, Anthony, 1981, quoted in Hughes, Caroline, *Dependent Communities. Aid and Politics in Cambodia and East Timor*. Ithaca: Cornell Southeast Asia Program, 2009.

—'Culture, Community and Territory'. *International Affairs* 72, 3 (1996): 445–58.

—*Myths and Memories of the Nation*. New York: Oxford University Press, 1999.

Stanton, Gregory, *Blue Scarves and Yellow Stars: Classification and Symbolization in the Cambodian Genocide* [Online] lecture notes distributed in Faulds lecture at Warren Wilson College, Swannanoa, North Carolina, March 1987, p. 4. Available at: http://www.genocidewatch.org/images/AboutGen89BlueScarvesandYellowStars.pdf [accessed 15 September 2013].

Thompson, James, 'From the Stocks to the Stage', in Michael Balfour (ed.), *Theatre in Prison: Theory and Practice*. Bristol: Intellect, 2004, pp. 57–76.

—*Digging up Stories: Applied Theatre, Performance and War*. Manchester: Manchester University Press, 2005.

—'Performance, Globalization and Conflict Promotion/Resolution: Experiences from Sri Lanka', in Helmut Anheier and Yudhishthir Raj Isar (eds), *Conflicts and Tensions. The Cultures and Globalization Series*. London: SAGE, 2007, pp. 296–305.

—*Performance affects. Applied Theatre and the End of Effect*. London: Palgrave Macmillan, 2009.

Thompson, Ashley and Prenowitz, Éric, 'Un Théâtre Épique non Aligné', in Soko Phay–Vakalis and Pierre Bayard (eds), *Cambodge, Mémoire de l'Extrême*. Paris: Université Paris 8, 2011, p. 24.

Winston, Joe, *Beauty and Education*. London: Routledge, 2010.

Chapter 6

Breed, Ananda, 'Performing Gacaca in Rwanda: Local Culture for Justice and Reconciliation', in Yudhishthir Isar and Helmut Anheier (eds), *Cultures and Globalization Series*. Los Angeles, USA: Sage Publications, 2007, pp. 306–12.

—'Discordant Narratives in Rwanda's Gacaca Courts', in Maddalena Campioni and Patrick Noack (eds), *Rwanda Fast Forward: Social, Economic, Military and Reconciliation Prospects*. Basingstoke: Palgrave, 2012.

—*Performing the Nation: Genocide, Justice, Reconciliation*. Chicago: Seagull Press, 2014.

Fujii, Lee Ann, *Killing Neighbors: Webs of Violence in Rwanda*. New York: Cornell University Press, 2009.

Ingelaere, Bert, 'From Model To Practice. Researching and Representing Rwanda's "Modernised" Gacaca Courts'. *Critique of Anthropology* 32, 4 (2012): 388–414.

Miles, Malcolm, *Herbert Marcuse: An Aesthetics of Liberation*. London: Pluto Press, 2012.

The Norwegian Helsinki Committee (NHC). *Prosecuting Genocide in Rwanda: The Gacaca System and the International Criminal Tribunal for Rwanda*. Report II/2002. Oslo: NHC.

Rusagara, Frank K. 'Gacaca: Rwanda's truth and reconciliation authority'. *The New Times*, 16 May 2005, http://allafrica.com/stories/200505170174.html.

Uvin, Peter, 'The Introduction of a Modernised Gacaca for Judging Suspects of Participation in the Genocide and the Massacres of 1994 in Rwanda'. Unpublished discussion paper prepared for the Belgian Secretary of State for Development Cooperation, 2000.

Villa-Vicencio, Charles, *Walk with Us and Listen: Political Reconciliation in Africa*. Washington DC, USA: Georgetown University Press, 2009.

Chapter 7

Appadurai, Arjun, *Modernity at Large: Cultural Dimensions of Globalization.* Minneapolis, MN: University of Minnesota Press, 1996.

Berlant, Lauren, *The Queen of America Goes to Washington City: Essays on Sex and Citizenship.* Durham, NC: Duke University Press, 1997.

Brook, Peter, *The Empty Space.* Victoria: Penguin Books Australia, 1968.

de Certeau, Michel, *The Practice of Everyday Life.* Berkeley: University of California Press, 1984.

C&T Theatre, Online, URL: http://www.candt.org [accessed 18 February 14].

Guattari, Felix, *The Anti Oedipus Papers.* Los Angeles: Semiotext (E), 2006.

Habermas, Jürgen, *The Structural Transformation of the Public Sphere: An Inquiry into a Category of Bourgeois Society.* Cambridge: Polity Press, 1962.

Hartley, John, *The Uses of Digital Literacy.* St. Lucia: Queensland University, 2009.

Hickey-Moody, Anna. *Youth, Arts and Education.* Routledge: London, 2012.

Hoggart, Richard, *The Uses of Literacy: Aspects of Working Class Life with Special Reference to Publications and Entertainments.* London: Chatto and Windus, 1958.

Kelly, Peter, 'Youth at risk: processes of individualisation and responsibilisation in the risk society'. *Discourse* 22 (2001): 23–34.

—'Governing individualised risk biographies: new class intellectuals and the problem of youth at risk'. *British Journal of Sociology of Education* 28, 1 (2007): 39–53.

Rheingold, Howard, 'Using participatory media and public voice to encourage civic engagement', in Lance Bennett (ed.), *Civic Life Online: Learning How Digital Media can Engage Youth.* Cambridge, MA: The MIT Press, 2008, pp. 97–118.

Richardson, Rene, *From Uncle Tom to Gangsta: Black Masculinity and the U.S. South,* Athens, GA: University of Georgia Press, 2007.

Riley, Sarah, More, Yvette and Griffin, Christine, 'The "Pleasure Citizen": Analysing Partying as a Form of Social and Political Participation'. *Young* 18, 1 (2010): 33–54.

Rock Eisteddfod Challenge Online, Available http://www.rockchallenge.com.au/ [accessed 11 April 2011].

Rodgers, Richard and Hammerstein, Oscar, 'My Favourite Things'. *The Sound of Music*, Twentieth Century Fox, 1965.

Sandercock, Leonie, *Cosmopolis II: Mongrel Cities in the Twenty-First Century*. London: Continuum, 2003.

Savage, Glenn and Hickey-Moody, Anna, 'Global Flows as Gendered Cultural Pedagogies: Learning Gangsta in the 'Durty South'. *Critical Studies in Education* 51, 3 (2010): 277–93.

Styan, John, *Modern Drama in Theory and Practice*. Cambridge: Cambridge University Press, 1981.

Tait, Gordon, 'Shaping the "At-risk Risk Youth": Risk, Governmentality and the Finn Report'. *Discourse* 16, 1 (1995): 123–34.

—'What is the Relationship Between Social Governance and Schooling?', in Bruce Burnett, Daphne Meadmore and Gordon Tait (eds), *New Questions For Contemporary Teachers: Taking a Socio- Cultural Approach to Education*. Frenchs Forrest: NSW Pearson Education Australia, 2004, pp. 13–24.

Te Riele, Kitty, 'Youth "At Risk": Further Marginalizing the Marginalised?' *Journal of Education Policy* 21, 2 (2006): 129–45.

Turner, Graeme, 'Critical Literacy, Cultural Literacy, and the English School Curriculum in Australia', in Susan Owen (ed.), *Richard Hoggart and Cultural Studies*. London: Palgrave Macmillan, 2008, pp. 158–70.

Warner, Michael, 'The Mass Public and the Mass Subject', in Craig Calhoun (ed.), *Habermas and the Public Sphere*. Cambridge, MA: MIT Press, 1992, pp. 377–401.

—'Publics and Counterpublics'. *Public Culture* 14, 1 (2002): 49–90.

Williams, Raymond, *Resources of Hope: Culture, Democracy, Socialism*. Verso: London 1989, pp. 3–14.

—*Culture and Society*. New York: Columbia University Press; first published 1958; London: Chatto and Windus, 1963.

—*The Long Revolution*. Harmondsworth: Penguin; first published 1961; London: Chatto and Windus, 1965.

—*Communications*. New York: Barnes and Noble, 1966.

Willis, Paul, *Learning to Labour*. Aldershot: Gower, 1977.

—'Cultural Production is Different from Cultural Reproduction is Different from Social Reproduction is Different from Reproduction'. *Interchange* 12 (1981): 48–67.

—*Common Culture*. Open University Press: Milton Keynes, 1990.

—*The Ethnographic Imagination*. Polity: Cambridge, 2000.

Chapter 8

Barthes, Roland, *Critical Essays*. Evanston: Northwestern University Press, 1972.

Boal, Augusto, *The Aesthetics of the Oppressed*. New York: Routledge, 2006.

Bowell, Pamela and Brian Heap, 'Drama on the Run: A prelude to mapping the practice of process drama'. *Journal of Aesthetic Education* 39, 4 (2005): 58–69.

—'Drama is not a Dirty Word: Past Achievements, Present Concerns, Alternative Futures'. *Research in Drama Education* 15, 4 (2010): 579–92.

—*Planning Process Drama: Enriching Teaching and Learning*. London: Routledge, 2013.

Britzman, Deborah P., *Practice Makes Practice: A Critical Study of Learning to Teach*. New York: State University of New York Press, 2003.

Cahill, Helen, 'Re-thinking the fiction-reality boundary: investigating the use of drama in HIV prevention projects in Vietnam'. *Research in Drama Education: The Journal of Applied Theatre and Performance* 15, 2 (2010): 155–74.

Freire, Paulo, *Pedagogy of the Oppressed*. UK: Penguin Books, 1972.

Goffman, Erving, *Frame Analysis: An Essay on the Organization of Experience*. Cambridge, MA: Harvard University Press, 1974.

Heap, Brian, 'New Reals: Drama in Education as a Process of Realization'. Unpublished Diss. U of Newcastle upon Tyne, 1984.

—'Process Drama: An Investigation into the Paradox of Negotiating Fictional Contexts for Meaningful Learning'. Unpublished Doctoral Thesis: University of the West Indies, Mona, Jamaica, 2011.

—(ed.), *Caribbean Quarterly: The IDIERI Papers* 53. 1. 2007.

Heathcote, Dorothy, *Collected Writings on Drama and Education*. Eds. Liz Johnson and Cecily O'Neill. Evanston: Northwestern, 1991.

—Personal written communication with the author. 28 June 2008.

Neelands, Jonothan, *Creating Democratic Citizenship through Drama Education: The Writings of Jonothan Neelands*. Ed. Peter O'Connor. Stoke on Trent: Trentham, 2010.

—'Three Theatres Waiting: Architectural Space and Performance Traditions', in Juliana Saxton and Carole Miller (eds), *The Research of Practice, The Practice of Research*. Victoria: IDEA Publications, 1998.

Nettleford, Rex, (ed.), *Jamaica in Independence: Essays on the Early Years*. Kingston, Jamaica: Heinemann Caribbean, 1989.

Prendergast, Monica and Juliana Saxton, *Applied Theatre: International Case Studies and Challenges for Practice*. Bristol: Intellect, 2009.

Styslinger, Mary E., 'Relations of Power and Drama in Education: The Teacher and Foucault'. *Journal of Educational Thought* 34, 2 (2000): 183–99.

Teale, Polly, *After Mrs. Rochester*. London: Nick Hern, 2003.

Epilogue

Belfiore, Eleonora, 'On bullshit in cultural policy practice and research: notes from the British case'. *International Journal of Cultural Policy* 15, 1 (2009): 343–59.

Frankfurt, Harry G., *On Bullshit*. Woodstock: Princeton University Press, 2005.

Omasta, Matt and Dani Snyder-Young, 'Gaps, silences and comfort zones: dominant paradigms in educational drama and applied theatre discourse'. *Research in Drama Education* 19, 1 (2014): 7–22.

Index